Searching for the Bright Path

Indians of the Southeast

SEARCHING FOR THE

Bright Path

The Mississippi Choctaws

from Prehistory to Removal

James Taylor Carson

University of Nebraska Press

LINCOLN & LONDON

Acknowledgments for the use of previously
published works appear on page xiv.

∞

First Nebraska paperback printing: 2003
Library of Congress Cataloging-in-Publication Data
Carson, James Taylor, 1968–
Searching for the bright path: the Mississippi Choctaws
from prehistory to removal / James Taylor Carson.
        p.   cm.—(Indians of the Southeast)
Includes bibliographical references and index.
    ISBN 0-8032-1503-7 (cl.: alk. paper)
    ISBN 0-8032-6417-8 (pa.: alk. paper)
    1. Choctaw Indians—History—Sources.
    2. Choctaw Indians—Social life and customs.
        3. Choctaw Indians—Relocation.
4. Ethnohistory—Mississippi.   5. Mississippi—
    History—Sources.   I. Title.   II. Series.
            E99.C8C33   1999
    976.2'004973—dc21   99-12949
                    CIP

FOR KARLA

CONTENTS

ILLUSTRATIONS

Series Editors' Introduction

CHANGE and persistence are key problems for historians. We are trained to expect change in the human experience, and our research into the records of the past reveals evidence of such change and suggests ways to interpret its causes and consequences. But students of Native American history must balance that evidence, often so overwhelming that we see little else, against the lessons anthropologists teach about persistence, especially the persistence of culture. The challenge for ethnohistorians thus becomes one of defining change, measuring its depth, and explaining the coexistence of both persistence and change. The appearance of change, we discover, is far from the whole story. James Taylor Carson has constructed this interpretation of preremoval Choctaw history around the twin themes of persistence and change. Persistence is culture, flowing out of the Mississippian past and providing a link that explains essential elements of Choctaw ethnicity. Four elements of Mississippian culture—chiefly political organization, gendered division of labor, matrilineal kinship, and Mississippian cosmology—constitute what Carson argues was the "moral economy" of the Choctaws. These elements become Carson's interpretive framework. In his view the changes in Choctaw history during the volatile eighteenth and nineteenth centuries, although in some ways dramatic, become more apparent than real as the fundamental elements of Choctaw culture persist. He reminds us that things are always more complicated than they seem.

We are especially pleased to offer Carson's *Searching for the Bright Path* as the newest volume in the series Indians of the Southeast.

Theda Perdue
Michael D. Green

Acknowledgments

THIS BOOK would not have been possible without the guidance of Michael D. Green and Theda Perdue. I went to the University of Kentucky to study the Native American Southeast and have been richly rewarded for doing so. They allowed me the space to pursue my research and writing on my own but pushed me further than I would have dared to venture. By balancing rigorous criticism with generous support, they have taught me not only how to write history but how to teach it. And I will carry these lessons with me for the rest of my academic life.

Others also share a measure of responsibility for the work that follows. To Lance Banning I owe appreciation for close reading and criticism of other scholars' work and for the ebb and flow of historiographical debate. Karl Raitz opened my eyes to the importance of a geographic understanding of the lived past, and I benefited considerably from his perspective. Dan Usner and Richard White provided insightful critiques of the manuscript, and their input challenged me to argue more clearly, more concisely, and I hope more effectively.

A number of other organizations and individuals have contributed to the project. Financial support from the Pew Program in American Religious History at Yale University relieved me of my teaching duties and enabled me to devote a full year to preparing the manuscript. Mark Knoll and the other participants in the 1998 spring Pew Fellows conference were generous in their criticism. The Phillips Fund of the American Philosophical Society and a grant from the Graduate School of the University of Kentucky enabled me to visit far-flung repositories. I am grateful to the staffs of the M. I. King Library, University of Kentucky; the Oklahoma Historical Society, Norman; the Gilcrease Institute of American History and Art, Tulsa; the Western History Collections of the University of Oklahoma; the Southern Historical Collection of the University of North Carolina, Chapel Hill; the Mississippi Department of Archives and History, Jackson; the Alabama Department of Archives and History, Montgomery; and the Cain Archives, Millsaps College, Jackson,

Mississippi. I am also indebted to the Newberry Library of Chicago, whose fellowship program allowed me to spend time there becoming familiar with their impressive collections and talking with people of similar academic inclinations.

I would also like to thank Professor Peter Walker, who set me on to history, my friends at Tulane University—Charles Chamberlain, Walter Hickel, and James Moses—and my colleagues at the University of Kentucky—Tim Garrison, Greg O'Brien, Jennifer Petit, Rowena Ruff, and Ella Drake—as well as Bethany Chaney, who watched this project develop from scribblings on cocktail napkins to the printed word.

Portions of this work have appeared previously in the following articles and essay and are used here with the publishers' permission: "Horses and the Economy and Culture of the Choctaw Indians, 1690–1840," *Ethnohistory* 42 (summer 1995): 495–513; "State Rights and Indian Removal in Mississippi, 1817–1835," *Journal of Mississippi History* 57 (February 1995): 25–42; "Native Americans, the Market Revolution, and Culture Change: The Choctaw Cattle Economy, 1690–1830," *Agricultural History* 71 (winter 1997): 1–18; and, "From Corn Mothers to Cotton Spinners: Continuity in Choctaw Women's Economic Life, 950 A.D. to 1830 A.D.," in *Women of the American South: A Multicultural Reader*, ed. Christie Anne Farnham (New York: University of New York Press, 1997), 8–25.

Finally, as I began this project my wife entered law school. Her demanding schedule made it possible for me to set up my own stringent schedule, and we fed off one another's hard work, intellectual curiosity, and crises of confidence. It is to Karla that I dedicate this work.

Searching for the Bright Path

The Flight of Oakatibbé

I love the whites—I was always a friend to the whites. I believe I love their laws
better than my own. Loblolly Jack laughed at me because I loved the whites,
and wanted our people to live like them. But I am of no use now.
I can love them no more. My people say that I must die. How can I live?

OAKATIBBÉ, quoted in William Gilmore Simms, *The Wigwam and the Cabin*

OAKATIBBÉ stood out among the forty or so Choctaws who picked cotton
on Colonel Harris's plantation. Not only was he a full head taller than
the rest, but of the three men who stooped among the long rows of
fluffy white bolls, he was the only one who was neither aged nor infirm.
Choctaw men and women regarded agricultural labor as women's work,
a task inappropriate for healthy male hunters and warriors, and for his
efforts Oakatibbé earned a measure of scorn to go along with the few
dollars he collected at the end of the working day.

One Saturday evening Oakatibbé and the other workers lugged their
bulging baskets of cotton up to Colonel Harris's cabin to be weighed.
While the planter dutifully noted who had picked how many pounds,
a locally prominent Choctaw man named Loblolly Jack expressed his
displeasure with the colonel's scales and attempted to tip the balance in
his wife's favor. Oakatibbé spotted Loblolly Jack's trick and accused the
"rascal dog" of being a cheat. The two men drew their knives, only to be
stopped by the colonel, who sent one of his slaves to fetch his shotgun.

Oakatibbé and Loblolly Jack had a long history of personal enmity, and
when they resumed the argument in a local tavern just down the road from
the plantation, their heated words escalated to blows. The brawl spilled
out of the dramshop and onto the street, and at some point in the fray

Oakatibbé fatally stabbed Loblolly Jack in the chest. As was customary among the Choctaws, the death had to be avenged, and Oakatibbé knew that members of the dead man's clan would expect to execute him the next day.

The popular novelist William Gilmore Simms was visiting Colonel Harris at the time, and he took great interest in the murder. He spun the incident into a short story that was published in *The Wigwam and the Cabin*, a collection of tales about life on the American frontier. Having apprised himself of the situation and having spoken with Oakatibbé, he could not fathom why Slim Sampson, as Oakatibbé was known to his American friends, would allow himself to be executed at the hands of a people Simms viewed as primitive savages. To Simms, Sampson personified the progress Anglo-American "civilization" was making among the Choctaws of the early nineteenth century. Surely, the novelist thought, Slim Sampson would not submit to the execution.

In preparation for his punishment the next morning, Oakatibbé spent the night composing the death song he would sing before he died—a song that, in Simms's words, arranged his "narrative of the past, in proper form for the acceptance of the future."[1] Simms and Harris, however, pleaded with him to flee. To this end Harris gave the doomed man a horse, which Oakatibbé reluctantly accepted. "Go to bed, Kurnel. Your horse will come back," were the last words he spoke before he galloped into the night.[2]

Aside from the murder he committed, we know very little about Oakatibbé. We know nothing of his childhood or of his home life. We do not even know where he fled that night. But we do know that he worked for cash like an American, dressed like an American, and may have even drawn spiritual succor from Christian sermons. For all outward appearances, however, Oakatibbé was not an American. He was a Choctaw, and the story of his tragic life captured in the trials of one person the struggle of all Choctaws, and indeed all Native Americans, to adjust to life in postcontact America. Besieged by an Anglo-American culture that held entirely different values as well as tremendous economic, military, and political clout, Native Americans continually had to refuse, refute, or adapt to the intrusions of missionaries, traders, politicians, and settlers. What had been a way of life for the Choctows before Columbus became after contact and colonization a culture in contention with what the European invaders regarded as "civilization."

From their means of subsistence to the gods they worshiped, Native Americans witnessed enormous changes in their lives in the decades that followed the European colonization of North America. Students of Native American history have spent the better part of this century trying to untangle which parts of native culture changed substantially, which changed slightly, and which might not have changed at all. To date, scholars have a good idea of the extent of cultural change and persistence among native peoples, but there are still many issues to investigate and many questions to pose. Why did cultures change or persist in the ways they did? To what purposes were the changes aimed? And what can the changes tell us about how Native Americans viewed their past, present, and future as well as their own sense of identity?

The seven chapters that follow constitute an attempt to answer these questions by looking at one culture, the Choctaws', over time, in this case nearly eight centuries. It is not a story of progress and decline, of resistance and survival, or of persistence and change. It is a story of adaptation and reckoning, a search for what one prominent Choctaw of the early nineteenth century called "the straight bright path."[3]

To find out what the path was and what the search for it entailed, I have turned to a historical method called ethnohistory, a particular approach to source materials and theoretical models that over the past few decades has revolutionized the way historians have interpreted the Native American past. There is, however, a tension in ethnohistory between those who emphasize the persistence of cultures over time and those who focus on the changes that occur. To reconcile the two often mutually exclusive approaches involves synthesizing change and persistence into an interpretation of culture as a historical process.[4] At the same time, we need to remember that culture does not exist independent of the people who make it or of the environment that sustains it. In short, culture is a sort of lived social history in which the received patterns of past beliefs and behaviors converge on the contingencies of life in the present.

Defining culture is a tricky business. I have built my understanding of it around anthropologist Clifford Geertz's advocacy of an interpretive theory of culture. Geertz defines culture as a "historically transmitted pattern of meanings embodied in symbols, a system of inherited conceptions expressed in symbolic forms by means of which men [and women] communicate, perpetuate, and develop their knowledge about and attitudes toward life." He differentiates culture into several layers, from the deeply buried core beliefs of a people to the more superficial but no less important behaviors that transmute beliefs into actions like eating, praying, and fighting. "Our double task," Geertz writes, "is to uncover the conceptual structures that inform our subjects' acts . . . and to construct a system of analysis in whose terms what is generic to those structures, what belongs to them because they are what they are, will stand out against the other determinants of human behavior."[5]

Geertz cautions against two things. First, the search for continually deepening levels of thought and belief can distract the investigator from important surface events and influences. The pains and pleasures of daily life cannot be forgotten for the sake of locating the principles this life rests on. Second, a "thick" description of the subject culture must avoid what anthropologist Alfred Kroeber called the "superorganic," an understanding of culture in which "the march of history . . . is independent of . . . particular personalities."[6] In contrast to the superorganic model, thick description must not reify culture as an explanatory device divorced from the vagaries of human personality. Rather, the role of the individual must be considered important. Certainly one's culture influences one's choices, but it does not determine them. Other noncultural factors like imperial rivalries, Protestant missionizing, or personal experience can also affect people's beliefs and behaviors. The task at hand, as Geertz outlines it, is to understand how temporal and environmental factors interacted with cultural imperatives to shape the individual choices that together form a people's history.

Putting the individual at the center of interpretations of culture, however, is still problematic. Nearly a decade ago ethnohistorian William Simmons lamented that his colleagues had a "tendency to deny individual consciousness an active role in culture theory," and his criticism still rings true.[7] To incorporate the individual fully into an interpretation of culture, we must examine culture as a moral system.

Morality constitutes the intuitive and evaluative processes through which people translate into specific behavior their understanding of their relation to their culture, to their fellow human beings, and to their environment. One of the pioneers in this kind of approach, labor historian E. P. Thompson, argued in his study of capitalism and economic exchange that the capitalist marketplace refracted both the moral concerns of the workers and the profit motives of the bosses into what he called a moral economy—a system that sanctioned as proper or rejected as improper the outcomes of economic interaction.[8] Whereas Thompson wrote that the market was "a junction-point between [different] social, economic, and intellectual histories," I would argue that the frontiers of contact between Europeans and Native Americans were likewise junction points where dramatically different geographic, social, economic, political, and ideological histories met. In a more comprehensive sense, colonization touched off a moral struggle whereby each group strained to place the other within accepted categories of belief. Choctaw culture therefore can be thought of as a grid that individuals carried in their heads and hearts and into which they fed received customs, personal knowledge, and perceptions of the present in order to determine appropriate and proper courses of action. Based on such an understanding of culture, we can begin to appreciate why certain Choctaws accommodated European or American culture on some occasions and resisted it on others.[9]

The Choctaw story is especially complicated because it involves not one culture but several—the indigenous one plus a French one, an English one, a Spanish one, an African one, and an American one. How various cultures interact constitutes one of the most important fields of ethnohistorical investigation. Traditionally such concerns have fallen under the rubric of acculturation theory, the permutations of which stand in direct proportion to the number of its proponents. Anthropologist Alexander Lesser, for example, drew several of his conclusions about acculturation from his study of the Pawnees. It was, he wrote, "the ways in which some cultural aspect is taken into a culture and adjusted and fitted to it."[10] Other scholars have added that the acculturative relationship must be reciprocal, that the donor culture and the recipient culture exchange influences.[11] Most recently, in the hands of two psychologists, Hope Landarine and Elizabeth A. Klonoff, acculturation has come to mean not a mixture of cultures within an ethnic group but the persistence of "traditional" practices by a minority group as judged against their participation in the cultural activities of the dominant group.[12] Implicit in the more recent conceptions of acculturation is that cultural adaptation and change as a result of contact with another culture in some way reflect the relative balance of power between donor and recipient. But the equation between power and acculturation is misleading. According to its critics, acculturation theory overstates the invasive properties of the dominant culture and consequently diminishes the crucial roles

indigenous peoples play in picking and choosing innovations.[13] Power
in the context of culture therefore ought not to be gauged in comparative
geopolitical terms, for when a society produces outlooks and achieves
outcomes comprehensible in terms of *its own* culture and not that of
the politically or economically predominant other, then the society, the
individuals, and the culture in question have power.[14]

Yet restoring individuals to center stage in the drama of cultural
history needs to be balanced by a historically framed understanding of
the bigger picture. British sociologist Anthony Giddens has dedicated
the past two decades to reconciling the specific short-term actions of the
individual with the long sweep of time in a theory he calls "structuration."
Giddens considers individuals crucial agents in social and cultural change
because while social systems condition and constrain human behavior, the
outcomes of individuals' behaviors return in full to shape the operation
and constitution of the social systems.[15]

To explicate the links between time, culture, and the individual,
Giddens divides the past into three discrete segments. The first he
borrowed from Fernand Braudel and the French scholars of the *Annales*
school. The slow processes of geographical, environmental, and social
change that occur across generations constitute what Braudel called the
"long duration." The second period, what we might in contrast call the
"short duration," lasts the life span of an individual. Looking at the short
duration lets us begin to piece together how the processes of the long
duration shaped and were shaped by the actions of individuals. Third
is event time, where specific interactions between individuals produce
contingent outcomes.[16]

The purpose of such an approach is to make allowances for the disparate
nature of sources available to the ethnohistorian. Owing to the problems of
extrapolating individual thought and behavior from the archaeological
record, chapter 1 draws together nearly six centuries of prehistory to
establish a baseline from which to gauge the long duration of Choctaw
history. The eighteenth century, the short duration in this book, is
somewhat easier to examine because source materials that reveal glimpses
of the Choctaw side of things are fairly abundant. As chapters 2 and 3
show, we can begin to understand why individuals did the things they did,
but doing so still requires that we explain much of their actions in terms of
their culture rather than their personality. Only in the nineteenth century,
the third period of event time, is the source material sufficient to reveal

why certain Choctaws acted as they did and how their actions evolved out of the historical legacy they had inherited from their forebears. Chapters 4, 5, 6, and 7 examine economic, political, and religious change and persistence as well as explore how different leaders fashioned different solutions to the impending removal crisis of the 1830s. Laying the three layers of time and of interpretation atop one another makes it possible to differentiate the deep structures of Choctaw culture that endured over the long duration from the superficial manifestations of the structures that characterized life in the short duration. And it illuminates the relation of events and individuals in time to culture over time.

By building on the theoretical work of Geertz, Thompson, and Giddens we can begin to further understand the "whys" that follow the "whens" and "whats" of ethnohistorical inquiry. We will also see that although the Choctaws experienced an enormous range of changes in the ways they governed themselves, fed themselves, and thought of themselves and their place in the world, certain basic features of their culture persisted. What persisted did not do so because of the latent powers of inertia; rather, things persisted because they still made sense and still explained the world and its workings to Choctaws in ways that resonated with what they believed was proper and true.

Was Oakatibbé the exception to the rule as he turned his back on the laws of his culture and fled into the oblivion of the night? In the end we must explain not only why he embraced certain aspects of Anglo-American culture, but why he fled when everything he had learned in his life told him to stay. Oakatibbé, Loblolly Jack, and the thousands of other Choctaws who had come before them were all looking for "the straight bright path" that led to a righteous life and to the salvation of their world. That was what made them Choctaws. Who would blaze the trail and where it would lead concerned everyone. And whether adjusting to the postcontact world involved cultural adaptation (picking cotton for cash), cultural conservation (demanding revenge for the death of a kinsman), or cultural dislocation (fleeing the scene of a murder), there were choices that all Choctaws had to make.

CHAPTER ONE

The Mississippian Foundations
of Choctaw Culture, 950–1700

> Many generations ago Aba, the good spirit above, created many men, all Choctaw,
> who spoke the language of the Choctaw, and understood one another. These came from the
> bosom of the earth, being formed of yellow clay, and no men had ever lived before them.
> CHOCTAW CREATION STORY, told in David I. Bushnell Jr.,
> *The Choctaw of Bayou Lacomb, St. Tammany Parish, Louisiana*

ON THE EDGE of a cow pasture just off State Road 789, northeast of
Philadelphia, Mississippi, stands one of the hundreds of large Indian
mounds that are scattered throughout the Deep South. This particular
mound is called Nanih Waiya, the leaning mound, and for the Choctaw
people there is no more important place on earth. Sometime in the ancient
past Nanih Waiya gave birth to the Choctaws. Out of the subterranean
womb of the Great Mother crawled the "beloved people," and they lay on
her belly to dry themselves in the warm rays of their Great Father Aba,
the sun. Afterward Aba promulgated his law. He divided the Choctaws
into two great families, or *iksas,* and established the social conventions
and rituals whereby the new people would enjoy a secure and prosperous
existence on earth. Before returning to his home in the sky, Aba kindled
a sacred fire that he left burning in his stead as an earthly reminder of
his power. The sun god had chosen the Choctaws as his people and the
land around the mound as their world, and so long as they followed his
law, they would remain on the bright path to a righteous life. Should they
stray from the path, however, and follow the dark one, the monsters who
haunted the boundaries of their world would invade their land, bringing
destruction and despair.[1]

It is not clear what kind of people these first Choctaws were, for their archaeological legacy still lies buried under the forests, fields, and small towns of rural east-central Mississippi.[2] In the absence of hard data, ethnohistorians must resort to both upstreaming and downstreaming, that is, comparing the archaeological record of the prehistoric Mississippians, the culture that preceded the Choctaws, with the historic record of the Choctaws to arrive at some approximation of what the proto-Choctaws might have been like.[3] Because of the nature of the archaeological record we can never be sure exactly what prehistoric people thought or believed or how their cultures were organized. Nevertheless, unless ethnohistorians try to bridge the gap that divides prehistory from history, we can never come to grips with the problems of cultural continuity and discontinuity in the postcontact era.

It is important to bear in mind that we are not in search of a Mississippian cultural template to impose on the historic Choctaws. We are looking at the Mississippian tradition to see if certain of its basic cultural structures persisted over the centuries and survived in Choctaw culture. As Charles Hudson, the leading student of southeastern Indian cultures, has described the disastrous impact of European colonization that preceded the rise of the historic Indians of the American South, "We can perhaps use the analogy of a two-story house in a tornado, where the small, ornate upper story is blown away, leaving all the lower rooms more or less intact."[4] How historic groups rebuilt the upper story and renovated or added on to the lower varied from place to place and from time to time.

After Christopher Columbus's landfall in the Caribbean, countless Europeans coasted the shores of the American Southeast in search of slaves to sell, ores to mine, and lands to settle. One of the first encounters between an indigenous society and Europeans occurred in Florida. With a hail of arrows the Calusas beat back Juan Ponce de León's attempt to settle Florida and took his life into the bargain. Other Spanish attempts to colonize the peninsula followed some years later. In 1565 Pedro Menéndez de Avilés founded St. Augustine on the east coast and initiated a prolonged period of contact between Europeans and native Floridians. As a consequence of the contact, a host of diseases, what historian Alfred Crosby has called "virgin soil epidemics," spread among the Florida Indians, who lacked immunity to smallpox, measles, influenza, and other common Old World maladies. The Timicuan population, for example, fell from an estimated 722,000 in 1515 to just over 62,000 in 1625. For Florida as a whole demographer Henry Dobyns has calculated that the native population declined by 95 percent during the first century of contact.[5]

Archaeologists Marvin Smith and Ann Ramenofsky tell a similar tale of disease and death for the Mississippian peoples who inhabited the southern interior after Hernando de Soto and his men bullied their way through the region between 1539 and 1543. Violent conflict between the armored Spanish column and native warriors occurred throughout the march, and the casualties and the collateral damage sustained by towns, homes, and fields sapped the ability of chiefdoms like Coosa, in present-day Alabama, to sustain themselves. When in 1559 Tristán de Luna attempted to build a colony on the Florida gulf coast, a small party of soldiers made their way to Coosa, where they found the chiefdom considerably weakened by its contact with Soto. The chief of the tottering polity pleaded with the Spaniards to help him subdue a recalcitrant tributary chiefdom and thus restore a measure of Coosa's former glory.[6]

The ultimate impact of contact and depopulation, however, is open to debate. Henry Dobyns has written that depopulation led to substantial cultural discontinuity for native peoples between the pre- and postcontact eras. Marvin Smith, however, has proposed that consequent changes in Native American culture must be understood as "deculturation." Smith does not argue that postcontact Indians had less culture than their predecessors. Rather, he suggests that prehistoric cultures simply changed in terms of their aesthetic traditions, social customs, and political and economic organization. In other words, from personal adornment to settlement patterns, the polished culture of the prehistoric Mississippians dulled to a dim reflection of its original brilliance.[7]

In the aftermath of contact many native peoples were no longer viable economic, social, and political entities, and throughout the region remnant groups amalgamated into multiethnic confederations. The Catawbas of South Carolina offer a striking example of the process of amalgamation. Despite the many tongues spoken by the constituent peoples of the Catawba nation and subtle differences in their material cultures, they drew on a common Woodland tradition to unite as a historic people. Far from weak, they enjoyed a period of great power in the Carolina Piedmont. Likewise the Mississippian remnants of the great chiefdom of Coosa and others that Soto had visited combined to form a heterogeneous confederation that became known as the Creek confederacy.[8]

The Choctaws too were an amalgam of remnant Mississippian groups. One group, the Burial Urn people, noted for their underground burials in urns or with a bowl capping the head of the deceased, emerged out of the remains of the Bottle Creek chiefdom of the Mobile delta and of the Moundville chiefdom that had collapsed about the middle of the fourteenth century. The composition, color, and design of their pottery in particular reveal strong lines of continuity between the Mississippian tradition and their own despite the loss of the former's more elaborate stylistic elements. The Burial Urn people probably fled westward to escape the epidemics that followed the Soto expedition's circuitous route, and they provided the original populations of the Concha and Chickasawhay towns of the Southern division of the Choctaws and of the Inholahtas, the Eastern division of the Choctaws.[9]

As they crossed into present-day east-central Mississippi the Burial Urn people met with a scattering of "prairie peoples" who had lived to the northwest and with the remnants of the Plaquemine people who had lived to the southeast in the Yazoo River Valley. (See fig. 1.) Not much is known of the prairie peoples other than that they were associated with the Nanih Waiya mound site and with the Mississippian era Sorrells and Summerville sites. They contributed to the historic populations of the Chickasaw and Chakchiuma Indians as well as to the Western division of the Choctaws—the Imoklashas. The Plaquemine people possessed a hybrid culture that resulted from the mixture of general Mississippian influences and specific local practices. They evolved into the Six Towns of the Southern division. The coming together of the Burial Urn people, the prairie peoples, and the Plaquemine people thus created the Choctaw confederacy.[10]

Face-to-face contact between Choctaws and Europeans, however, did not occur for another century and a half until 17 October 1699, when a Choctaw man and twelve Pascagoulas visited the Biloxi colony that Pierre Le Moyne, Sieur d'Iberville, had planted on the gulf coast. In the summer of 1700 Iberville returned to Louisiana and met with two Choctaws on board his ship *Renommé*. By questioning the visitors and other Indians of the gulf coast, the French commander learned of a grouping of culturally related peoples known collectively as Choctaws, the "men of the Tombigbee River." Although politically disunited, the Choctaws shared a common baseline of Mississippian culture that consisted of four "deep" structures: chiefly political organization, matrilineal kinship, a gendered

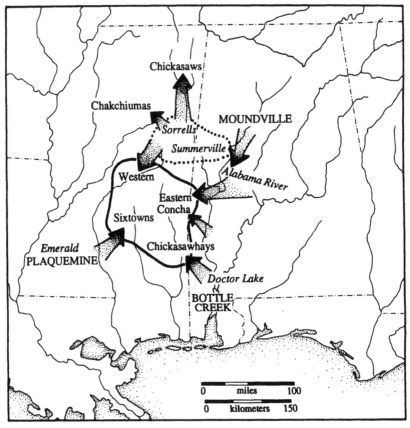

Fig. 1. Formation of the Choctaw confederacy, 1500–1700. Reprinted from *Choctaw Genesis, 1500–1700* by Patricia Galloway, by permission of the University of Nebraska Press. © 1995 by the University of Nebraska Press.

division of labor, and a complex cosmological system based on the sanctity of the sacred circle and the rules and rites necessary to protect it from foreign invasion.[11]

With the exception of the cosmology, none of the other three structures was uniquely Mississippian. Chiefly politics were common around the world, matrilineal kinship can be found among numerous historic North American tribes, and a gendered division of labor is common to many native cultures. The commonness of the three structures, however, should not diminish their particular importance to the case at hand. Just because the Choctaws and the Iroquois, for example, shared similar gender conventions regarding work does not mean that the history of gender and work in each group was the same. Moreover, such general categories are not intended to represent a detailed picture of Mississippian culture. Instead, they are meant to be taken as basic categories of analysis that can help draw certain links between any historic group and its prehistoric predecessors. Only by rooting the ethnohistory of native societies in a theoretical approach characterized by relatively ubiquitous categories of analysis can we begin to appreciate the remarkably diverse histories experienced by groups that, on the surface at least, appeared quite similar.

Chiefly politics characterized the governments of Mississippian societies. Although chiefdoms come in three general types, they should be seen as points along a broad continuum of political organization and authority rather than as discrete categories. At one end of the spectrum simple chiefdoms incorporated a few towns or kinship groups into a polity governed by a chief but with little differentiation between chief and commoners. Intermediate chiefdoms combined several towns or kinship groups into a polity that developed under the guidance of a powerful chief who was differentiated by birth from the common population. Complex paramount chiefdoms like Coosa and Moundville had achieved the greatest level of organization. They integrated numerous simple and intermediate chiefdoms into a multiethnic polity in which the lesser chiefs paid tribute to the paramount chief, who consolidated the polity by placing relatives in positions of power throughout the chiefdom.[12]

Chiefs derived their power in part from their control of the chiefdom's economic resources. The nature and extent of the control, however, have been widely debated. In 1962 anthropologist Elman Service defined a chiefdom as a political system characterized by a reciprocal pattern of exchange. The chiefs received tribute from the commoners in the form of corn, meat, or other foods and redistributed it according to need, whether feeding the people as part of the day-to-day business of government or placating rivals and rewarding allies at sumptuous feasts.[13] Another student of southeastern chiefdoms has proposed that chiefs helped "mitigate natural and cultural disasters" by redistributing stored food in times of distress. Whereas families could feed themselves under normal conditions, droughts, hurricanes, early frosts, or warfare often forced the population to draw on the communal resources that the chief held in his charge.[14] In addition to collecting food surpluses, chiefs commanded community labor at various times. They organized workers to build mounds and other public works, maintained stables of artisans to produce high-quality goods, and fielded armies to expand their power and defend them from all comers.[15] So long as the chief redistributed subsistence goods and the population continued to provide food and labor, his rule was secure. But if the reciprocity of the relationship broke down, so too would the chiefdom.

Other scholars have challenged the centrality of redistribution of subsistence resources as a defining characteristic of Mississippian chiefdoms. Archaeologists Christopher S. Peebles and Susan M. Kus have concluded that redistribution of subsistence goods neither united independent communities into chiefdoms nor universally characterized the prehistoric chiefdoms of the Southeast. Subsequent investigations of the Summerville chiefdom in the Tombigbee River Valley by John Blitz have supported Peebles and Kus's argument that Mississippian chiefly power was not predicated on redistribution of corn, meat, and so forth.[16]

Despite debate over the nature of the chiefs' relation to subsistence goods, scholars agree that they exerted decisive control over the flow of exotic prestige goods within and between chiefdoms. Shell gorgets inscribed with religious imagery, catlinite pipes, copper celts, and eagle feathers are some of the exotic goods that circulated throughout the Mississippian Southeast. Chiefs deployed them as sacred objects to support an ideology of chiefly control that was justified by the polity's public religion and ceremonial aesthetic.[17] The prestige goods enabled them, in the words of one archaeologist, to "make decisions based on their own political agendas while acting within another set of cultural norms to which they owe[d] their access to power."[18] As with subsistence goods, however, interruptions in the flow of exotic prestige items imperiled the chiefs' government.

Each of the Choctaw divisions shared certain fundamental characteristics with intermediate chiefdoms. Chiefs differentiated from commoners by birth governed the Eastern and the Western divisions and the Concha, Chickasawhay, Six Towns clusters of the Southern division. In the 1740s a French observer made detailed observations about the nature of the Choctaw social and political hierarchy. Within each division, a "grand chief" presided over a contingent of peace and war chiefs. Below each of these chiefs were the *tascamingoutchy*, who were junior to the war chiefs, and the *tichou-mingo*, who were junior to the peace chiefs. In addition to the hierarchy of political offices, the male population was divided into four orders that allowed for some social advancement based on merit: whether women were likewise divided was not recorded. At the highest level were the chiefs, or *minkos.* "Beloved men" ranked second, and warriors were third. The fourth category was reserved for men who had not engaged in warfare or who had killed only a woman or a child.[19]

"Chiefdoms," one archaeologist has written, "are first and foremost kin-based societies," and kinship, the second structure of Choctaw culture, tied Choctaws together across divisional boundaries as the different chiefs could never do.[20] Unfortunately, the archaeological record of Mississippian societies does not reveal the details of their kinship organization, but historical documents of the early contact period indicate that they probably followed the same general conventions as did the historic Choctaws.

Choctaw kinship was matrilineal, and it affected everything from descent to land distribution and use. Just as the nation identified with the "Great Mother" mound, children identified with their mothers' clans. Within the clan, the mother and the maternal uncles, not the biological father, raised children to adulthood. Since habitation was matrilocal, husbands moved in with their wives' families. Clan rules also patterned social behavior outside the family and the home. Marriage between clan members was taboo, and each clan was responsible for avenging the deaths of members. Among most southeastern peoples matrilineal clans were important social groupings, but historical Choctaw sources are either contradictory or ambiguous on how many clans there were, how they functioned, and how they influenced political and social organization.[21]

There is more evidence to describe the operation of the two Choctaw *iksas,* or moieties—large groupings of individual clans. Moiety members, like clan members, shared kinship ties and obligations and certain social, political, and ritual responsibilities. Like the Creeks and the Chickasaws, the Choctaws had two moieties. The war chiefs came from the red *iksa,* and their counterparts, the civil chiefs, came from the white one. In addition to defining political roles, the Choctaw moieties were responsible for avenging the murder of fellow *iksa* members. At feasts members of the two groups ate separately, and men and women had to marry into the other *iksa.*[22] Archaeologist John Blitz has proposed a direct link between the Choctaw moieties and the Mississippian tradition. The prevalence of the colors red and white in Mississippian artwork, he argues, suggests that Mississippian societies may have also been divided between red moieties linked to warfare and white moieties linked to civil government.[23]

Funerals offered the most conspicuous operation of the moiety system. At their earliest contact with Europeans, Choctaws did not bury the dead. Instead they constructed a wooden scaffold fifteen to twenty feet tall directly opposite the door of the deceased's home. The body was laid out atop the scaffold, covered with a blanket, and allowed to decompose. The period of decomposition constituted a time of transition between life and death, and while the flesh rotted the spirit of the deceased wandered about the town in an anxious state. To placate the fretful spirit, relatives left food outside the home and kept a fire burning to ward off the chill of night. Mourners cried loudly to make it clear that they felt the loss.[24]

When it was sufficiently rotted, bone pickers of the opposite moiety from the deceased took down the body, for it had finally passed from life to death. While the spirit journeyed to the afterlife, the bone pickers stripped the decayed flesh from the bones with fingernails grown long especially for the task and threw the fetid remains into a sacred fire. They painted the skull red, bundled the bones in a box made of cane, and presented the package to the deceased's clan for interment in the town bonehouse. After the interment, a great feast was held to end the mourning. First one *iksa* would mourn while the other danced, and the following day they would switch roles.[25] Death thus highlighted both the kinship differences and social interdependence of the moieties, while the bonehouses established the long-standing claims of lineages, towns, and moieties to the land Aba had given them.[26]

While chiefly government defined the political order and matrilineal kinship characterized many social relations, gender divisions structured the Mississippian and the Choctaw economies. Some theorists have used the phrase "gender stratification" to describe the division of labor between genders and the greater prestige that was usually attached to male work and the lack of prestige accorded female work.[27] In the case of the Mississippians and the Choctaws, "stratification" rings hollow because there is no evidence that women's work as farmers was held in lower esteem than men's work as hunters and warriors, or vice versa. For these reasons scholars now use the term complementarity to describe gender relations among most Native American societies. Activities like hunting and fighting, for example, carried men far and wide and brought them into contact with outsiders. Women, however, lived their lives in the fields and households that made up the many towns and chiefdoms of the Mississippian countryside.[28]

How men and women in complementary societies partitioned economic as well as political power and influence is one of the most pressing questions confronting students of Native American history. Because of their association with government and warfare, men controlled diplomatic affairs and dominated political offices. Vested with the official power to make decisions on behalf of the communities they represented, men held what scholars have defined as "authority." Lacking access to formal expressions of power, women possessed "influence," the power that came with control of houses, domestic property, and land.[29]

Abundant archaeological evidence shows that women farmed the land in Mississippian times. For example, the Birger figurine excavated from Cahokia, a Mississippian site in western Illinois, depicts a kneeling woman encircled by a snake, a symbol of fertility and the Underworld, into which she has sunk the blade of her digging stick. (See fig. 2.) Another figurine associated with the Spiro site in Oklahoma depicts a woman preparing to pound corn in a mortar. Carbon dating has placed at roughly the tenth century the time when corn became the staple for several groups living in the Lower Mississippi Valley. The crop grew best in alluvial areas where Mississippian farmers had access to sandy, well-drained soils that could be worked easily with digging sticks, so towns tended to congregate on floodplains.[30]

The remnant groups that made up the Choctaws had fled inland away from the river floodplains, so they had to settle for less fertile soils. Nevertheless corn was their staff of life, and women continued to enjoy a special relationship with the plant. According to Choctaw oral tradition, corn came to them from a crow that had flown up from the south. The bird dropped a grain at the feet of a little girl, who asked, "What is this?" Her mother came to investigate and determined that it was corn. "In this way," the story told, "the forefathers of the Choctaws got their seed corn."[31] After the men had cleared the fields, Choctaw women raised one corn crop in family gardens and a second in communal fields that ran along the creek and river bottoms near their towns.[32] One historian has estimated that women harvested two-thirds of the Choctaw diet from their fields. Not surprisingly, an English traveler described them as a "nation of farmers."[33]

Just as Mississippian artifacts portray women as farmers, they portray men as warriors. Fighting and hunting complemented one another and organized much of male life. In the fall and winter groups of men

Fig. 2. Birger figurine, 1100 A.D. This figure is reproduced with the permission of the Illinois Transportation Archaeological Research Program, University of Illinois.

set out from their homes to hunt white-tailed deer, bears, and other animals. Frequently they established temporary hunting camps in the borderlands that surrounded their towns, where the women who had accompanied them cooked meals and dressed the skins of the slain animals. At home women made the bones, antlers, hides, and meat of the deer into tools, clothing, and food. The men's relationship with animals, however, extended beyond hunting. In a ball game similar to lacrosse that the southeastern Indians considered the "little brother to war," men illustrated the relationship dramatically by affixing wildcat tails to the backs of their breechclouts and tying white bird feathers to their ball sticks. The players believed such decoration imbued them with the ferocity of the wildcat and the swiftness of the bird.[34]

Men applied the lessons learned on the ballfield to their forays on the battlefield during the spring and summer. Warriors fought to avenge deaths and to expand the power of their chiefdoms by conquering neighbors and forcing them to pay tribute to the chief. To better their prospects in conflict, Choctaw war chiefs tapped into Aba's power by using stuffed animal skins to provide divine guidance for the war parties. Should the talisman fall "or any other ways be disordered in position," wrote one European observer, "the expedition is frustrated." Success in warfare meant an increase in prestige and power, whereas defeat or cowardice in battle marked a man as unworthy. "He loses prestige," wrote Jean-Bernard Bossu, "[and] no one has any further confidence in his leadership."[35]

The war chiefs who relied on stuffed animal skins to guide them to victory believed, as did all Choctaws, that metaphysical forces influenced the outcome of every action. Reconstructing a belief system from artifacts is fraught with difficulty, but the few historic accounts of Mississippian religion point to certain similarities with Choctaws' worldview. Sun worship, specific cosmological motifs, concerns over purity and pollution, and the belief that humans could use metaphysical forces for their own ends characterized the cosmology of the Mississippians and of the Choctaws and constituted the fourth structure of Choctaw culture.[36]

The world the Mississippians lived in was structurally complicated. They divided the world into three levels. The Upper World was home to the sun, whose fiery light brought order to the world. In contrast, the Underworld was home to the moon, water, and disorder, the antitheses of the sun's fire and order, as well as the creative powers of fertility. This World stood between the fire of the Upper World and the water of the Underworld, and its survival required a balance between the sun and the moon, the powers of order and of creation, and the forces of light and of darkness. In more practical terms, if the corn crops flourished in the Mississippians' and in the Choctaws' fields, they owed the bounty to a perfect balance between the warm rays of the Upper World and the fertile earth of the Underworld.[37]

Choctaws sought to manage cosmological imbalances and disorders through magic and religion. The term magic has pejorative connotations, but it should be taken to mean action directed to produce a specific and limited end through the use of metaphysical powers. Its operation was confined to the sacred circle in which the Choctaws lived, a place where their social and cultural conventions defined the parameters of acceptable and unacceptable social conduct. Magic was, in effect, a social discourse through which witches and doctors waged an interminable struggle over the community's health and good fortune. Daily life was thus acted out in moral spaces where average folk tried to follow Aba's law, witches sought to break it, and doctors sought to combat the efforts of the witches.[38] During his tenure with the culturally similar Chickasaw nation in the 1740s, trader James Adair witnessed an old man using magic to secure his house "from the power of the evil spirits . . . and from witches, and wizards who go about in dark night, in the shape of bears, hogs, and wolves, to spoil people."[39] To counter the malevolence of witches and wizards and the threats that lurked in the forms of animals, doctors used herbal medicines and rituals. Magic thus directed action that brought the agent psychological if not material satisfaction. For this reason the expectations and behaviors associated with magic were completely different from the public and communal values of religion.[40]

Whereas magic explained isolated events, religion was connected to the broader patterns that ordered the sacred circle in which the Choctaws lived.[41] Aba was the most important figure in Choctaw religion, and as archaeologist Chester DePratter has noted, it comes as no surprise that a society dependent on farming would regard the sun with such awe. Known also as Hushtahli, Sun as Divine Mover, and Ishtahullo Chito, Great Sun Priest, Aba oversaw and ordered the Choctaw world through his earthly agent, sacred fire. Indians followed numerous rules when kindling, tending, or extinguishing fires, and as James Adair remarked, they were "firmly persuaded that the divine omnipresent Spirit of fire and light resides on earth, in their annual sacred fire while it is unpolluted."[42]

To avoid polluting themselves, their world, and their fires, Choctaws followed numerous taboos. Most concerned individuals in transitional states, such as menstruating women. During their menses, Choctaw women segregated themselves from town life and lived in huts built specifically for the purpose. What went on in the huts in unknown, but ethnohistorian Patricia Galloway has theorized that they were meeting points for large numbers of women who undoubtedly performed special rituals.[43] When a woman began her stay in the hut she kindled a new fire, because taking some of the fire that burned in her own house would pollute it. Should she violate the sacred fire, Choctaws believed sickness would spread throughout the land. Men avoided contact with such women at all costs because, as one Frenchman noted, "the men think that if they approach a menstruating woman they will become ill and will have bad luck in battle." As the vital force of life, blood had the potential to pollute everything if it was not managed carefully.[44]

The stain of pollution, however, could be removed through religious ritual. Each year, when the first corn crop ripened, Mississippians and their historic descendants gathered at annual green corn ceremonies to absolve themselves of the pollution they had caused by breaking Aba's law.[45] Evidence for the Choctaw celebration of the green corn ceremony is contradictory. According to James Adair, the Choctaws of the 1740s had made "no annual atonement for sin" for several years. Antoine Simon Le Page du Pratz seconded Adair's remarks some years later, observing that the ceremony had lapsed "since their numbers have been greatly diminished." Whatever effects disease, slave raids, or other consequences of contact with Europeans might have had, the Choctaws appear to have resurrected the ceremony by the latter half of the eighteenth century, if indeed it had ever fallen into disuse. In 1773 William Bartram heard that Choctaws held the celebration. "When a town celebrates the [green corn ceremony]," the naturalist recorded, "they collect all their worn-out cloths and other despicable things, sweep and cleanse their houses, squares, and the whole town, of their filth." The ceremony may have lapsed again by the early nineteenth century, because Reverend Alfred Wright claimed that the Choctaws "have heard of what is termed the *green corn dance* among the Creeks, but deny having any knowledge that such a practice existed among themselves." Wright, however, also regretted that a "difficulty in ascertaining their ancient traditions, arises from their unwillingness to divulge them, especially to foreigners."[46] Despite the ambiguous history of the ceremony among the Choctaws, its symbolism nonetheless occupied a central place in their belief system. According to nineteenth-century Choctaws, the ceremony was "a sacred religious duty" that "was held in honor of, and to conciliate and secure a continuation of favors from the great sun."[47]

Several other ceremonies involved imagery similar to the green corn ceremony and served to solidify the Choctaws' relationship with Aba, the sanctity of their sacred circle, and their sense of a common identity and history. The night before ball games men and women gathered around sacred fires that may have represented their hometowns or clans. While the women sat in circles around the fires and sang, the men stood in an outer circle and set a musical cadence with their *chichicouas*, gourd rattles filled with hundreds of small pebbles.[48] Some of the ceremonies they performed might have included the turtle dance or the tick dance. "A life in the wilderness," sang the turtle dancers, "with plenty of meat, fish, fowl and the [turtle dance], is far better than our old homes, and the corn, and the fruit, and the heart melting fear of the dreadful [Europeans]." The tick dance celebrated a Choctaw ambush of a European exploring party early in the contact period. To commemorate their victory over the boatload of Europeans, the first tick dancers traced out a sacred circle in the high grass on the riverbank adjacent to the boat and symbolically stomped on the ticks that crawled in the grass within their circle.[49]

The recurring themes of sun, fire, and circles in religious ceremonies point to strong links between Choctaw and Mississippian cosmology, particularly the division of This World into two distinct places: the sacred circle that encompassed the Choctaws' homes, fields, and familiar surroundings and the outside world that was characterized by disorder and profanity and inhabited by dangerous creatures. In particular, the circle and cross motif, perhaps the most prominent motif in Mississippian art, transcended religion and served as a schematic map of the Choctaw universe. The circle, an image of the sun, described the limits of the Choctaw sacred circle. The cross represented the four cardinal directions, each of which had meaning. The north was home to cold weather, and the south gave rise to warm weather. Light emerged in the east and disappeared into the west, the land of darkness. The cross that overlay the circle represented the order that was subject to Aba's power and maintained by his people's proper behavior.[50]

The circle and cross motif cropped up in all sorts of daily activities. Rainmakers, for example, drew on the image to ensure rainfall. After a spell of drought, the rainmaker left the inhabited settlements for the dark, uncultivated, and uncontrollable forest. Here, beyond the limits of human habitation, he ritually recreated the ordered world of the sacred circle by clearing brush and debris from a circular piece of ground and marking the circle with a symmetrical cross. He then stood over the image and for four days and four nights invoked the powers of the wind and water spirits to restore the rain.[51]

The floor plan of winter homes further replicated the symbols conjured by the rainmaker. The homes consisted of a circular wattle-and-daub wall topped by a conical thatched roof. Support structures inside the round dwelling partitioned the living space into four equal parts. A fire flickered in the middle of the house where the women cooked, and its light illuminated various activities. When the family gathered to eat, they partook from the same bowl and sat in a circle, again confirming the basic order of life.[52]

Outside the rainmaker's circle and beyond the confines of home lay the disorder of the forest. Similarly, outside the sacred circle loomed the outside world, a place where the regular rules of life no longer applied.

Passage through the stark boundaries that separated the sacred circle from the outside world entailed a simultaneous transformation from order to disorder. Men caught in this transitional state, like menstruating women, had to isolate themselves before and after crossing the boundaries of the circle because of the dangerous powers that attached to them. Before leaving their towns to wage war, warriors spent several days performing certain rites to secure divine favor and ensure that their passage into the outside world would be successful. After they returned from fighting, they confined themselves in communal sweat lodges to purify themselves with medicine and to regain the balance they had lost in shedding blood. To signify the end of the state of war and the reclamation of balance, they were daubed from head to foot with white pigment. When traveling out of the nation to go to Mobile for trade and councils, men also stopped at a place called Boukaille to put on their war paint before they entered the European outpost. The rituals that accompanied the passing of boundaries between the two worlds reflected the Choctaws' conception of the region as a highly differentiated place and stressed the importance of respecting these boundaries to maintain order in their world.[53]

The importance of boundaries and the circle and cross motif cropped up most frequently in the decoration of ceremonial gorgets worn by Mississippian chiefs or priests in sacred ceremonies. Figure 3 depicts such a gorget, and it shows that the space beyond the orderly sacred circle was filled with horrible anomalous creatures who embodied the chaos and power of the outside world. By mixing the Underworld (a serpent's body), the Upper World (an eagle's wings), and This World (a panther's head), the creatures violated the separation of the planes that was necessary if balance was to be maintained. Moreover, the representations of male and female genitalia in the circular and elliptical designs that covered their serpentine bodies suggests the equally terrible consequences of mixing genders. Such monsters offered the people a terrifying reminder of the need to follow prescribed social conventions to save their world and themselves.[54]

From the sleepy rivers and fetid swamps that represented pathways between This World and the Underworld to the dark arboreal embrace of the forests beyond the pale of human habitation, the outside world that surrounded the Choctaws was home to many terrible creatures.[55] Those who ventured beyond the circle's safe confines could expect to encounter monsters like the Nalusa Falaya, the Long Evil Being. Its beady eyes, set

Fig. 3. Mississippian gorget, Spiro Mound. This figure is
reproduced with the permission of the Missouri
Archaeological Society.

in a small, shriveled head, peered over a protruding nose and searched
the night for hunters. When it spotted prey the monster crept up behind
hunting parties and called to them. Those who turned to look fainted
from fright at the sight of its face, and Nalusa Falaya pricked them with a
magic thorn to transform them into evil beings. Less dangerous was the
Kashehotopalo, which juxtaposed gender and species in a truly hideous
form. Perched on the legs of a deer, a man's trunk extended from the waist
and was topped by an evil-looking head. From its wrinkled mouth came
a woman's cry that terrified all who heard it. Other creatures infested the
thickets and waters around the Choctaw circle, creatures that with one
glance could force travelers to lose their way or draw them into pools and
streams for a bewitched life in the Underworld.[56]

Much as the border monsters could use their powers to manipulate
Choctaws, so too could Choctaws take from them miraculous powers to do
both good and evil. Kwanokasha lived in a cave in a "rough and broken
part of the country." Although a man, he was no larger than a small
child. Perhaps his size aided him in his quest, for he traveled the forest in

search of young children. When he captured a victim, Kwanokasha took the boy or girl to his cave, where three spirits lived. Each spirit presented a different gift: one extended a knife, the other held out poisonous herbs, and the third offered "good medicine." A child who took the knife would grow up to be a murderer. One who fancied the poisonous herbs would "never be able to cure or otherwise help others." If the child chose the medicinal herbs, the spirits would teach him or her to be a doctor. Afterward the child returned home and grew up to be either a criminal, a failure, or a doctor.[57]

The powers associated with transitional states, with crossing borders, and with interaction with witches and anomalous creatures lent the Choctaw world a dynamism that demanded constant vigilance. To maintain balance between the three worlds and to ensure order within the sacred circle, chiefs had to redistribute goods, men and women had to follow the rules of kinship and do the work appropriate for each gender, and all Choctaws had to avoid polluting themselves and their society and to propitiate Aba.

Europeans challenged the delicate state of affairs that characterized life in precontact America, what one historian has called the "Indians' Old World."[58] Reporting a conversation with Amoroleck, a Mannahoac Indian of the Virginia Piedmont, English adventurer John Smith wrote that "they heard we were a people come from under the world, to take their world from them."[59] Post-Mississippian peoples like the Choctaws and the Chickasaws knew as much. In the 1740s, the Terrapin Chief, a Chickasaw war leader, implored the Choctaws to join his people to resist the encroachments of English traders and settlers and to protect "their holy places, and holy things, from the ambitious views of the impure and covetous English peoples."[60] The Underworld was running amok, and the Choctaws' subsequent struggle to maintain the balance and purity of the sacred circle in the face of European colonization brought their culture into open conflict with an alien way of life. To defend themselves and their world, they sought to mediate and to manage contact with the Europeans and the disorderly powers they had brought with them—powers that, if not checked, threatened to abrogate the sacred charter made between Aba and his children at the foot of Nanih Waiya and to divert them from the bright path on which the sun had set them.

CHAPTER TWO

The Emergence of a
Choctaw Polity, 1700–1805

> The Choctaw nation is divided into three districts; each district governed by a
> head chief, and various subordinate chiefs or captains. Each district is politically
> independent of the other and they are bound by no other tie than that of
> kinship and a common origin. Neither of the three head chiefs considers
> himself responsible to the others, and they acknowledge no common ruler.
> James McDonald to Thomas L. McKenney, 27 April 1826

SOMETIME in the sixteenth century the Choctaws emerged from the destruction and death that had followed the Spanish exploration of the Southeast. Europeans did not return to the region in force until 1699, when Pierre Le Moyne, Sieur d'Iberville, founded Fort Maurepas, also known as Fort Biloxi, on the gulf coast of present-day Mississippi. The Choctaws regarded his arrival with a mixture of trepidation and relief. The abandoned towns, empty homes, and overgrown fields that dotted the countryside were grim reminders of earlier epidemics brought by European sojourners. But at the same time, Chickasaw slave raiders were making life miserable for the Choctaws. Since the 1690s English traders had armed the Chickasaws with flintlock muskets and urged them to raid the Choctaws and other groups for slaves, which the English transported back to Charles Towne for shipment and sale to plantations in the Caribbean. The Choctaws could counter the raids only with bows and arrows. Both the Choctaws and Iberville perceived the conflict as an opportunity for the French to assert their presence in the region and confound English aspirations to dominate the interior of North America, and they acted accordingly.[1]

In the fall of 1701 a group of Choctaws sought French support for their struggles against the Chickasaw slave raiders. In response, Iberville

26

dispatched Henri de Tonti to both groups in early 1702. Worn down by years of fighting, the Choctaws needed guns to survive, and they welcomed as something of a savior the lone Frenchman who had come to their towns. After finishing his business among the Choctaws, Tonti journeyed north to the Chickasaws and convinced several chiefs to follow him to Mobile. Three Choctaw chiefs representing the three divisions joined the party on its return through the Choctaw towns, and they accompanied Tonti and the Chickasaws to Mobile. On 26 March 1702 Iberville welcomed both delegations with gifts of two hundred pounds of gunpowder, two hundred pounds of bullets, twelve guns, and assorted other goods. In spite of the gifts, Iberville failed to pull the Chickasaws into the French orbit, but the conference nonetheless signaled the engagement of an imperial struggle over the Lower Mississippi Valley. The French entered the fray on the side of the Choctaws, and generous gifts of guns, gunpowder, and bullets restored the regional balance of power.[2] Well-armed Choctaw warriors turned back the Chickasaw raiders, and they called their new weapons *tanampo,* after the verb *tanampi,* "to be at war."[3]

What Iberville had failed to see, however, was that the three Choctaw chiefs did not represent a cohesive political entity. Among the people known as Choctaws, the Western Imoklashas, the Eastern Inholahtas, and the Southern Conchas, Chickasawhays, and Six Towns functioned as autonomous intermediate chiefdoms. Although culturally similar and related through kinship, in the absence of any overarching form of political organization, each group pursued its own interests in its own ways, and the chiefs of each polity based their relationships with the French and the English on the same principles of reciprocal exchange and chiefly authority that had characterized the government of Mississippian chiefdoms, except that guns, ammunition, and cloth had replaced shell gorgets, copper celts, and catlinite pipes as the currencies of chiefly power.

To obtain goods, chiefs had to offer Europeans two things—marketable commodities like deerskins, and soldiers to fight the wars of the colonial powers. Not surprisingly, the chiefs joined in the European struggles for empire, but Iberville and the officials, traders, and military men who followed him never fully understood the fractious and often violent competition between the chiefs for access to and control of European trade goods. What they viewed as native perfidy instead represented the chiefs' cogent and rational plans to play off European interests and augment their power in the process.

Native Americans used play-off strategies throughout North America wherever more than one European power vied for their support. Chiefs who followed the strategy played one interest against another to obtain favorable trade concessions and to forestall the ability of either power to impose its will on them or their commoners. Play-off, however, rarely produced harmony among native societies. Rival factions coalesced around different trade interests, and the consequences could be disruptive and often violent. Still, as long as there were multiple partners for trade and alliance, the strategy could be effective.[4]

By the end of the eighteenth century the French, the English, and the Spanish had retreated from the Lower Mississippi Valley, and the Choctaws confronted alone the expansionist United States. At the same time, leaders had begun to cede large swaths of their homeland to pay off the debts incurred by their play-off policies, and American settlement of the region brought an end to the diplomatic strategy. Chiefs had to devise new strategies for concerted political action that required a level of cooperation they had never before attained. Faced with the piecemeal dissolution of their homeland, by the early 1800s the divisional chiefs began to conceive of the Choctaws as more than a congeries of culturally related kinsmen, and the cycle of chiefdom formation that had reached its nadir in the sixteenth century began to rise again.

The gifts with which Iberville had welcomed the Choctaw chiefs to Mobile in 1702 established the patterns of exchange and support that characterized the Franco-Choctaw relationship throughout the first half of the eighteenth century. To the French the gifts laid the foundations of an alliance whereby the Choctaws would provide them with military aid, food, and deerskins. Defense and provisions were essential to the survival of the fledgling colony, but the Indian trade, as Iberville's experience in New France had proved, would make Louisiana an important part of the Sun King's empire—or so he hoped. Iberville's brother, Jean-Baptiste Le Moyne, Sieur de Bienville, estimated that the Choctaws alone could provide fifteen thousand skins a year, but his optimism proved unfounded.[5]

The Choctaws were more interested in reciprocity than in profit, and to them the alliance fulfilled many of their expectations. Having come from a patrilineal society, Iberville declared himself the "father" of his Choctaw "children" in hopes of establishing a firm line of authority and obedience between him and his charges. In the matrilineal society of the Choctaws, however, fathers were hardly the stern paternal figures that Iberville had in mind. Choctaw fathers indulged their children with gifts but left discipline and control to the mother and her brothers. Unaware of the particular kinship role played by Choctaw fathers, Iberville expected them to follow his every dictate. The Choctaws, however, expected Iberville to give them gifts.[6] Bienville in particular was galled by "the insolence with which they pretended to consider as tribute the presents which the King is so kind to grant them."[7]

The kinship discourse between the French and the Choctaws centered on annual visits paid by the Choctaws to the colonial governor in Mobile, where the fictive kinsmen exchanged gifts and renewed friendships. Chiefs took back to their towns guns, cloth, glass beads, and other goods and distributed them to their constituents as a demonstration of their power and generosity. For those who received the goods in exchange for their support of the chief, the items conferred the prestige essential to a range of successful social interactions. According to one French observer, for example, to show their fitness for marriage young men had to give glass trade beads to their prospective bride's mother and a breechclout to her maternal uncle.[8]

Just as chiefs used gifts as expressions of political authority, they exerted firm control over the French traders who came into their towns and over the distribution of their trade goods. Traders who traveled into the nation entered the house of the town chief, whose wife probably offered *tomfulla*, a hospitality dish made of fermented corn that Choctaws commonly shared with visitors. Afterward the chief and the trader silently smoked tobacco together, and the host asked his guest, "You are come then?" On receiving an affirmative reply, the chief informed the townsfolk that a trader had arrived, telling them what he had brought to trade and what the exchange rates would be. In 1721, for example, Choctaws could purchase a foot's length of limbourg cloth for four dressed deerskins, while a musket cost twenty skins. To ensure the trader's complicity in his role as a broker, chiefs often gave important traders a portion of the gifts they had received from colonial officials, which the traders then sold for their own profit.[9]

Chiefs used trade to bolster their authority and prestige, but the French sought to use it to manipulate them. By consolidating the distribution of trade goods in the hands of a few leaders the French called "medal chiefs," colonial officials believed they could create a hierarchy of chiefs dependent on their largesse and amenable to following their orders. Accordingly, in 1738 Bernard Diron d'Artaguette, the commandant of Mobile, encouraged each chief to share trade goods and gifts "only with his relatives or his partizans."[10] The policy caused problems, however, because the French trade was concentrated in the Eastern division and the Concha towns of the Southern division, to the exclusion of the Western division and the other town clusters in the south.[11]

The disparity in price and quality between French and English goods further complicated matters. "In the campaign that was made against the Chickasaws," Bienville reported in 1736, "the Choctaws took advantage of the need that we had of them to ask [me] to put the trade with them in merchandise on the basis of that which they carry on with the British." French prices were so high, chiefs argued, that they "could not obtain enough peltries to procure what was necessary for their wives and children."[12]

Complaints about expensive French goods and threats to turn to the English signaled that the chiefs were engaging the Europeans in a "play-off." Eastern chiefs had generally overseen the alliance with the French, but in times of war the French also patronized chiefs and warriors from the Western division. During the several campaigns against the Chickasaws in the 1730s and 1740s, colonial officials paid warriors one gun, one pound of powder, and two pounds of bullets for every Chickasaw they scalped. One Western warrior in particular, Red Shoe, parlayed his success in the Chickasaw wars into a position of power whereby he challenged the peacetime trade monopoly of the Eastern chiefs. But Red Shoe sought a more liberal trade than the French could offer, and the Eastern chiefs were reluctant to share the trade with him. Faced with such opposition, he attempted to make peace with the Chickasaws and establish a relationship with the English traders stationed in their towns.[13]

In the fall of 1734 Red Shoe and a group of his partisans journeyed to Carolina to dine with colonial officials and discuss trade. The talks came to nothing, so after his return he and Alibamon Mingo, chief of the Chickasawhays, invited four English traders into the Choctaw towns and offered an escort of warriors to protect their train of packhorses. But such impromptu arrangements failed to satisfy Red Shoe. In 1738 he and eight other Western chiefs set out again for Charles Towne, where they successfully concluded a "Treaty of Peace and Commerce" with the governor that opened up a more regular and systematic trade.

For whatever reason, however, Red Shoe and Alibamon Mingo began to bicker over the new trade soon after the first goods began to flow into their towns. Red Shoe headed back to Charles Towne to sort things out and to reassure the governor of his fealty, but his imperial benefactors withdrew their support. On arriving in the Western towns he denounced the English and ordered his warriors to plunder the traders and their trading posts.[14]

Not surprisingly, Red Shoe's fitful relationship with the English angered Bienville, and in 1740 he withheld the war chief's gifts during the annual meeting in Mobile. "Affected with disgrace and with the prospect of losing . . . the authority he had in his own nation," one French official noted, Red Shoe tried to regain French favor by attacking the Chickasaws. Bienville rewarded the chief's about-face by restoring his gifts and presenting him with a medal, but the governor was hardly convinced of Red Shoe's commitment to the French.[15] Bienville warned his successor, Pierre de Rigaud, Marquis de Vaudreuil, about Red Shoe's unwillingness to abandon his hopes of English trade, and Vaudreuil took every opportunity to humiliate Red Shoe and belittle his authority. When the chief failed to attend yet another conference in Mobile, Vaudreuil cut off his supply of presents.[16]

Ostracized by the French governor, Red Shoe again sought an exclusive alliance with the Chickasaws and the English. Not all Choctaws, however, shared his attraction to the English. In spite of an earlier interest in trading with their former foes, Alibamon Mingo and several Eastern chiefs resented the upstart war leader's interference in their relationship with the French and his threat to their power. The most influential war chief in the Eastern division, Chokoulactas, sided with Alibamon Mingo, and the two men cast their lot with Vaudreuil against Red Shoe and his allies in the Western towns and in the Six Towns.[17]

As the two factions pursued different courses of action, the tensions of the Anglo-French rivalry in North America came into play, making a dispute between chiefs into a colonial affair of considerable dimensions. Unwilling to lose Indian clients to their opponents, each colonial power urged its Choctaw allies to make war on the others. The kinship bonds between the divisions, however, militated against open civil war. Instead of killing one another, Choctaws focused their hostilities on other native groups allied with either the French or the English. But warfare through surrogates failed to satisfy French and English ambitions to wound one another's colonial enterprises. At the urging of colonial officials and traders, the Choctaws grudgingly began fighting each other.

The hostilities stemmed from a 1746 meeting between Red Shoe and a Chickasaw chief named Mongoulachas Mingo at which they renewed a peace they had concluded at the end of 1745. The accord proved ineffective, however, because the Eastern chiefs refused to abide by it. Indeed, Chokoulactas led a sortie against the Chickasaws in the summer of 1746, and on 4 August he followed up the attacks by ordering the murder of a Chickasaw diplomat and his wife who had gone to the Western division to firm up the flagging peace between those Choctaws and the Chickasaws.[18]

To assure their new Chickasaw and English friends of his fidelity, one of Red Shoe's allies, Matahachito, countered Chokoulactas's assassinations by ordering the murder of three Frenchmen, an act the chief likened to killing rats that had come to eat his chickens. The order was carried out on 14 August 1746, and Red Shoe dispatched portions of the scalps to his allies to prove his loyalty and his power. In retaliation for the murders, Vaudreuil demanded the heads of the three Western chiefs he believed were responsible—Matahachito, Abekimataha, and Opayechito—and he ordered Alibamon Mingo to kill Red Shoe. Revenge on outsiders was a normal part of life, but retaliation against fellow "beloved people," no matter their political persuasions, for the deaths of outsiders was unprecedented. Alibamon Mingo understandably refused to kill either Red Shoe or any of his supporters, but Vaudreuil continued to pressure him to avenge the traders' deaths. To this end the governor threatened to withhold merchandise from the chief until Red Shoe was dead.[19] Despite the harm such a move would do to Alibamon Mingo's prestige and authority among the Chickasawhays and the Eastern Choctaws, the chief continued to "speak well" of the French.[20]

The Western chiefs, meanwhile, "declared war against the French" and began to look for a regular supply of guns, ammunition, and other goods from traders based in Savannah and Charles Towne.[21] In April 1747 Red Shoe's brother Pooscoos led fifteen chiefs to the South Carolina capital to renew the treaty Red Shoe had agreed to seven years earlier. On 18 April Pooscoos concluded a new agreement whereby the English pledged to supply the Western towns in exchange for the capture of the French outpost Fort Tombecbé. Soon several English traders set out for the Western towns, and the advantage gained by Red Shoe's faction raised the stakes of the conflict. In June 1747 Red Shoe helped lead one of the caravans from Carolina to his home village of Conchitto, and on the night of the twenty-third, while the caravan rested, someone sneaked up on the sleeping chief, stabbed him in the stomach, and slipped away unseen. Who killed the chief is unknown, but his death ignited bitter warfare between the two factions, and over the next two years each side razed the other's homes and burned their fields.[22]

The Eastern chiefs were hardly enthusiastic about the war. They despaired of having to kill "their blood," "their relatives," and "their friends," but they held the upper hand throughout most of the conflict. In a rare reversal of form it was the English and not the French who were slow to deliver supplies and ammunition to their Indian allies.[23] Delegations from the Western towns regularly visited Charles Towne to beg for more guns and ammunition. Pooscoos, who succeeded Red Shoe as leader of the anglophile faction, feared that without the goods his supporters would abandon him and turn to the French. Without weapons the Western warriors could not fight effectively, and the Eastern warriors decimated Pooscoos's forces. In December 1749 a triumphant Alibamon Mingo presented Vaudreuil with the scalps of one hundred Western warriors as well as the skulls of three of their most prominent chiefs to silence the crying blood of the three dead Frenchmen. Soon thereafter Vaudreuil's offer to pardon the anglophile faction convinced many to end the war. A squad of French marines led a final assault on the Western towns that had refused to surrender and brought the war to a conclusion on 15 November 1750.[24]

Though peace had come to the Choctaws, neither division was prepared to forsake its autonomy and unite with the other against the Europeans. Chiefly power had become so enmeshed with European trade that the leaders could repudiate neither the French nor the English without destroying the political order that had evolved coevally with colonization. Instead, each division resumed the play-off game. The victorious Eastern chiefs reaffirmed their relationship with the French and named Vaudreuil's replacement, Governor Kerlérec, "King of the Choctaws and greatest of the race of the [Inholahta] which is the finest and the oldest."[25] Meanwhile the defeated Western leaders continued to meet with English traders among the Chickasaws.[26]

The outbreak of the Seven Years' War in 1755, however, put an end to the French trade and, for the time being, to the play-off. English corsairs took to the seas and sank or captured countless French ships bearing cargo intended for the Eastern Choctaws. The chiefs complained of the resulting dearth and began attacking the French settlements throughout the colony, which they thought was refusing to pay them tribute. Governor Kerlérec was at a loss. "They must be conciliated," he argued to the French government, "cost what it may."[27]

While Kerlérec cast about for supplies, leaders from all three divisions met with British officials to request a more liberal trade. In July 1759 three hundred Choctaws came to the Upper Creek town of Waulyhatchey to complain that the French could no longer supply their needs, and they invited the English to build trading posts in their towns. In exchange the Choctaws promised to house and protect the English traders and to fly the Union Jack over their homes. Some months later, in the fall, another group of chiefs met with English traders in the Creek town of Okfuskee, where the Choctaws made it clear to Edmund Atkin, the English superintendent of Indian trade, that they wanted to expand their relationship with the English.[28] "We desire," said one of the Choctaws, "you will not suffer Goods to be stopt from coming. . . . the paths are white." To the English, a people the Choctaws believed had "come from under the sun rising," the assembled chiefs presented a lit pipe to smoke as well as a white wing and white deerskins to prove their peaceful intentions.[29]

The Choctaws present at the meetings in Waulyhatchey and Okfuskee soon got their wish. England never invaded Louisiana during the Seven Years' War, but it defeated French armies in Québec, in the Caribbean, and in India. As part of the 1763 Peace of·Paris that ended the conflict, France ceded to England all of Louisiana east of the Mississippi River, which England organized as the province of West Florida. Spain, also defeated in the conflict, relinquished the Florida peninsula to England. But in a secret negotiation France turned over to Spain all of Louisiana west of the Mississippi River as well as the Island of Orleans where New Orleans was situated.[30]

The English moved quickly to secure an alliance with the powerful Choctaws and assert some control over their new territory, but they too were under the mistaken impression that the Choctaw people constituted a nation. James Colbert, an English soldier who lived among the Chickasaws, traveled to the Western towns in July 1763 to discuss the English accession of the region. The chiefs greeted him with open arms, but their Eastern and Southern counterparts refused to extend their hands in welcome, for their French allies were still in possession of Mobile. In November of that year, however, representatives of the Eastern division went to the town to hear, much to their dismay, the French governor surrender Louisiana to Robert Farmar, the new English commandant of Mobile. Without the French, the Eastern chiefs accepted English dominion, but they cast an eager eye toward the new occupants of New Orleans, the Spanish. Meanwhile, a second Red Shoe set out for a conference to meet with John Stuart, the English superintendent of Indian affairs in the Southern colonies, to negotiate the terms of a formal alliance.[31]

On behalf of the Western division, Red Shoe II and another warrior, Shapahooma, made the long trip to Augusta, Georgia, where Cherokees, Creeks, and Catawbas also had gathered. They must have been gratified to hear Stuart ask them, "Do you wish for anything more than to be plentifully supplied with Goods by the White People?"[32] As a chief Red Shoe II wanted nothing more, and he gladly signed a treaty that pledged friendship between the Choctaws and the English and established regulations for the conduct of their trade. At the close of the talks Stuart promised the two Western Choctaws that English traders from Mobile would be in their towns before their return.[33]

English traders quickly fanned out through the three divisions. Unlike the French, who had failed to profit from the Choctaw trade, the English insisted that they make money from it. One trader projected a windfall of sixty thousand pounds sterling.[34] "You must advise your people to be Industrious and good Hunters," John Stuart urged an assembly of Choctaw chiefs and warriors in Mobile, in order to provide the empire with valuable deerskins. The English further sought to make the Choctaws dependent on them for the guns, kettles, hoes, cloth, and other goods that eventually replaced many household items of native manufacture. "From this day forward," Stuart declared, "you are to look upon yourselves as dependent upon the generosity and Benevolence of the Great King George."[35]

At a conference in Mobile in 1765 the chiefs continued to jockey for position. Alibamon Mingo pressed his claim to be chief of the Choctaws. "I have made an alliance," the venerable chief declared, "with the other Race of Imongoulache [the Western division], and we have agreed that our Talk Should be one." His assertion, however, bore little resemblance to the actual state of affairs among the chiefs, because the other leaders present wasted no time redrawing the traditional lines of division. The Western leader Red Shoe II, who likened the English

to a "new" fire that he hoped would "always burn clear," named West
Florida governor Johnstone "Support of the Imoklasha," to symbolize the
primary relationship of the English and the Western towns. A chief from
the Eastern division later awarded the English agent to the Choctaws,
a Frenchman named Montault de Monberaut, the name "Support of
the Inholahta."[36] Even though the French had departed the Lower
Mississippi Valley, the English alliance struck at Mobile failed to suppress
the deep factional divisions, and the chiefs who left Mobile returned to a
nation that existed only in the eyes of the English.[37]

Despite the considerable differences on the divisional level between
the East, West, and South, chiefs in all the towns confronted many of the
same problems with the English traders. Like his French predecessors,
John Stuart hoped to control the Choctaw trade so that it promoted rather
than frustrated the Crown's imperial designs, but chiefs complained
regularly about traders' abuses. The rum trade in particular had elicited
considerable complaint from Choctaw chiefs for one reason—rum traders
refused to follow the protocols that previously had governed relations
between chiefs and traders.[38] "When the clattering of the Packhorses Bells
are heard at a distance," one chief regretted, "our Town is immediately
deserted. Young & old Run out to meet them Joyfully Buying Rum!
Rum!" It "pours in upon us like a Sea from Mobille," added another.[39]
Captain Houma believed rum had replaced chiefs as the centers of society;
he likened the commoners who participated in the trade to "a parcel
of chickens" who had lost their first "hen," the chief, and found a
new one, the rum trader.[40] Still, commoners looked to their chiefs to
ensure the fairness of the English trade. Inaccurate weights, unscrupulous
traders, and ineffectual colonial oversight, however, operated against
even the most conscientious leaders, and their power waned accordingly.
Illepotapo, a "great medal chief" of the Six Towns, complained to John
Stuart in 1772, "My warriors reproach me & ask why I who am their Chief
do not obtain Justice for them? this makes me asham'd & diminishes my
Consequence in the Nation."[41]

In response to such complaints, John Stuart rewrote the Indian trade
regulations, mandated the use of standardized weights and prices, and
prohibited the extension of credit to Indian hunters beyond the value
of thirty pounds of dressed deerskins. He further deemed debts over the
limit unrecoverable. Stuart also bowed to the wishes of several chiefs
by criminalizing the rum trade, but such measures failed to reverse the

damage the trade was doing to the chiefs. The rum trade had proliferated beyond anyone's control, and even those chiefs who had welcomed the English alliance rued the trade and saw their authority weaken further as the English doled out medals, gorgets, and commissions to whomever they thought might be useful to their interests.[42]

While many chiefs watched their power and influence diminish, several leaders in the Southern and Eastern towns hatched a plan to sack Pensacola and drive the English out of the region. The English were especially concerned that francophile Choctaws had found a sympathetic ear in the Spanish governor of New Orleans, Bernardo de Gálvez, who employed former French officials as traders, agents, and translators to the Choctaws.[43] The Spanish thought they had secured an ally, but the Choctaws hoped only to use the governor to procure trade goods and thus restore the equilibrium of the play-off system. Having been promised presents from the Spanish since 1763, Southern and Eastern chiefs began to demand tribute from New Orleans, "threatening war if denied."[44] To quiet their discontent Gálvez invited over three hundred chiefs, captains, and commoners from the Southern and Eastern towns to New Orleans in 1778, where he showered them with gifts and warm pledges of friendship.[45]

Sharp criticism and censure awaited the chiefs who had met with Gálvez when they returned home. Public harangues by anglophile chiefs and English agents led several men to withdraw their support of the Spanish. Others stood fast. Said one warrior named Red Topknot to Captain James Colbert, "Two people love us[.] [W]ho ever gives us the most will be the most Regarded so I would advise you to give presents Superior to the Spaniards."[46] Far from greedy, Red Topknot knew that his political authority in the nation depended on the quantity of goods he could obtain from Europeans. Although hispanophile chiefs endured harsh criticism over the next couple of years, their alliance with the Spanish paid great political dividends. Spanish medals, commissions, and goods, admitted English agent Farquhar Bethune, "give weight and influence in this nation."[47]

To dissuade the Choctaws from supporting Spain, John Stuart argued that only the English could check American expansionism. If the chiefs continued their fractious ways, he threatened, "Your country will soon be overrun by [Americans], and when they get the better of you they will enslave you and your Families."[48] Choctaws like Red Topknot, however, did not perceive diplomacy in the same stark terms. Chiefs raised in a Mississippian political, economic, and religious tradition that emphasized balance and reciprocity preferred to retain the flexibility of play-off rather than commit to the kind of unquestioning allegiance Stuart demanded.

A dramatic change in English policy, however, frustrated Red Topknot's and others' plans to extract more concessions from the English. As superintendent of Indian affairs in the Southern colonies, John Stuart had run up enormous expenditures. In December 1778 Parliament launched an investigation into his accounts and the affairs of his department that led Lord George Germain to decide that Stuart had to be reined in. In the meantime Stuart died, and Germain dissolved his office and divided the Southern superintendency into two districts. He instructed Alexander Cameron, whom he had appointed superintendent of the Mississippi district, to cultivate the English interest among the Choctaws and to limit his expenses to a small annual budget. In another cost-cutting move, Germain ordered Cameron to stop giving the Choctaws gifts.[49]

Cameron had served under Stuart, and he was accustomed to the liberal budgets of his predecessor's tenure. Knowing the Choctaws would not approve of Germain's policy changes, he asked his superior to reverse the decision. To support his request, Cameron described the Choctaws as a "poor ragged Sett" in dire need of English gifts, but the plea stirred little sympathy in Whitehall.[50] A disconsolate Cameron became convinced that without gifts Choctaw support of the English in the troubles between England and its American colonies would probably not be forthcoming.[51] When rumors of a Spanish invasion of West Florida circulated among them, support for the English plummeted even further because several chiefs began to fear that if the Spanish won they might be angry with those Choctaws who had stood firmly by the Union Jack. Fighting the Spanish, remarked one Choctaw, would be like "extinguishing the sun."[52]

In the contest between the Spanish and the English for a Choctaw alliance, one astute English agent remarked that "a penny more bought the whistle."[53] Though some chiefs in the Western towns remained allied to the English, a shortage of arms, ammunition, and trade goods undermined their position. Most of the chiefs allied themselves with Governor Gálvez, whose rapid invasion of West Florida made good on their predictions of a Spanish victory. In 1779 Gálvez captured Natchez, and after quelling a revolt by its English citizens he trained his sights on Mobile and Pensacola. The former fell easily, but at the latter the

Spanish force encountered heavy resistance by 350 warriors under the leadership of a rising Western chief named Franchimastabé, who had come to be known as the "English chief." He had participated in the defense of Natchez and had elected to continue to fight for the English in exchange for a large number of presents. After his warriors rebuffed the initial Spanish assault, however, General Campbell, the man in charge of Pensacola's defenses, refused to reward the warriors, and they returned to their towns angry about the general's high-handed behavior. When the Spanish rejoined the attack, they overwhelmed Pensacola's puny red-coated garrison. The Paris treaty that ended the American Revolution recognized Spanish control over the land conquered from the English and placed the Choctaws under the jurisdictions of both His Catholic Majesty's empire and the United States of America.[54]

A number of chiefs from the other divisions attempted to discredit Chief Franchimastabé and those of his followers who had fought for the English. They insisted to the Spanish that the anglophile leaders not be given any medals until they surrendered the scalps of the Spanish soldiers they had killed, a demand that would have stripped Franchimastabé and his supporters of the prestige that attached to victory in warfare. Consequently Franchimastabé and his right-hand man, Taboca, spurned an offer to go to Mobile and receive Spanish goods and instead made plans to travel to Savannah, where warriors of the Eastern division had already gone in search of American presents.[55]

The departure of the English from the Lower Mississippi Valley upset the previous pattern of factionalism that had characterized the Choctaws' response to colonization because the long-standing affiliations of the Eastern, Southern, and Western towns lost their historical force. In a sense the slate had been wiped clean, and in the postrevolutionary scramble for trade goods, the divisions raced against one another to set up new and profitable alliances.

Spain made the first overture for Choctaw support. In July 1784, at the invitation of the Estevan Miró, governor of Spanish Louisiana, 185 chiefs and captains representing all three divisions came to Mobile to discuss affairs, and they wasted little time in demanding to be supplied with goods by the Spanish. Miró was more than happy to comply, and the governor signed a treaty of mutual friendship and support with the assembled chiefs. The Spanish empire, however, was hardly an efficient business operation, and supplying the Choctaws proved difficult.[56]

The federal and state governments were equally anxious to cultivate ties with the Choctaws because they feared Spain's influence over the Southern Indians. In the summer of 1785 the state of Georgia dispatched two agents, Nicholas Long and Nathaniel Christmas, with $3,000 worth of goods to woo the Choctaws over to the American side. In October Congress followed up Long and Christmas's mission by sending an invitation to the Choctaws requesting a formal meeting with delegates from the three divisions.[57]

Taboca led a party of chiefs from the Western towns and a few towns in the Southern division to meet with American commissioners at Hopewell, South Carolina, to discuss a possible alliance. Cherokee and Chickasaw chiefs also planned to attend and negotiate treaties with the United States. The Choctaw party set out in the fall of 1785, but winter came early that year. Snowstorms and ice made the journey to Hopewell difficult. After traveling for two and a half months, the delegation arrived at Hopewell in December.[58]

On 3 January 1786 Taboca and the others signed a treaty with the United States that pledged friendship between the two nations, marked the boundaries of what the Americans considered the "Choctaw nation," and established various rules to enforce crimes committed by Americans against Choctaws and by Choctaws against Americans. After the treaty talks the chiefs made clear their desire for trade goods and their expectation that the Americans would supply them.[59]

"Our nation is much in want of clothing Arms & ammunition," implored Chief Taboca, and others expressed a similar wish to "be supplyed by your traders as early as possible."[60] The American commissioners therefore inserted into the treaty the right for the United States to select parcels of Choctaw land on which to build trading posts. Apparently the interpreter John Pitchlynn failed to make this provision clear to the chiefs, and the stipulation came back to haunt Taboca. But he was glad to hear the Americans promise to negotiate with the Chickasaws a cession of land near Muscle Shoals in present-day Alabama, where the federal government would build a trading post to supply the two nations.[61] In closing, the men and women who had accompanied Taboca to Hopewell painted their bodies white and performed a dance that brought order to the foreign place and consummated a peaceful relationship with the Americans. Afterward the chief covered his hands with white clay and presented the treaty commissioners with an eagle feather to signify the opening of a straight path between the sacred circle and the United States. He entrusted the American commissioners with some of the sacred fire he had brought from his home, and he told the commissioners that he expected to "take some of yours."[62]

While Taboca exchanged fire with the United States in the falling snow at Hopewell, Franchimastabé pursued a relationship with the Spanish in New Orleans. He led 150 Choctaws to meet Governor Miró "to extend the hand to the Spaniards," one observer remarked, "and deliver to Your Lordship the medals of the English."[63] Acutely aware of the redistributive role he had to play, the chief informed the governor that "when i get presents for myself i would wish for all my Nation to Get there part as well," and he expected Miró to assent to his demands.[64] Colonial officials, however, resented what they perceived as the chief's avarice. "His impertinences," wrote one Spaniard, "merely spring from a desire to receive more presents."[65]

Despite Franchimastabé's request for a fair trade and fair prices, the Spanish were slow to respond, and he considered hooking up with American traders. In November 1787 a Spanish agent named Juan de la Villebeuvre journeyed to West Yazoo, Franchimastabé's hometown, to evaluate the situation and to mollify the disgruntled chiefs. One of Franchimastabé's supporters, a war chief named Mingo Huma, plainly stated the aspirations of his confreres: "We do not care to deal with any of the whites except those who bring us goods, powder and shot." Nevertheless Chatenoqué, the chief of the Six Towns in the Southern division, was less enamored of the Janus-faced policy of the Western chiefs. "Accept these overtures," he advised Franchimastabé; "listen no more to the flattering words of others." Having made clear his adamant opposition to trading with the United States, Chatenoqué pledged his support to Spain.[66]

Notwithstanding the lack of consensus among Western and Southern chiefs regarding the Spanish alliance, the difficulty of acquiring goods, especially when compared with the heady days of the English trade, seems to have enabled Choctaw chiefs to gain control of the rum trade. Unwilling to trade alcohol willy-nilly, the Spanish and Choctaws agreed to cease the vending of rum by individual traders.[67] Apparently their efforts were successful, because the Spanish correspondence contains none of the complaints about rum traders that fill the English documents. Indeed, the ban worked so well that the Choctaw chiefs imposed their control on the availability of alcohol and carefully regulated its distribution. "The Choctaw chiefs," one Spanish official wrote, "ask me for [rum] all the time." Not surprisingly, they used their access to rum to further solidify their political authority.[68] In one case a local chief named Red Shoe sent his nephew and two other relatives to procure two barrels of rum "to give to his warriors who [in return] are going to build a hut for him."[69]

Just as the chiefs had asserted a measure of control over the rum trade and rejoined the play-off system, global economic trends were undermining the stability of the deerskin trade on which the entire strategy rested. When the value of deerskins began to plummet in the late 1780s, Governor Miró ordered that prices for goods be kept at correspondingly low levels in order to placate chiefs who were already complaining about the high cost of Spanish merchandise. The governor's orders, however, seem not to have been carried out, and continuing high prices drove some Choctaws to ask the Creeks for permission to travel through their lands to trade skins in Georgia, where Choctaws believed they could obtain a more favorable rate of exchange. But the Creeks, mindful of their neighbors' predicament, refused the request.[70]

Besides high Spanish prices, the Choctaw chiefs grew increasingly dissatisfied with the tight-fisted conduct of their traders. John Joyce and John Turnbull of the firm Mather and Strother had refused to extend credit to the Choctaws, much to the chagrin of the chiefs, who needed it to obtain goods. The men instead preferred to deal only with European traders they felt they could trust. Taboca, knowing full well of Franchimastabé's ongoing efforts to secure an American trade, spoke out vociferously to the Spanish against Joyce and Turnbull's refusal to extend credit to him and his supporters. Unwilling to suffer such insulting treatment any longer, Taboca, without the blessing of Franchimastabé, set out for Philadelphia and New York, where he spoke with Benjamin Franklin and George Washington about opening a more regular trade to the Western Choctaws.[71]

Though their colonial administration was at times inefficient and unresponsive, Spanish officials made a sincere effort to reform the Indian trade so as to shore up their strained relationship with the Choctaws. The governor abrogated Mather and Strother's monopoly of the Choctaw trade and offered it to Panton, Leslie and Company, the firm that controlled the Creek trade. Reorganization of the trade was not enough, however, because the nature of politics in the Lower Mississippi Valley was changing. In 1789 the state of Georgia allowed a combine of land speculators to purchase title to twenty-five million acres of land near the Yazoo River, much of which belonged to the Choctaws. A year later the state government rescinded the sale, but for the time being the Spanish government feared the worst. To block American expansion into the area, they planned to build a fort at Nogales, or the Walnut Hills, which stood at the junction of the Yazoo and Mississippi Rivers, near present-day Vicksburg.[72]

Under the direction of Manuel Gayoso de Lemos, the governor of Natchez, work crews began clearing brush and opening roads on 2 April 1791. The next day a chief named Iteleghana emerged into the clearing and asked Gayoso de Lemos what the Spanish were doing. After taking some food, Iteleghana gave all appearances of being satisfied with the work and with Gayoso's explanation, and he slipped back into the forest.[73] He quickly relayed word of the Spanish fort to Franchimastabé, and the chief and Taboca dispatched a letter to Gayoso de Lemos. "We thought," the chiefs stated, "that you were our friends and that you loved us. . . . What right have these men to take our land?"[74] They insisted that a Spanish settlement at the Walnut Hills infringed on their traditional hunting grounds.[75]

One month after the construction of Fort Nogales had begun, Stephen Minor, a Spanish agent, traveled to the Choctaw nation to discuss the cession of the Walnut Hills. Though the Spanish had assumed that the English claim to the region had passed to them after the American Revolution, Gayoso de Lemos did not want to risk alienating the allies he needed so much. To the assembled throng Minor painted a rosy picture of the proposed fort and trading post. Choctaw hunters, he argued, would be able to simply drop off their skins at the post rather than suffer the inconvenience of carrying them to the traders in their towns. What Minor had failed to realize was that such a plan was anathema to chiefs, who needed to scrutinize the conduct of the trade and to oversee the distribution of goods. Franchimastabé explained to Minor that the Choctaws had plenty of horses to carry their skins back to their towns and that they preferred to continue to trade with the traders who lived with them there. The traders who were present to hear the talks roundly seconded the chief's rebuttal, because they knew the post would undercut their business.[76]

The council's refusal to consider the cession prompted Gayoso de Lemos to invite them to Natchez the next year to discuss the topic further. Franchimastabé refused to countenance the cession, but when the governor promised to open the doors of the city warehouse to the Choctaw and Chickasaw chiefs who had gathered for the negotiation, support for the cession swelled. Still the Western chief refused to agree, so he deferred to the Chickasaws, whom Franchimastabé considered his elder brothers. On 14 May 1792 the leading chiefs of the Western division and the Chickasaws signed the Treaty of Natchez whereby they ceded the Walnut Hills to Spain. Franchimastabé had saved face by not openly supporting the cession, the fort was finished without incident, and John Turnbull opened a small store within its walls.[77]

For good reason Franchimastabé opposed Turnbull's operation. He feared hunters would trade their skins at the fort beyond his oversight and that consequently they would be unable to discharge the debts they owed the traders who lived in the Choctaw villages, traders who had married into the families of the chiefs and who underwrote their political authority.[78] "That Plase," Franchimastabé said, referring to Turnbull's new store in the fort, "Makes our White Peopple that Supploys us with Goods Pore."[79] The strong, indeed intimate, relations between traders and chiefs' families reflected the extent to which Choctaws had incorporated Europeans into indigenous patterns of alliance and exchange. Since the Choctaws were matrilineal, the children born of unions between Choctaws and traders were accorded full membership in their respective clans and moieties, but at the same time their fathers considered them their kin and heirs.[80]

Among the traders who married into the Eastern division was Nathaniel Folsom. While Folsom's family was traveling through the Choctaw towns sometime in the 1770s, he had a disagreement with his father and ran away to work for a trader named Welsh. He later struck out on his own and settled in the town of Boktukla where "the great French king" lived. Who the great king was is unclear, but it was probably Pooscoos II, because Folsom married two of his nieces and fathered with them twenty-four Choctaws. Other traders married into the Western division. Louis LaFleur was a Canadian who came to Mobile in 1792 to work for Panton, Leslie and Company. To improve his trading prospects, he married the two Choctaw daughters of an old French trader named Jean Cravat, Nancy and Rebecca Cravat. Ebenezer Folsom, the brother of Nathaniel, was also a Panton, Leslie and Company trader who married into the Western towns. He and his wife had a daughter named Sophia Folsom whom John Pitchlynn, another trader, married.[81] In the south the most prominent trader family was the Juzons. Charles Juzon entered the nation in the late eighteenth century and, as he put it, "connected myself with a sister of a chief of the southeast district."[82]

The traders' marriage ties to Choctaw chiefs and their opposition to the post at Nogales made them poor agents for empire, but it was the chiefs who most seriously challenged Spanish attempts to control the Choctaws. Contrary to what one historian has written, the Choctaws had not "unwittingly found themselves pawns in a three-cornered international rivalry which drained them of their integrity, honor, and independence."[83] Indeed, Taboca and Franchimastabé had decided to throw their support behind the Spanish after weighing the difficulties of obtaining American goods, especially since the Creeks had refused them permission to travel through their land. Taboca visited Gayoso de Lemos in Natchez shortly after the signing of the Natchez Treaty to reaffirm his friendship and to assure the governor that "the Spaniards have my Heart, and I do not intend to go anywhere else than to this government."[84] Whether or not the promise was sincere, Taboca had reason to contract the play-off strategy at this time. Talks of the land cession he had unwittingly made at Hopewell had undermined his and Franchimastabé's popularity, and they tried to distance themselves from the Americans lest their followers suspect their motives. According to Creek chief Alexander McGillivray, Franchimastabé had sent a deputation to him "expressing his anger and disgust, and offering to join us in opposing the Americans."[85]

The Americans nevertheless persisted in their efforts to win the Choctaws' favor. William Blount, governor of the territory south of the Ohio River, dispatched Anthony Foster and David Smith to the Choctaws to persuade the chiefs to come to Nashville for a conference. The agents arrived on 19 June 1792, and representatives of all the divisions convened to hear the talk. Foster opened the discussion with a solemn ceremony that had become a regular part of the play-off game. He presented Franchimastabé and Thloupouye Nantla, the chief of the Eastern division, each with a uniform, a set of armbands, and a medal that made plain the men's importance. During Foster's talk with the assembled chiefs, Turner Brashears, a trader and interpreter in the Spanish service, broke into the meeting with a party of drunken warriors and dispersed the council.

Afterward Franchimastabé, knowing full well that his and Taboca's power was, for the time being, tied to the Spanish, turned his American medal over to Iteleghana, who delivered it to Gayoso de Lemos in Natchez. Thloupouye Nantla, however, kept his medal. When it came time to meet with Blount in Tennessee, the chiefs of the West, at Franchimastabé's behest, stayed home, but those of the East followed Thloupouye Nantla and his shiny silver medal to the American settlements on the Cumberland River.[86]

On 7 August 1792 the Nashville conference opened, and Blount informed the two dozen headmen from the Eastern towns who had made the trip that he hoped to reaffirm the principles of the Hopewell agreement and to disburse a number of presents "as a final proof of the sincerity and friendship of the President and of the United States."[87] John Pitchlynn interpreted the governor's remarks to the Choctaw delegation, and he returned their greetings to the governor. Thloupouye Nantla expressed his satisfaction at meeting the governor in, as he put it, "the middle ground" between the Choctaws and the Americans. A war captain named Tunnathoemah likewise remarked on the importance of coming together in the "mid-land" that filled the gap between the sacred circle and the United States.[88]

After the Nashville talks, Eastern Choctaws began to trade regularly with Americans. Over one hundred warriors traveled to settlements in present-day northern Alabama to exchange deerskins and other goods. The captains who led the parties received eight blankets apiece and the common warriors four. Reports of the munificence of American traders circulated throughout the towns, and it appeared that the efforts of Thloupouye Nantla had paid off. "They are," one Spanish agent reported to Gayoso de Lemos, "praising the Americans to the skies, saying that they did not speak harshly to them, and did not ask to buy land of them as they had been told."[89]

The Western towns, however, were farther from the American settlements, and Franchimastabé and Taboca steered their trade toward Spanish factors based in Mobile, Natchez, and New Orleans. To establish Spanish influence over the Eastern towns more firmly, Governor Francisco Luis Héctor, Baron de Carondelet, ordered Juan de la Villebeuvre to call a council, which Thloupouye Nantla failed to attend. The commissioner persuaded the councilors to sign a treaty that gave Spain the land surrounding the old French trading post Fort Tombecbé. Carondelet hoped to use the post to provide the Eastern towns with goods and wean them from the American trade.[90]

Emboldened by Villebeuvre's success, Carondelet decided to try to create a confederation of Southern Indians that would be dependent on Spain for goods and able to help the Spanish resist the United States. In October 1793 representatives of the Creeks, Cherokees, Chickasaws, Tallapoosas, Alabamas, and Choctaws met with Gayoso de Lemos to hammer out the details of the confederacy. Franchimastabé, Taboca, and Pooscoos II headed the Choctaw delegation. In return for promises of trade, the Indian nations pledged to defend one another as well as Spanish Louisiana from encroachment by the United States.[91] In honor of the occasion, Carondelet renamed Fort Tombecbé Fort Confederación. Though the Spanish crown conceived of its Indian confederates as vassals and viewed the treaty as the linchpin of Spanish hegemony in the region, sojourners among the Choctaws were quickly disabused of such feudal notions. Villebeuvre remarked, "We are not their masters; they do whatever they like."[92]

Having experienced American generosity firsthand, the Eastern chiefs were unwilling to pledge either their military support or their trade to the Spanish. Moreover, the gifts and prestige that came with close ties to the Americans did not go unnoticed in the Western and Southern towns, and the feeble saber rattling going on behind the decrepit walls of Forts Nogales and Confederación did little to counter Spain's sagging reputation among the Choctaws as a weak power. One Choctaw complained to a Chickasaw chief that the Spanish had given them only "four blankets & four flags to a town," and others had grown weary of high prices and meager presents.[93] In retaliation for Spanish penury, Pooscoos II instructed warriors to kill the cattle herds of Juan de la Villebeuvre and a Spanish trader named Simon Favre.[94]

As the relationship with Spain unraveled, the Western and Southern chiefs returned their attention to the American trade. In April 1795 Franchimastabé and Taboca took a large party of men from the Southern and Western towns to trade at the settlements in northern Alabama where Thloupouye Nantla's men had been going for years, and they received generous amounts of goods.[95] But while the Choctaws lashed out at the Spanish among them and enjoyed the fruits of the American trade, diplomatic negotiations between Spain and the United States were afoot that brought the whole play-off system crashing down.

In 1795 American diplomat Thomas Pinckney negotiated with the Spanish the Treaty of San Lorenzo, which established a formal boundary between the United States and His Catholic Majesty's empire. In Louisiana the treaty mandated the Spanish evacuation of northern West Florida, including Natchez, and Forts Nogales and Confederación, and it secured for the United States free navigation of the Mississippi River.[96]

To survey the new boundary between the United States and the Spanish possessions, in late 1797 Andrew Ellicott traveled to Natchez, where he encountered Choctaw hostility toward his mission. Contrary to the advice of Governor Gayoso de Lemos, Ellicott ran up an American flag at his camp on the outskirts of Natchez. Offended by the stars and stripes and by Ellicott's officious behavior, Indians in the area began to circle the American camp and brandish their knives. Rumors raged that they would attack during the night, but Gayoso intervened and put a stop to the Indians' threatening behavior. Ellicott later heard that the Choctaws feared the United States would claim their land and drive them off by force of arms, but he dismissed such fears as fantasies inspired by Spanish propaganda.[97] The Spanish, however, had not totally distorted the Americans' objectives. Shortly after Ellicott concluded his mission, the federal government organized the former province of Spanish West Florida into the Mississippi Territory with the expectation of settling the region.[98]

The Treaty of San Lorenzo redrew the boundaries of the Lower Mississippi Valley, but it also dramatically altered the balance of power in the region. Confined to a rump of West Florida and New Orleans, the Spanish had lost their claim to the Choctaw homeland, and with the Spanish out of the picture the Americans had little incentive to continue to give generously to the Choctaw chiefs. When Franchimastabé returned to the northern Alabama settlements in 1797 to trade he did not receive the customary allowance of clothing and other goods. Instead he had to beg for a coat and a horse "to carry him back to his Nation."[99]

When the Spanish pulled out of the Choctaw towns they brought the play-off system to a sad and sorry end. Unable to continue to manipulate Spanish and American interests, the chiefs confronted alone the New Republic. In 1801 the United States negotiated with chiefs from all three divisions the Treaty of Fort Adams, which affirmed American sovereignty over the land around Natchez and Fort Nogales, and American commissioners pressured the chiefs to accept the opening of the Natchez Trace through their towns. Together Oakahummé, who had succeeded his uncle Franchimastabé as chief of the Western division, Pooscoos II, and others acknowledged the arrival of a new "great father."[100]

Meanwhile, the repercussions of the politics of play-off ensnared the chiefs in the credit trap. Shortly after the Fort Adams talks, Panton, Leslie and Company began to insist on payment for the Choctaws' substantial purchases of bullets, guns, powder, and cloth on credit. Because the Choctaws could not settle their debts, which totaled over $46,000, Panton, Leslie and Company demanded a land cession to retire them. William Panton had long believed that the sale of land was the only viable way for Indians to extinguish their debts, and he pressed the federal government for remuneration.[101] Instead of sanctioning a land cession by the Choctaws to a company serving Spanish interests, the federal government held treaty talks with the Choctaws to quiet Panton. Under the terms of the 1805 Treaty of Mount Dexter, they ceded a substantial portion of southeastern Mississippi to the United States for $50,500, and the cash they received for the land went to retire their debt.[102]

The treaties of 1801 and 1805 signaled a change from the colonial politics of play-off to the American shell game of sovereignty, land cessions, and removal. As leaders from all three divisions gathered at the treaty conferences and were held corporately liable for the debts and the land of each division, they could not help but come to see their mutual interest in opposing the further aggrandizement of the United States. Treaty talks with the United States did not single-handedly spark a nationalistic fire among the Choctaws, but they did crystallize a sense of common purpose among the chiefs. Thus when the warrior Tecumseh visited the Choctaws in 1811 and urged them to take up arms against the United States, the chiefs of the three divisions answered with a resounding no! Although they had resented the land cessions, the chiefs hoped to earn the respect of the United States by fighting under its banner, just as a warrior would do for his chief.[103]

It would be several years before the Choctaws created a complex chiefdom to replace the intermediate chiefdoms that constituted the confederacy of the eighteenth century, but the lessons of play-off had been well taken. Though chiefs had retained control over their local jurisdictions and over the European trade throughout the 1700s, politics at the divisional level had changed from a bitter and competitive rivalry to a more general community of interests. There were still no institutional or formal mechanisms for organized cooperation between the divisions at the close of the colonial period. But by the early nineteenth century there were slight stirrings of a more national consciousness. Still, as of the early 1810s, there was no such thing as a Choctaw nation.

CHAPTER THREE

Change and Persistence in Choctaw Culture, 1700–1805

Learn their language and swap for their useful things, but cultivate
no further intimacy with them. They are a dangerous people.
"The History of the Chahta Nation," as told by
Chahta Immataha to Gideon Lincecum

IN SPITE of the political boundaries and quite different political histories
that divided the Choctaws into Easterners, Westerners, Conchas, Chickasawhays, and Six Towners, they shared a common culture. And the ways
they adopted into their culture the "useful things" that they received
from the "dangerous people," like the guns Iberville gave to the Choctaw
chiefs in 1702, differed little from town to town.

The introduction of European manufactures among Native Americans
has often been interpreted in the light of dependency. Scholars have
argued, for example, that trade upset indigenous patterns of work and
exchange and that Indians abandoned native tools, vessels, and clothing
for stronger and better European goods on which they became dependent.[1]
For the Choctaws, one need look no further than one warrior's plea to
John Stuart in 1772; "We are . . . incapable," he asserted, "of making
necessaries for ourselves, our sole dependence is upon you."[2]

But not all European goods introduced to the Choctaws in the eighteenth century inculcated dependency. Cattle, horses, pigs, and chickens
and new plants in fact helped them restore a measure of the economic
and political independence that had been mortgaged to the colonial
powers of the Lower Mississippi Valley through the play-off politics
of the eighteenth century. Choctaws adopted nonnative flora and fauna

on their own terms and used them in ways that reflected their distinct modes of thinking. Men's and women's economic roles expanded with the availability of new goods and broader trading opportunities, but their respective relations to the animal world and the plant world, and to the town and countryside, showed little or no significant alteration.

Contact with Europeans affected men and women in different ways. A recent archaeological investigation of some historic sites has suggested that the warrior who complained to John Stuart about dependency probably spoke only for himself and his fellow warriors. The quantities of European artifacts found at sites increased dramatically in the late eighteenth century, but the profusion of potsherds throughout the period suggests that the degree of dependency may have been a function of gender. Women manufactured pottery, and the persistence of the tradition throughout the century suggests that women were less dependent on European trade. In contrast, men who had at one time made their own bows, arrows, hatchets, and knives were extremely vulnerable to dependency because they could neither manufacture nor repair their firearms since they lacked the necessary blacksmithing skills.[3]

The spread of European goods preceded an even larger tide of settlement in the Lower Mississippi Valley that not only challenged the beliefs and values that gave purpose to the lives of Choctaw men and women but posed a grievous threat to the plausibility of their cosmology. The pantheon of anomalous creatures that before contact had lived at the margins of the sacred circle in effect gained new and powerful members. Traders and colonial officials refused to remain in the dark forests and swampy sinks of the native landscape, and as the population of settlers increased steadily throughout the eighteenth century, they breached the circle. Their square homes, obtrusive fences, and disregard for Choctaw conventions elicited a violent response from warriors, who sought to drive the homesteaders back to the colonial enclaves whence they had come.

At the same time a countervailing force came into play that threatened to upset not only men's ability to defend their circle from the outside world but their ability to earn prestige and material goods in their accustomed ways. After the end of the Seven Years' War Europeans grew less willing to employ native levies to fight one another, and Choctaw men resented the chill that descended on the region's geopolitics after the 1760s. Moreover, the deerskin trade had also picked up speed after 1763, and Indian hunters so decimated stocks of white-tailed deer in the region that by the early

1800s the animal population verged on collapse. To fulfill their traditional roles and responsibilities, men had to find new ways to demonstrate their social and economic worth. Drinking and raiding offered two viable and popular alternatives to hunting and warring, but they also embroiled the Choctaws in conflict with European and American settlers.

Neither the French, the English, nor the Spanish had been able to force the Choctaws to toe their respective imperial lines because of the efficacy of the chiefs' play-off policies. But after the American Revolution and the subsequent Spanish withdrawal from the region, things changed. Unlike the Europeans, who had seen the Choctaws as clients, the United States government considered them subjects who needed to be "civilized." Policymakers hoped to teach the Indians to work, dress, and worship like Anglo-Americans, and the federal government took several steps to implement the plan. But the haughty paternalism of the United States blinded Americans to the fact that Choctaws were capable of adapting on their own terms to the changing world of the eighteenth and early nineteenth centuries. In 1801 the chiefs of the three divisions who met with American commissioners at Fort Adams to cede land made it clear in their talks that they had agreed among themselves to a reformist economic agenda that fit within the strictures of their culture and morality but that also attempted to meet the demands of the situation in which they found themselves. From the meeting with Iberville in 1702 to the American accession of the Lower Mississippi Valley in the early 1800s, the Mississippian structures that patterned the Choctaws' culture and economy enabled them to adapt to what one scholar has termed the "Indians' New World" while at the same time they struggled to avoid being colonized.[4]

Choctaws had their first contact with European material culture through other native middlemen. Their experience with livestock, for example, came by way of the Caddo Indians, who by 1690 had acquired horses and cattle from neighboring Indians farther to the west.[5] Contact with livestock, like contact with other items, forced Indians to think not only about what they might do with them but about what names to give them. What different groups called horses and cattle reveals much about their conception of how the animals fit into their cultures and into their economies. In fact many societies that lived in and around the Lower Mississippi Valley considered horses and cattle as goods that were integral to and indeed inseparable from their trade with the Spanish in New Mexico. The Caddos, to name one group, called horses *cavali,* a derivative of the Spanish word *caballo.* Other tribes, including the Osages, Wichitas, Cherokees, and Creeks, as well as those speaking the Mobilian trade dialect that was the lingua franca of the Lower Mississippi Valley, also used a Spanish loanword, *vaca,* for cattle. The persistence of the Spanish loanwords further suggests that the animals failed to assume an important place within the different Indians' cultures in the early years of contact. Indeed, the two terms constructed cattle and horses as exotic prestige goods that bound the Indians to their European trading partners.[6]

The Choctaws had not participated in the early cattle trade, but they too had long experience with the animals. A standard Choctaw source reports that cattle were not introduced to them until after the American Revolution, but linguistic and artifactual evidence shows they had contact with the animals much earlier.[7] In 1701 Jesuit priest Jacques Gravier recorded during his travels through the valley that the Indians used the term *vaca* for cattle, and it appears that by the 1730s cattle were becoming a regular fixture on the Choctaw landscape. About eight miles outside Mobile, the French soldier Guillaume Régis du Roullet crossed a small river named Bouk ouaka Hopohka, or "bayou where cattle pasture." In contrast, the French called it Mill River, which reflected their altogether different conception of the river's use.[8] Perhaps Choctaws free-ranged cattle in the canebrakes that lined the languid streams of the gulf coast for trade with the nearby French colonists. Whether or not they herded the animals, they used a variety of cattle products. Warriors and hunters carried powder horns made of cattle horn, and women fabricated winter cloaks from cowhides complete with long bovine tails. The impact of cattle on Choctaw material culture and landscape nevertheless was small and in no way comparable to the effect of horses.[9]

Unlike the loanword Choctaws used for cattle, their own term for horses reflected the animals' place and value in their culture. Father Gravier noted in his conversations with his sources that they called them *isuba,* from *isi holba,* "deer resembler." The earliest meetings with horses came when hunting parties ventured across the Mississippi River in the seventeenth century and saw Caddo or Osage horses, which they shot and ate. Accepted initially into the Choctaw diet, horses were soon integrated into their culture and economy, for a trade network comprising Caddos, Wichitas, Avoyelles, and Spaniards introduced enormous numbers of horses into the Southeast.[10]

Unlike cattle, which could only be eaten, horses provided the means to rapidly expand the scope and intensity of hunting expeditions and to change hunting from a subsistence to a commercial activity. Men rode horses to distant hunting grounds, and women, who formerly had to carry the game shot by the men back to the villages on their backs, began to use the animals to fetch the carcasses. Women also drove horse trains laden with provisions when they accompanied their husbands on the long hunting journeys in late fall and early winter.[11]

The horse-powered deerskin trade with the French and the English stimulated changes in the Choctaw landscape. Footpaths became horse trails, and routes previously used for intervillage and international communication expanded their function to serve as conduits for the mushrooming deerskin trade. During a trip between Mobile and the Choctaws in 1732 Régis du Roullet reported the incorporation of *isuba* into two place-names. The first, Conchak ou Soubaille ("canebrake where a horse drowned"), perhaps commemorated the unfortunate loss of a horse by a Choctaw man or woman. The second, Bouk ite Tchuie Souba ("bayou where there is a tree that marks a horse trail") indicated the steady passage of horses and goods between Choctaws and French colonists.[12]

Whereas cattle and horses made their way to the Choctaws via a native trading network that reached into New Mexico, pigs and chickens seem to have been deposited directly in the Lower Mississippi Valley by the Spanish and the French. In 1686 the Spaniard Marcus Delgado set out from San Marcos de Apalachee in Florida and traveled through present-day Alabama, where he left pigs with some of the native groups that inhabited the gulf coast. In 1701 a French colonial official remarked that Spaniards had recently visited the Tohomé and Mobile nations and left with them a stock of pigs so that when settlers came to the area there would be ample supplies of fresh meat. They named the animals *shukhushi.* Chickens probably debarked from French ships, but they proliferated rapidly in the region. Father Gravier remarked that the towns of the nearby Houmas were home to more chickens than the villages of France.[13]

For Choctaws, pigs and chickens were wholly different from cattle and horses because they fed not on grass or cane but on the refuse that accumulated around the towns. "These animals eat filth," Choctaws explained to the French, and to eat them would have violated dietary and religious taboos.[14] Not surprisingly, English naturalist Bernard Romans reported, "Of their fowl and hogs they seldom eat any as they keep them for profit."[15] Who looked after the pigs is unknown, but Choctaw women rather than men tended the chickens, perhaps because much of the "filth" surrounding Choctaw homes and towns was associated with the offal of household production. Women periodically collected their fowls to sell in Mobile and New Orleans, but purchasers had to be careful not to tell the vendors that they intended to eat the birds or to kill them in the vendors' presence.[16]

Besides selling poultry in colonial towns, women also benefited from the substantial European contributions to the plant world. Peach trees were among the first adaptations women made to the Mississippian sister crops of corn, beans, and squash. Bernard Romans added that "they have carried the spirit of husbandry so far as to cultivate leeks, garlic, cabbage and some other garden plants, of which they make no use, in order to make profit of them to the traders."[17] Profit in the sense that Romans meant was a relatively new development for women. Formerly women had welcomed visitors to their towns and homes with gifts of food, but they began trading victuals to traders, soldiers, and travelers in exchange for paint, beads, and other small items.[18]

When women swapped a bunch of leeks for a string of beads or when men used horses to increase the number of skins they could carry to the European traders, they participated in what historian Daniel H. Usner Jr. has called the "frontier exchange economy." Whereas an earlier generation of historians characterized such exchanges as informal and therefore as less important aspects of economic exchange and production in the American colonies, Usner has restored the trade in food, handicrafts, and services between Indians, settlers, and slaves to the center of a regional system of social and economic interaction. The trade addressed primarily the subsistence needs of its participants, and it brought Indians and colonists together in ways that far exceeded the limits of diplomacy and alliance.[19] Nevertheless, although the power of native traders in the frontier exchange economy enabled them to control their adoption and incorporation of European goods, the settlers who made up the other side of the trade could not be as easily managed.

The Choctaws' cosmology had evolved out of a Mississippian model that valued order and balance. It is clear that they had regarded the French as "dangerous people," and that when they looked at the expanding city of New Orleans they saw Balabanjer—the "town of strangers"—but how they incorporated Europeans into their cosmology is less clear because no Choctaw maps of the colonial world have survived the rigors of time.[20] Two Chickasaw maps from 1737 are extant, however, and they suggest how the culturally and linguistically related Choctaws might have viewed their sacred circle, its place in the region after contact, and where the strangers fit in the new scheme of things. (See figs. 4 and 5.)

To the Choctaw mind's eye the Southeast consisted of an undifferentiated space in which discrete sacred circles symbolized different nations. More an indication of political relationships than of physical proximity, the distances from circle to circle distinguished close friends from passing acquaintances. The broken paths that traversed the empty spaces signified hostile relations, while uninterrupted trails spoke of peaceful relations. The Chickasaw maps, moreover, captured neatly in the circle the delimitation of the nation from the outside world, but they also commemorated the sites of European battles and marked the opening of European trading paths.[21]

The maps' themes of indigenous order and European intrusion were acted out daily in the course of trading, negotiating, and living with Europeans. In 1729 Diron D'Artaguette refused to allow Red Shoe I to come to Mobile for his annual presents, which outraged his ally Mingo Chito. The irate chief flung his medal into a nearby stream, returning French power to the watery source of chaos and instability whence it had come. Anxious to repair the damage caused by Artaguette's rash actions, Iberville sent Régis du Roullet to meet with Mingo Chito. The chief and his retinue welcomed the Frenchman, and they smoked the calumet in an open space enclosed by four mighty trees, but the actual negotiations were to take place in the town's sacred square. To Roullet's amazement, Mingo Chito would not allow him to walk across their squareground. One of the principal "honored men" approached and beckoned him to climb aboard his back. Roullet did so, and the man scurried across the squareground while others shielded the conspicuous Frenchman from the peering gaze of the sun. Once he had been deposited at the chief's feet, the talks began, the breach between the chief and the French was repaired, and Mingo Chito had his son retrieve his medal from the stream.[22]

Just like the Nalusa Falaya and the other anomalous creatures that inhabited the borders of the Choctaw world, the French could pollute the Choctaws' sacred circle, but they could also provide powers that the Choctaws hoped to harness for their own use. Black-robed Jesuits offered

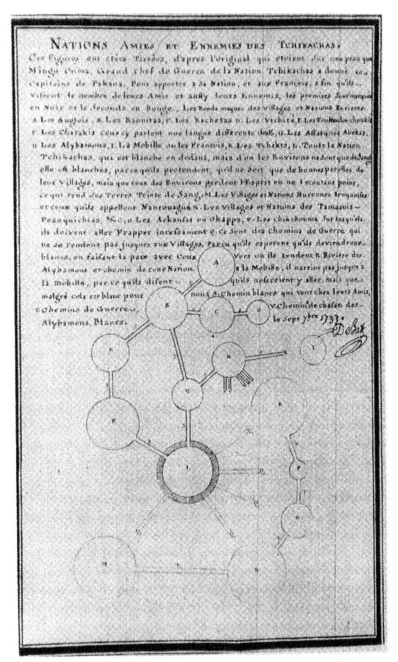

Fig. 4. Map of the Chickasaws and surrounding nations by Alexandre de
Batz, 1737. "Nations amies et ennemies des Tchikachas," COL C13A,
vol. 22, folio 67. Published with the permission of the Archives
nationales, Centre des Archives d'Outre-Mer, Aix-en-Provence, France.

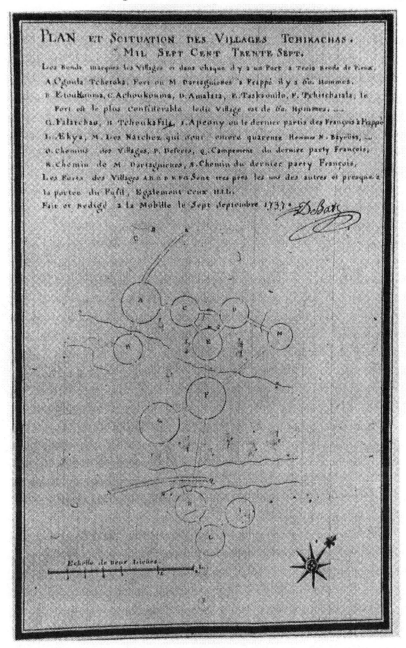

Fig. 5. Map of the Chickasaw villages by Alexandre de Batz, 1737. "Plan et situation des villages Tchikatas," COL C13A, vol. 22. Published with the permission of the Archives nationales, Centre des Archives d'Outre-Mer, Aix-en-Provence, France.

the most conspicuous access to the powers of the outside world, and the Choctaws initially held the missionaries in such high regard that from time to time Choctaw men stole their sacred paraphernalia for use in their dances and ceremonies.[23] Others sought power directly through the priests. One young man who had spent an entire hunting season without killing a deer asked Father Nicolas Lefevre to baptize him. After the hunt was over, the man returned to the town where Lefevre lived. Having failed to change his luck, he informed the startled Black Robe that "his medicine was worthless" and that he wished to be "debaptized."[24]

In the early years of colonization, the Choctaws found the English far more dangerous than their French allies. In the winter of 1730– 31 an epidemic struck the Choctaws, and some chiefs charged that the sickness had arrived in their towns in limbourg cloth that the English had infected with a medicine made of cane sugar and traded to the Choctaws through Chickasaw middlemen. Sent, one chief claimed, "for the purpose of making all the Choctaws die," the epidemic only confirmed suspicions that the malevolent magic of the English lay behind "all the misfortunes [that had] happened to their nation."[25] In fact, Choctaws drew parallels between the English and the four creatures that danced around the circle and cross motif on the gorget shown in figure 3. They refused, English trader James Adair reported bitterly, to allow "the English the name of human creatures:——for the general name they give us in their most favorable *war-speeches,* resembles that of a contemptible, heterogeneous animal."[26] Alibamon Mingo had even been taught as a youth that "wherever the English went they caused disturbances for they lived under no Government and paid no respect either to wisdom or station."[27] The British were, in short, the opposite of "beloved people": they were "accursed people."[28]

The non-Indian population of the Lower Mississippi Valley grew ever more threatening to the Choctaws as its numbers increased. By the 1770s the Spanish began to encourage settlement with generous offers of land grants and civil immunity to Americans who accepted their offer. The colonial government hoped that prosperous farmers would transfer their allegiance to Spain and act as a bulwark against the encroachment of the United States. The trickle of newcomers that had come to settle under cover of Spanish law, however, soon swelled to an uncontrollable tide of immigrants who refused to extend their loyalty to His Catholic Majesty. In Mobile alone the civilian population rose from 300 in 1760 to over 1,400 in 1788, but Natchez experienced the most dramatic growth. During the early years of the Louisiana colony, Natchez had been noted for cultivation of tobacco and indigo. The French experimented with growing cotton there as early as 1725, but the success of indigo and tobacco and the difficulty of cleaning cotton limited its widespread adoption by farmers. By the end of the century, however, advances in ginning technology and improvements in cotton strains had led to a renewed interest in the plant. The rich alluvial soil surrounding Natchez was ideal for large-scale cotton cultivation, and the crop soon became the region's staple. With the cotton boom came thousands of settlers, and the town's population grew from 1,926 in 1788 to 4,436 in 1792. Plantation agriculture expanded along the bottomlands of several creeks and rivers, and aspiring nabobs followed them into the Choctaw domain.[29]

Word of the cotton boom spread rapidly to the east. Individuals who had traveled to Mississippi to scout out opportunities returned home with tales of immense yields of two to three bales of cotton per acre, which was staggering compared with the several acres it took to make a bale in the exhausted fields of South Carolina and Georgia. Since conventional wisdom had "the Indians . . . leaving for other hunting grounds," prospective immigrants reasoned that settlement would be an easy affair.[30] Little did they expect to find themselves unloading their wagons and building their cabins in a climate of conflict and hostility. As one settler soon learned, "There were at least three hundred Indians to one white man, and for peace sake we would submit to [their] invasions."[31]

Individual chiefs and warriors fought the invasion as best they could. "The Indians," one Spaniard wrote, "burn down all the . . . fences of [the settlers] without paying any attention to their remonstrances." Spanish efforts to put a stop to the raids only amused the angry Indians. One official remarked, "When I have remonstrated with them for these injuries, they have done nothing except laugh."[32] The laughter, however, belied the seriousness of the problem of American expansion. In a meeting with Francisco Cruzat, the Spanish governor of St. Louis, a delegation of Choctaws, Cherokees, and Chickasaws protested that "the Americans put us out of our lands, forming therein great settlements, extending themselves like a plague of locusts."[33]

The Choctaws had chosen well the simile of a plague to describe American expansion, for in the meantime numerous disasters had visited their land. Droughts ruined the corn crops of 1792 and 1793 and produced widespread famine. Desperate families flocked to Fort Confederación, where Commissioner Villebeuvre doled out badly needed corn and rice. To make matters worse, an epizootic killed most of the Choctaws' horses in 1792. Worst of all was a gradual change that had taken place in the environment of the Lower Mississippi Valley at the end of the eighteenth century. While everyone suffered through the lean years, men in particular faced a serious threat to their accustomed way of life, for their ability to hunt and to fight was in steady decline.[34]

When the French left the region in 1763 it triggered a long, slow process that threatened to destroy the men's way of life. After the Seven Years' War the need for client warfare such as had occurred between the Chickasaws and the Choctaws vanished because the English hoped to turn a profit from the deerskin trade rather than throw good money after bad in conflict with the Spanish. At John Stuart's urging the deerskin trade expanded rapidly, but the men missed the days when they could divide their time equally between hunting and fighting. One party of hunters asked John Stuart why he did not use them as mercenaries, as the French had done. The American Revolution, however, did enable Choctaw men to prove themselves on the battlefield once more. Not surprisingly, on several occasions young men overruled the older chiefs who had preferred to follow Spanish and American advice to remain neutral in the conflict. Nevertheless, in spite of Franchimastabé's success at Pensacola, the Americans' subsequent struggle to turn small colonial towns like Mobile and Natchez into viable and profitable settlements made regular warfare a thing of the past. Rather than concede defeat to the new order, Choctaw warriors found two ways to retain their traditions and prerogatives. By drinking rum and by raiding the farms of European and American settlers, they engaged in "safety valve" behaviors that mitigated internal strife, focused hostilities and tensions beyond the borders of their world, and enabled young men to stake traditional claims to manhood in altogether new ways.[35]

The English oversaw an expanding rum trade. Unlike guns, cloth, and other durable goods for which Choctaw demand was relatively inelastic, alcohol was a cheap item for which English traders hoped demand would be infinite. Their plan worked, one scholar has argued, for "the Choctaws quite simply, hunted for liquor."[36] Why Indians drank in the quantities they did, however, is still unclear. One recent study of Indians and alcohol in early America offers several explanations. "Perhaps,"

Peter Mancall concluded, "Indians . . . drank as they did because they, like most colonists, enjoyed the sensations created by alcohol. Perhaps Indians drank . . . because the world they knew was crashing down around them."[37] Attributing their apparent thirst to a state of cultural deprivation in which they expressed their frustration with the postcontact world is problematic, however, because although men and women of all ages drank rum, chiefs and colonial officials identified young men as the most conspicuous and troublesome consumers of alcohol. The rum problem was not general. Rather, it was tied to a particular generation, and its causes were specific and concrete.

Choctaws called alcohol *oka homi* and *oka humma*. The former, "bitter water," described the taste, but the latter, "red water," linked alcohol to the color of warfare.[38] Disaffected young warriors who had fewer opportunities than their ancestors to fight in wars figured most prominently in accounts of alcohol use and related violent behavior. Much to the chagrin of chiefs anxious to maintain peaceful relations within and outside their towns, drunken warriors fought among themselves and attacked settlers and destroyed their property. In April 1771 John Stuart wrote to the governor of West Florida that Choctaw chiefs wanted the importation of rum into the nation stopped because they had lost all "government of their Young Men & Warriors [who were] perpetually quarrelling and killing each other."[39] Neither the chiefs nor the colonists could tolerate the disruptive behavior for long, particularly when it spilled over into aggression toward colonial homesteads.

To obtain alcohol, young warriors frequently raided settlers' farms, stole horses, and exchanged them with English traders for kegs of rum "dashed" with water. The liquor-for-horses trade appears to have occurred beyond the oversight of the chiefs, occasioning complaints from them as well as colonists. In an attempt to stifle bootlegging, the English government of West Florida enacted laws to suppress the exchange of horses between Choctaws and Europeans.[40]

The Americans, however, sanctioned the warriors' horse raids. The 1786 Treaty of Hopewell had reserved for the Choctaws the right to punish illegal American squatters on their territory "as they please," and under cover of this clause, warriors eager to earn prestige confronted hundreds of American settlers.[41] Two hundred families who had settled the Tombigbee Valley represented typical targets. They had initially established homes and fields outside the Choctaw boundary but, territorial official Ephraim Kirby wrote, "for want of good land, [they] have effected most of their cultivation upon ground where the native right remains unextinguished."[42] In an encounter with one squatter, a war chief gave the "usurpers of these lands" two weeks to remove themselves and their property from the Choctaw domain. If they failed to heed his warning, he promised to "return with my warriors . . . to compel all of your people to evacuate this territory."[43]

Squatters who refused to retreat paid the consequences. In the fall of 1802 eight warriors raided Daniel Grafton's farm outside Natchez and killed or wounded all his work oxen.[44] John Hutchins, the son of an early settler, remembered that the Choctaws had destroyed everything his family "could not carry on our backs in retreat."[45] Other Americans living in the vicinity complained regularly about Choctaw depredations on their herds and about the bloated carcasses of slaughtered cattle that littered the countryside.[46]

Just as raids were intimately linked to warfare, so too were they connected to changes in the hunting economy. By the last decades of the eighteenth century, Choctaw hunters had overhunted the stock of white-tailed deer that lived in the Choctaw borderlands. "Game is so scarce," reported Bernard Romans in the 1770s, "that during my circuit through the nation we never saw any."[47] Men fully appreciated the dilemma, and the depletion of deer stocks in the region threatened their ability to sustain themselves and their families. Because horses, like deer, could be eaten or traded, desperate hunters turned to Americans' pastures for new quarry. In one exchange of words with Winthrop Sargent, the governor of Mississippi Territory, Choctaw men made clear the new state of things. Observing that their "Country, once affording abundance, had become desolate by the hands of a People who knew not but to increase their Wretchedness," the governor wrote, " . . . they were determined in future to Consider our Domestic animals as fit Objects for the chase."[48] If hunters could not hunt deer, they could at least train their guns on "deer resemblers."

Historian William McLoughlin has linked horse raiding among Cherokees in the late eighteenth century to the loss of status faced by men whose opportunities to engage in warfare had likewise diminished. He argued that the growing prominence of horse raiding signaled the breakdown of the Cherokees' culture.[49] It is more appropriate to consider the horse raid as an adaptation and transformation of male culture at a time when the expectations of male behavior could no longer be met by traditional means. Young men growing to maturity in a society where the normal means of social, economic, and political advancement were no longer present had to create new means if they were to improve their status and maintain their culture. Indeed, Choctaw men so valued the raids that they incorporated the words for horses and cattle, *isuba* and *waka*, into the names conferred on warriors after victory in the field. By the early nineteenth century several men named Wakatubbee, "cow killer," and at least one man named Horse Hunter bore testimony to the importance of the innovative combination of warfare and hunting that enabled them to fulfill their moral obligations and become men.[50]

The fusion of hunting and warfare into raiding caused much consternation for territorial and federal officials. Sargent's successor, William C. C. Claiborne, lamented that although American settlers had suffered great "inconvenience" at the hands of Choctaw raiders, his feeble government could do little to stop them. Even Secretary of War Henry Dearborn regarded the Choctaws as "the most powerful Nation of Indians within the limits of the United States."[51] The terror inspired by the horse raids of the 1790s was nevertheless short lived. The 1814 Treaty of Fort Jackson, imposed by Andrew Jackson on the defeated Red Stick Creeks at the end of the Creek Civil War, opened much of Mississippi Territory to American settlement. The population of what became the state of Mississippi consequently soared from just over 30,000 in 1810 to 75,000 in 1820.[52]

As settlements grew, the federal government had to put an end to the raids and subjugate the Choctaws. Rather than utilize them either as military allies or as trading partners, federal leaders sought to change their culture in order to save them from what most Americans expected would be their inevitable extinction. To avoid the shame that would attach to causing the Indians' extermination, George Washington's secretary of war, Henry Knox, conceived of a new kind of Indian policy. Knox believed that the United States had to respect each Indian nation's sovereignty, and he urged that treaties be negotiated to acquire their land. But Knox and others also believed that the federal government had a responsibility to "civilize" Native Americans who, they presumed, could not maintain their "savage" lifestyle and still survive in close proximity to "civilized" people. Consequently federal Indian policy entailed two goals: "civilizing" the Indians and acquiring their land.[53]

Heavily influenced by the Enlightenment's emphasis on environmentalism and human perfectibility, federal leaders like Knox, Washington, John Adams, and Thomas Jefferson grounded their Indian policies in the assumption that changing the Indians' material conditions would transform their "savage" hearts into the souls of "civilized" men. By teaching them how to farm, to own private property, and to pray to the Christian god, the federal government aspired to raise them to the standards of contemporary Anglo-America. Ideally, policymakers believed "civilized" Indians could then be assimilated into American society on equal terms with Anglo-Americans.[54]

The second tenet of federal Indian policy—land acquisition—was expected to follow changes that occurred in the native cultures. As they adopted a yeoman farming economy, policymakers reasoned, Native Americans would no longer need the land they had formerly used for hunting. Federal officials justified land cessions by those who continued to hunt by reasoning that such cessions would force them to accept "civilization." After the government obtained title to the superfluous land, prosperous Americans who purchased and settled the land would provide an additional "civilizing" influence on their native neighbors. Congress and the president implemented the policy among the Choctaws in three ways: by passing protective laws, by posting federal agents, and by opening a federal trading house.[55]

To protect Native Americans from settlers' intrusions, Congress passed the Trade and Intercourse Acts, which prohibited the trade in alcohol between Americans and Indians, required traders to obtain federal licenses and to post bonds, and regulated the conduct of Americans among the Indians. Settlers, for example, could not hunt on native land, and they could not travel into the various nations without a pass signed by an agent of the federal government. Americans who committed crimes against Native Americans were to be tried as if they had committed a crime against an American citizen. Moreover, through the acts the federal government asserted its primary role in formulating policy and in mediating interaction between Native Americans and the United States. The laws were an impressive attempt to normalize relations, but enforcement was often lacking.[56]

The federal government dispatched agents to the various nations to oversee the enforcement of the Trade and Intercourse Acts and the implementation of the "civilization" policy. Secretary of War Henry

Dearborn charged one agent, John McKee, with persuading the Choctaws that farming and husbandry were "their best recommendation to the beneficence of the United States."[57] In 1803 Governor Claiborne urged McKee's replacement, Silas Dinsmoor, to reclaim the Choctaws from "a State of Savage ignorance." To this end, Claiborne expected Dinsmoor to teach them how to farm, raise livestock, and trade as well as to keep an eye on Spanish intrigues among them.[58]

To aid Dinsmoor in his mission, in 1802 the federal government built a trading factory for the Choctaws at Fort St. Stephens, a growing center of American population in present-day western Alabama. Although deerskins remained the single most lucrative item in the federally supervised trade, the substantial quantity of goods Choctaws purchased with cash suggests that other economic pursuits were challenging commercial hunting as the economic mainstay of the nation.[59]

Hunters took home from the post hoes, cotton cards, and other agricultural implements for their wives as well as whips, cowbells, and saddles for themselves, and they began to raise cattle and horses for sale on the open market. Though few cowhides were brought to the factory for trade compared with the number of other skins, in terms of value they rivaled bearskins as the second most important skin Choctaws traded. Unlike deer, bear, fox, and wildcat skins and beaver pelts, the cowhides were not destined for consumption in distant markets. Instead, the American factors and their slaves cut the hides into strips and used them to tie up the bundles of deerskins and other furs for shipment. The factors also used cowhides to shield the above-deck areas of the factory's two boats from any arrows and balls that might be shot at the crew. Another important commodity traded by men was tallow, but it never overtook beeswax in candle manufacturing because the latter was worth twice as much per pound. Cowhides and tallow only supplemented the vast array of goods that Choctaws traded at the United States factory, but they allowed hunters to incorporate cattle into the century-old deerskin economy and to continue the old hunter lifestyle in new ways.[60]

The shift from deer hunting to other commercial activities did not go unnoticed by the chiefs. When Franchimastabé acknowledged in 1792 that "the time of hunting and living by the Gun [is] . . . near its end," he articulated a growing consensus among the chiefs that they and their commoners had to find new ways to make a living.[61] In December 1801 American treaty commissioners asked several prominent chiefs to come to Natchez and negotiate a treaty. "We invite you," the American commissioners began, "to state to us freely the situation of your nation and what you wish on the part of your father the President to better your condition in trade, in hunting, in agriculture, manufactures and stock-rasing." After greeting the commissioners, several Choctaw chiefs responded to the Americans' query. Chief Homastubby of the Eastern division requested that the federal government send women to the Choctaws to "go among our half Breeds and teach them [to spin thread and weave cloth], and the thing will then extend itself one will teach another and [then] the whites may return to their own People again." Another Choctaw named Robert McClure reiterated an earlier request he had made for a cotton gin. "We half breeds and young men," McClure declared, "wish to go to work." Going to work in the American economy, however, was not limited to Choctaw women and biracial men who would take up farming, cotton cultivation, spinning, and weaving. In addition to asking the commissioners for plows and hoes for the women and the "half Breeds," Homastubby requested "a small set of Blacksmith Tools for a Red man."[62]

After all was said and done, the Choctaws got three sets of blacksmith tools, one for each division. More important, the chiefs at the conference, Homastubby of the East, Pooscoos II of the South, and Puckshunubbee of the West, had signaled a willingness to accept the material changes that had occurred in their culture over the course of the eighteenth century. Together they formulated a new plan whereby all Choctaws would participate in a revolution designed to replace the play-off economy of hunting, trading, and military service with one geared toward producing commodities for the emerging American market economy.

As Choctaw oral tradition had warned, the Europeans had indeed proved to be dangerous people, for their settlement of the Lower Mississippi Valley had threatened the security and sanctity of the sacred circle. They had, however, brought many useful things—horses, cattle, pigs, chickens, new plants, and a host of manufactured goods. The items wrought considerable changes in the Indians' material culture, but the morality that underlay it shaped the society's responses in ways consonant with age-old traditions. By the early 1800s the people and their culture had successfully accommodated and survived a century of contact and resisted for the most part the colonization of their land. Nevertheless, unlike equine "deer resemblers" or patches of leeks, American settlement could not be contained within ancient categories of belief. With settlement, the anomalous creatures that had always lived on the borders of the Choctaw world had entered the sacred circle, and they threatened to impose a new and alien way of life on the "beloved people."

CHAPTER FOUR

The Market Revolution, 1805–30

Choctaws know and are sensible that our white brethren ways are good, and we know that
we Choctaws must turn our gun into a plow, and work like as our white brothers do.
David Folsom to Elias Cornelius, 5 March 1820

AS THE chiefs of Franchimastabé's and Homastubby's generation passed
away in the late years of the eighteenth century and the early years of the
nineteenth, the task of overseeing economic reform fell to a younger cadre
of leaders. The sons of traders who had grown to maturity in the 1810s and
1820s were especially well placed to expand on the entrepreneurial efforts
of their fathers. David Folsom, the son of Nathaniel Folsom, was born in
1791 and attended only six months of common school, but he was well
versed in provisioning the travelers who frequented his father's tavern
on the Natchez Trace. Greenwood LeFlore, the son of Louis LaFleur,
was nine years younger than Folsom. He left his father's trading post
and plantation to live with an American family in Nashville. During
his five-year stay he learned English and fell in love with his first wife.
The boys, James and Peter, also grew up in a commercial milieu, the
considerable spread of their father, John Pitchlynn, and Peter lived for
a time with Andrew Jackson's good friend John Coffee in his home in
Alabama.[1] Having witnessed firsthand how market-oriented enterprises
and economies worked, the young men were well prepared to initiate the
transformation of the Choctaw economy from one based on reciprocity to
one predicated on buying, selling, and profit. The sons of traders, however,
were not the only Choctaws to adopt economic innovations. Rising chiefs

like Homastubby's nephew Mushulatubbee and Greenwood LeFlore's uncle Robert Cole as well as countless other individuals who were not raised to oversee a tavern or a plantation were equally prepared to reform the nation's economy.[2] "We cannot expect," Mushulatubbee succinctly declared in 1820, "to live any longer by hunting. Our game is gone."[3]

Instead of hunting, Choctaw men throughout the three divisions began to devote more attention to raising livestock while women sold produce and handicrafts to settlers, planted cotton alongside their corn, and began weaving and selling their own cloth. The Choctaws thus created a surplus-subsistence economy in which they followed the principle of safety first.[4] That is, they fed and clothed themselves first before selling in the marketplace what remained on hand. Their willing and active participation in the American market economy, however, does not mean they had become a market society. Unlike the Creeks and Cherokees, where market intrusions gave rise to class divisions and bitter socioeconomic strife, among the Choctaws bonds of kinship and the long-standing political relationship between chiefs and commoners militated against the formation of new class lines. Instead the old tensions between chiefs took on new guises.[5]

Owing to the adoption of innovative economic activities and the persistence of traditional social, political, and economic relations, the early-nineteenth-century Choctaws who participated in the market revolution evolved into what one historian has characterized as a "marketplace" society.[6] A marketplace society stands on a continuum between nonmarket and market extremes. For the transition from a nonmarket to a market society to occur, economic activity must be differentiated from the cultural meanings and behaviors that are related to economic production and exchange in nonmarket settings. When economic activity has been differentiated from social organization and cultural beliefs, one student of economics has written, demand, prices, and profit motive will provide the foundations on which the new economic system can operate.[7] In short, the nonmarket society must change from "buying and selling" to "living by buying and selling."[8] Choctaws in the early nineteenth century never completed the transition. Although they increasingly sought profit instead of reciprocity from trade with outsiders, they retained the gendered division of labor and production that had characterized their post-Mississippian economy, and they never became dependent on buying and selling to make a living. The nineteenth-century Choctaws became a marketplace society because they entered the market economy at fixed places and times, but in their homes, fields, and forests they remained attached to the traditional cultural meanings and behaviors that had characterized their precontact economy.

By the early nineteenth century the colonial frontier exchange economy that had linked the region's Indians, settlers, and slaves in a network of exchange and interaction had developed into a considerable trade that brought together Choctaws and Americans in the cities, towns, and countryside of the Lower Mississippi Valley. In New Orleans the number of women who sold vegetables in the sprawling town market and who wove cane baskets, mats, and sifters and made moccasins out of deerskin in their small camps on the outskirts of town impressed visitors to the Crescent City. In addition to the produce of their gardens and the work of their hands, women gathered scarce firewood and sold it in Mobile and other towns.[9] Among rural farmsteads, they offered "cooking vessels, pitchers, and trinkets" to their American counterparts.[10] Whether in the town markets, in their urban camps, or in the countryside, females seemed to be constantly employed in producing goods for sale.

Men, however, spent "their time in indolence and intoxication," according to one observer.[11] They "drink rum, or sit on the ground in a pensive posture doing nothing," noted another.[12] But for every traveler who saw men drinking rum, another described them carrying strings of birds, squirrels, venison hams, or perhaps pots of bear oil. Unlike women, whose labor was based in the home settings of the camps and the urban markets, men worked in the forests, where they hunted animals and gathered honey. When they were in the camps and markets, men used their time to relax, repair weapons, and drink, just as they would have done in the Choctaw towns.[13]

But not all economic opportunities lay in the bustling ports and sleepy hamlets of the Lower Mississippi Valley outside the Choctaw borders. The Indians did a considerable business selling to travelers on the Natchez Trace, which the 1801 Treaty of Fort Adams authorized to be constructed between Nashville and New Orleans, passing through the Choctaw towns. The treaty provided for taverns and ferries to be opened along the road. Americans like Josiah Doak and Noah Wall operated some of them, but most of the business of feeding and sheltering travelers fell to Choctaw entrepreneurs like David Folsom and Greenwood LeFlore.[14]

Travelers on the trace were not of one mind when it came to their Choctaw hosts. Martha Philips Martin remembered, "When ever we stopt, they treated us with great kindness, if you showed you had confidence in them."[15] Others complained frequently about the prices Choctaws charged and how avidly they pursued their business. On his way to New Orleans John H. B. Latrobe remarked that "hospitality exists everywhere, where food cannot be bought and sold. [But] a good market in the neighborhood always puts an end to it."[16] "Almost every Indian we passed," remembered the Reverend Jacob Young in 1807, "had something to sell, especially corn at two dollars per bushel, corn blades at a bit, pumkins for a quarter, and hickory-nuts, walnuts, [and] hazel-nuts for a bit."[17] Instead of being welcomed with an offering of *tomfulla*, nineteenth-century travelers could expect women running up beside their horses and wagons, offering their produce, and crying out "Bit. Bit."[18]

American settlers needed more than food and lodging to start their new lives, and they depended on Choctaws to sell or trade to them the cattle, horses, and pigs that were essential to establishing a successful small farm. One Alabama settler, Elisha Lacey, was surprised by Chief Mushulatubbee's "great many ponies, cattle and hogs," of which "he bought from the chief all the hogs he wanted."[19] Gideon Lincecum, who moved to Mississippi in 1818, recalled fondly, "We procured all our provisions from our Chahta neighbors on very good terms."[20] Lacey and Lincecum were far from isolated examples. Mushulatubbee was so successful at stock raising that cattle buyers from Alabama called at his home to ask for any animals he might sell, and, according to Agent William Ward, the Choctaws "generally supplied . . . the neighboring whites with pork and beef."[21]

Choctaws had raised pigs and horses in the early eighteenth century, but they did not begin to raise cattle until the 1770s. As they accumulated herds, they abandoned their towns and settled on scattered farmsteads where they could allow their cattle and hogs to roam free.[22] There is no evidence that they selectively bred their livestock, culled their herds, or used traditional land management techniques like burning to husband their animals. What features of their cattle complex can be discerned, however, bear a distinctly Anglo-American imprint.

"Crackers" from Georgia and the Carolinas settled near the Choctaws in the late eighteenth and early nineteenth centuries, and they imparted to them much of their cattle complex. At roundup times, Choctaw herdsmen gathered their cattle from the canebrakes, fields, and forests with loud cracks of the whip, herded them on horseback, and enclosed them in cow pens. Once penned, cattle could be driven down innumerable cow-paths to markets in surrounding American communities. To distinguish between herds, they branded their animals as was common practice among non-Indians of the region. Choctaw cowboys like Mushulatubbee, Puckshunubbee, Mastubbee, and Indian countrymen like John Pitchlynn and Charles Juzan bartered deerskins and cowhides for, among other things, saddles, bridles, spurs, whips, cowbells, and salt, which was essential for the animals' nutrition. Having mastered the accoutrements and techniques of the Anglo-American cattle complex, Choctaw men and women relied extensively on livestock to put the nation back on a sound economic footing. Stock raising, after all, fit perfectly within the regional market economy of the Lower Mississippi Valley and within the marketplace economy of the Choctaws. They could raise cattle, hogs, and horses with ease, and the demand for beef, pork, and horses in the Old Southwest remained constant because the region's planters generally devoted their acreage to cotton production rather than to livestock.[23]

Choctaw ownership of cattle, pigs, and horses was impressive. In 1828 the cattle herd numbered over 43,000 head, a ratio of 2.07 cows per person, which compares favorably with the 1840 ratio for the state of Mississippi, 1.8 per capita. The average price of a cow in 1828 was between $8 and $10, and fresh beef was worth four cents a pound. Based on these figures, the Choctaw herd had a maximum market value of over $300,000 on the hoof and several hundred thousand dollars when butchered for sale as fresh beef. Choctaw stocks of pigs and horses were equally valuable. With nearly four pigs per capita, there were upward of 85,000 swine living in and around their towns and farms. At an average price of $2.50 per animal, the pigs would have been worth nearly $212,500. The horse herd numbered approximately 15,000 in 1828, a ratio of 0.7 per capita, similar to Mississippi's 1840 ratio of 0.8 per capita. According to missionaries the average horse was worth $60, so the Choctaw horse herd may have been worth about $900,000. Comprising well over a million dollars worth of livestock, the Choctaw herds constituted a substantial portion of the regional economy.

Whether they owned herds of several hundred head or only a few animals, Choctaws, by all accounts, participated in the livestock economy.

Men and women owned their stock separately and impressed on their nephews, nieces, and children at an early age the value and importance of stock raising. One of Peter Pitchlynn's first duties as a child was to tend a herd of cattle, and generally sons and daughters received from their parents at birth a cow and a calf, a sow and a piglet, and a mare and a colt. As the child grew older, his or her herd would multiply and provide the owner with a sound source of income and subsistence in adulthood.[24] "These people," one observer remarked, "have stocks of horses, cattle, hogs, etc. some of them have *large* stocks, and appear to live plentifully."[25]

Realizing the economic importance of livestock, the chiefs and their subordinates, the captains, tried to stop American theft of Choctaw animals and to impose controls over the livestock trade with Americans. Two Choctaws complained in the summer of 1821 that an American had stolen some of their horses and sold them in Alabama. Little Leader, a captain, suffered a similar loss when an Alabamian stole two of his mares and two of his colts, and David Folsom lost a horse worth $60 to thieves. Nancy Gillet, known locally as "Big Nancy," went after American horse thieves who had stolen one of her horses while it grazed in her front yard; she chased them thirty-six miles before she lost them. Two Choctaw men who had seen the fleeing thieves thought nothing of the matter, for horse traders were regular visitors to the towns.[26]

Livestock theft was a particularly pernicious problem because Choctaws had difficulty obtaining justice. Agent William Ward was hardly zealous in his prosecution of American thieves, but more important, Mississippi and Alabama law prohibited Choctaws from filing suits in court and from testifying in court cases.[27] "How is a Choctaw to obtain redress," asked one Choctaw in a letter to Secretary of War John C. Calhoun, "when he is debarred, by the statutes of Mississippi, from giving his testimony in a court of justice?"[28]

In addition to thefts, American horse traders also caused problems for the chiefs because they traded whiskey for horses. David Folsom was especially scornful of the men "who sit near the edges of our country, who steal our horses . . . [and] who lay whiskey there."[29] But Choctaws were also responsible for the problems Folsom complained of. Men traded cattle for whiskey and retailed it "at a great advance" to their countrymen.[30]

Missionaries and chiefs alike singled out the trade in whiskey as a severe problem. Although federal law prohibited Americans from selling alcohol to the Choctaws, many chose to ignore it. "The laws of the United States are set at defiance," wrote missionary Cyrus Kingsbury, "The Indians' horses . . . are bought up, in open day, in the surrounding settlements, and poverty and wretchedness, and fighting and murder, are desolating the country."[31] Leaders decried the violence and poverty that they attributed to the trade and attempted to interdict the flow of whiskey into the nation. One captain from the Six Towns, Hwoolatahoomah, declared that he would destroy any whiskey brought into the nation by Choctaw warriors to trade for "blankets, guns, and horses."[32] Little Leader threatened to "take off [the] heads" of any persons in his neighborhood who had the temerity to peddle *oka humma.*[33] Councils everywhere followed suit, and for a moment the Choctaws were caught up in a teetotaling frenzy.[34] In the early 1820s the chiefs even organized a national police force known as the "light horse patrol" to patrol the whiskey traffic and to stop thefts of their livestock. Significantly, the force consisted of mounted men, which enabled Choctaw males to maintain a martial function in their society while they defended their nation's herds of pigs, horses, and cattle.[35]

Adam Hodgson, an Englishman who traveled through the Choctaw nation in 1820, witnessed firsthand the prosperity of the livestock economy. During his journey he visited two brothers who raised cattle for a living. The size of their herd, the lushness of their range, and the sturdy prosperity of their farm impressed the Englishman, and he decided to spend the night with them. As the sun set the cattle ambled in from the forest for milking, and Hodgson's host shot one for supper just as, a half century earlier, he might have killed a deer or turkey. That evening the Englishman sat down with the family for a meal of fresh beefsteaks. What escaped Hodgson's normally observant eyes, however, were the women who had milked the cows and cooked the steaks.[36]

The infrequent mention of Native American women in historical sources makes any study of their lives difficult and any conclusions tenuous, but linguistic evidence can open new lines of inquiry and suggest lines of argument and interpretation that otherwise would be overlooked for lack of sources. Anthropologists Mary Haas and Amelia Rector Bell have demonstrated that the Muskogee language family, to which the Choctaw language belongs, contains grammatical structures and vocabulary that differentiated in subtle ways the language the men spoke from the language the women spoke. By drawing on the Choctaw language and the few references to women and cattle in the documentary sources, one can offer a number of suggestions about women and the marketplace economy.[37]

Like male Choctaws, females incorporated cattle into their names, and the names reveal much about the complex intersection and discrete segmentation of gender roles in their culture and about men's and women's different relations to the same objects. Bell has argued that the Creek language differentiates gender according to definitions of male behavior. Creek men, for example, could not even refer to a woman by the word for woman. Instead they had to call her "food preparer" or "one who has a house." Accordingly, the woman "food preparer" can be understood only in secondary opposition to the primary male "warrior." One of the translatable female names that incorporated *waka*, Wakaihoner, meant "cow cooker." When contrasted to the male name Wakatubbee, which meant "cow killer," the names bear a striking resemblance to the pattern Bell describes. It seems cattle could define women in relation to men insofar as they performed a gendered function like preparing an animal that had been felled by their hunter husbands.[38]

That women owned cattle at all might seem to represent a fundamental contradiction of their culture, a transgression against their morality, because animals had traditionally been associated with men. But to Choctaw women cattle were not animals, they were plants. One Choctaw term for cattle—*alhpoa*—means literally "fruit trees such as are cultivated" and suggests a uniquely feminine linguistic construction of the value and utility of the animals. The fruit trees that proliferated among the Choctaw towns offered a sensible analogy to cattle for several reasons. Women tended both to extract valuable food, whether plums, peaches, or milk. The association of women with the great power of fertility also may have created a special relation between women and cattle because the animals' annual reproduction made them particularly valuable. Above all, for over a century orchards had been a part of the domestic landscape, and other cattle-related terms derived from *alhpoa* hint that this was becoming true for cattle as well. For example, *alhpoa aiimpa* meant pasture, and *alhpoa imilhpak* meant fodder. Both terms point to the careful tending that characterized women's horticulture as opposed to the neglect that marked the free-range herding practiced by the men.[39]

The linguistic construction of mobile cattle as stationary fruit trees may have enabled Choctaw women to adapt to the changes in their settlement patterns that occurred in the late eighteenth century. At that time families began moving out of their towns and settling on isolated farmsteads to raise livestock, and women had to abandon the orchards that had been an integral part of their landholdings and subsistence cycle. But because cattle were "fruit trees" women could, in a cognitive sense, take their orchards-cattle with them into the previously unsettled borderlands that formerly had been reserved for male hunting and fighting. Women were thus able to maintain what had been an important feature of stable town life in a new and forbidding environment.[40]

By designating cattle as fruit trees, women maintained a continuity with the past in the face of a changing present. In so doing, they also improved their prospects in the American market revolution of which they were a part. How often they sold or traded cattle is unclear, but in at least one instance a young woman used a cow to pay for her education. In July 1820 a thirteen-year-old girl tried to enter the Elliot missionary school, but the missionaries denied her admission because the school was already overcrowded. Reluctant to crush the girl's hopes of going to the school, her friends told her she needed some nice clothes to be accepted. Encouraged by the news, the girl determined to sell her cow for cash to buy clothes. Touched by her resolve, the missionaries agreed to take the girl in, and her uncle quietly offered to pay the cost of her schooling.[41]

What the missionaries mistook for youthful precocity, and what some might mistake for an everyday occurrence in the Old Southwest, in fact revealed two things: an accommodation between Mississippian morality and Anglo-American market sensibilities and how the cultural construct of language mediated relations between the two. The girl's conception of the cow as a good that could be sold for cash suggests that Choctaw children had begun to imbibe the lessons of the marketplace. But because she could conceive of the cow as a plant, she did not have to transgress her morality to raise and dispose of the animal. Unlike bourgeois Anglo-American women, who were being confined increasingly to their "separate sphere," or like other Native American women who during the market revolution found themselves trapped in the vicissitudes of the skin trade, Choctaw women could draw on their own culture to sanction innovative economic activities like stock raising and carve out a small place for themselves in the emerging American market economy.[42]

The Choctaw language enabled women to participate in the cattle economy without compromising their relation to farming. At the same time, women's supervision of the plant world made them agents of change in Choctaw horticulture, for it was women who adopted cotton cultivation from the American traders who lived in their midst. In 1800 Samuel Mitchell, the first federal Choctaw agent, disbursed cotton seed to his Choctaw neighbors and showed them how to plant it. Women took to the new crop quickly, and the white bolls spread from small patches at traders' homes and appeared alongside the corn, pumpkins, and squashes in their gardens.[43]

At home many women spun thread and wove it into homespun cloth, and they often produced surpluses. As early as 1801 the United States agent remarked that spinning was going on with "considerable spirit."[44] In 1817 missionary Elias Cornelius reported that federally supported mechanics in the nation had manufactured two thousand spinning wheels and several hundred looms for Choctaw use. "They raise cotton & manufacture it into cloth for their ordinary use," reported the good reverend.[45] Some years later Jedidiah Morse remarked that in 1820 women had spun and woven over ten thousand yards of cotton cloth in one year.[46] Another observer admitted, "I have myself bought many yards of cloth from full blooded Indians of their own make."[47] Apparently they did not always get full value for their products. According to one citizen of Mississippi, the women often were "cheated out of the proceeds" of their labors.[48] Nevertheless, the growth of the cloth economy from a subsistence to a commercial venture occurred rapidly, was profitable, and did not escape the wary eyes of the chiefs.

Not wanting Choctaws to develop trading patterns outside their oversight, the chiefs, led by Puckshunubbee, quickly endorsed cotton cultivation and the cloth trade. But the development of a marketable raw crop proceeded slowly. In 1818 only 238 pounds of cotton in the seed and five pounds of spun cotton were brought to the United States factory for trade, but by March 1822 the factory had in its possession 13,245 pounds of cotton in the seed.[49]

Most men could not farm cotton because such work was considered inappropriate for them. As Homastubby had acknowledged at the Fort Adams treaty talks in 1801, however, it appears that biracial men were free from such strictures. Why this was so is unclear. Nevertheless, prominent leaders, both full-ancestry and biracial, who depended on support from the commoners to underwrite their authority avoided the stigma that attached to male farming by purchasing slaves to do the work. Not surprisingly, the growth of the cotton economy paralleled the spread of slavery in the nation.[50]

In 1830 a federal census of the Choctaw towns revealed that of the 17,963 people who were enumerated only 512 were slaves. Contrary to historian Arthur DeRosier's assertion that Americans who resided among the Choctaws owned the most slaves, only twelve of the sixty-six slaveowners were Americans.[51] The fifty-four Choctaw owners mirrored the various strata of the slaveholding class found elsewhere in the South. Chief Greenwood LeFlore's holdings were by far the largest. His thirty-two slaves worked 250 acres of the Big Sand prairie in the Yazoo River Valley. His brothers William and Benjamin were not far behind with sixteen chattels between them.[52] To the east Chief David Folsom's ten slaves farmed his "considerable estate," which consisted of a house, barn, stables, and numerous outbuildings. Save for his dark-skinned labor force, one traveler remarked that "he reminded me of a hardy northern farmer."[53] Nearby, Joseph and James Perry relied on fifty-one slaves to tend their farms on Spring and Loociskoonah Creeks. Among those Choctaws who lacked European ancestry, Chief Mushulatubbee owned the most. His ten slaves cultivated thirty acres for him. Chiefs and their immediate families, however, made up only one-quarter of the native slaveowners. Their subordinates, captains like Joseph Kincaid, Little Leader, and Chatamataha, made up the bulk of the middling and small slaveowners. Perhaps slaveownership trickled down from the chiefs to the secondary level of the captains. In addition to the men, nine Choctaw women had slaves. Delila Brashears owned sixteen, the Widow Burris owned five, and Winney Batiest held two. Of particular note is Sally Tom, a free black. She owned one slave and appears to have presided over a small community of free blacks, whites, and African Choctaws in the Eastern towns near the old site of Fort Confederación.[54]

Choctaws typically bought their slaves from Americans who resided in or near the nation. A man named Morgan, for example, sent out word that he was eager to trade some slaves for either broken or unbroken horses. John Pitchlynn urged his sons James and Peter to round up their horses and take advantage of the opportunity.[55] Choctaws also purchased slaves from outsiders. Mushulatubbee bought six slaves—who turned out to be kidnapped freedmen from Kentucky or Tennessee—from some slave traders in Columbus, Mississippi, in exchange for 1,280 acres of land to which he was entitled.[56] Lacking legal standing in Mississippi, however, made slaveownership problematic. Molly McDonald purchased a slave in Alabama on credit. Though she had made payments for seven-eighths of the slave's price, one day the creditors demanded without prior notice that she make her final payment. When McDonald could not come up with the cash, the men repossessed the slave. Molly's son James wrote John C. Calhoun that the lack of a lien or mortgage was the root of the problem, and he pleaded with the secretary of war that by "the rules of reciprocity immediate compensation ought to be made."[57]

The slaves of Greenwood LeFlore's father, Louis LaFleur, perhaps represented the far-flung origins of the Choctaw slave population. Prince, LaFleur's driver, had been born among the Chickasaws in the 1780s. In the 1770s Catrene had arrived in New Orleans from the West Indies, where she had spoken French as her mother tongue. She was also proficient in Choctaw and English. Most of LaFleur's other slaves came from the Upper South. Rosa was an ardent Baptist who had lived in Tennessee, and Henry had been born in the Carolinas but grew up in Virginia.[58]

The lives led by Prince, Catrene, Rosa, and Henry probably differed little from the lives of slaves in other parts of the South. Among their many duties, they planted and harvested corn, built and repaired dwellings and outbuildings, herded livestock, and planted, tended, and picked cotton.[59] Based on Forrest McDonald's estimates for the South that one of every two slaves was a field hand and his estimates for per acre cotton production, the Choctaw slave force could have cultivated a maximum of 3,120 acres of cotton and produced at most a little over 500,000 pounds of ginned cotton. Whether or not the Choctaw slave force came close to reaching McDonald's estimates is impossible to say, but in 1828 Greenwood LeFlore's slaves and those of his neighbors alone raised 124,000 pounds of cotton.[60]

Next to the cultivation of cotton and the manufacture and sale of cloth, cotton picking ranked as the third most important activity in the emerging cotton economy. The case of Oakatibbé notwithstanding, early settlers of the region attempted to hire Indian men for the work, but their unwillingness to engage in the labor put an end to the experiment. Women, however, did work as itinerant farm laborers. After gathering their own crops of corn and cotton, Choctaw women, frequently accompanied by men, camped on the outskirts of plantations in Alabama, Mississippi, and even Kentucky to look for employment. While the men hunted, the women put their *kishi* baskets on their backs, looped the leather straps over their foreheads to hold the baskets in place, joined the slaves, and picked the planters' cotton before it rotted on the stalk. Women received blankets, cloth, handkerchiefs, and other manufactured items or cash wages for their work—usually one dollar for every hundred pounds they picked.[61] Itinerant cotton picking fit the seasonal rhythms of the Choctaw subsistence cycle and enabled many Choctaw women to earn wages or goods independent of their husbands and to participate in innovative economic activities while preserving the gendered structures of their culture.[62]

The proliferation of cattle, pigs, horses, cotton, and slavery in the towns signaled the Choctaws' acceptance of the basic commodities of the southern market economy. Choctaw material culture changed as well to reflect the sizable influence of American culture. As worm fences inched across the Choctaw landscape to protect fields from free-roaming hogs and cattle and square log cabins and corncribs replaced the round buildings of indigenous design, the landscape was dramatically transformed. Many Choctaws even wanted American furniture to fill their new homes. They were, wrote Cyrus Kingsbury in 1830, "already supplied in a manner not inferior to that of new settlers in our own country."[63] Mushulatubbee hired a trader from Alabama to build a new home for him. The cabin was built in the two-room dogtrot style common throughout the South, but it faced east so that the rising sun would shine in the windows every morning and remind the chief of Aba's presence.[64]

Clothing styles also expressed the juxtaposition of American styles and Mississippian meanings. Most Choctaw men continued to wear moccasins, but red cloth leggings and breechclouts as well as calico shirts had replaced buckskin garments. Silver armbands and wristbands as well as earrings and a nose ring completed the typical Choctaw male's outfit. Women also substituted for animal skins cloth that they had purchased or manufactured. Their scarlet skirts reached beneath their knees, and like the men they sported calico shirts and an array of silver jewelry. They wore their hair parted in the middle and braided behind, and in the part they traced a line of vermilion to represent the path of the sun.[65]

Under Aba's watchful eye, livestock and cotton had replaced deerskins as the Choctaws' chief commodities, and such products integrated the nation into the macroeconomic patterns of the American market economy. Not only did Choctaws raise the same things as Americans, but they lived in similar houses and wore some of the same clothes. To some leaders, however, the pace of change was too slow.

To accelerate the transformation of the Choctaw economy, David Folsom invited missionaries from the Boston-based American Board of Commissioners for Foreign Missions to come to the Choctaw towns and build schools, as they were doing among the Cherokees. In 1819 Folsom wrote to Elias Cornelius, missionary to the Cherokees, "Now lead us in this white path, that we may find the great joy and happiness as you do."[66] The same year Congress passed "an Act making provision for the civilization of the Indian tribes adjoining the frontier settlements," which appropriated $10,000 to support missionary endeavors. Thus funded, Cyrus Kingsbury, who had labored among the Cherokees at the Brainerd mission, embarked for Mississippi with his wife Priscilla and Loring Williams and his wife to "civilize" the Choctaws.[67]

In 1819 construction began on the first station, Elliot, on the banks of the Yallobusha River. Several factors recommended the site. Keelboats could navigate the river in high water, so the mission was intermittently accessible by boat. Furthermore, the Yallobusha flowed into the Yazoo River, which joined the Mississippi below the bluffs at Vicksburg and provided access to the markets of that town as well as of Natchez and New Orleans. The construction of Elliot also sparked a movement of the population of the Western division into the floodplains of the Yazoo and Yallobusha Rivers, where families expanded the livestock and cotton economies.[68]

The chiefs welcomed the arrival of the missionaries and the promise of schools. An initial donation of eighty-five cows and calves and $500 made by a council for the support of the missionaries inspired others to open their pockets. Chief Puckshunubbee of the Western division donated $200 for the schools and, with the support of his captains, pledged $2,000 of his division's share of the federal annuity to support Elliot over the next sixteen years. In the fall of 1819 Pushmataha, chief of the Southern towns, contributed a like amount "to be applied to the support of a school & Blacksmith's shop in [his] district." Mushulatubbee followed the lead of the other two chiefs, and even John Pitchlynn chipped in with a cash loan of $200 and ten shares of the Mississippi Bank worth about $1,000. He told Cyrus Kingsbury to sell the shares and pay him back when he could. By the time the American Board missions closed in 1831, the Choctaws had donated over $65,000 of a total operating cost of $147,920.[69]

To justify the generous support offered by the Choctaws, Kingsbury responded to requests to start other missions. In 1820 he began a second one, Mayhew, near the home of John Pitchlynn. Built on Oaktibbeha Creek twelve miles above its junction with the Tombigbee River, the station had good access to two important centers of the Choctaw urban trade, St. Stephens and Mobile, Alabama. Both Elliot and Mayhew were situated with relatively sure access to markets, yet they were connected to each other only by horse trails. David Folsom's home, Pigeon Roost, lay roughly between the two stations, and he asked the missionaries to build a road by his home that would connect them. With Folsom's help the missionaries cleared a sixty-mile connecting road in two months. After the road's completion, a wagon loaded with two thousand yards of cloth manufactured in Tennessee traveled down the Natchez Trace onto the new road and delivered the cargo to Elliot. The demonstration of the breadth of markets and the commercial possibilities that could now be tapped augured well for the station's role in promoting the development of the marketplace economy. And that Folsom sat astride the route connecting the two stations placed him in an enviable position.[70]

In addition to expanding access to outside markets, the stations provided important marketplaces. Because of illnesses among the missionaries and a shortage of American laborers, the missionaries hired Choctaws and their slaves to pick corn, tend the fields, herd their cattle, and lend a hand in constructing the dormitories, kitchens, barns, schoolhouses, and sheds at the stations. Such opportunities could be lucrative: the Choctaw herdsman the missionaries hired received an annual salary of three hundred dollars. Choctaws also traded their surplus meat, produce, and handicrafts to the missionaries for a variety of goods or sold them for cash. But the cost of renting slaves from the Choctaws proved prohibitive. After much debate and soul searching, the missionaries bought their own chattels.[71]

The economic development that accompanied the missions was but a beneficial outgrowth of their primary purpose—to teach young children how to read, write, live, and pray in the American market economy. The schools, however, were not dominated by biracial children as some scholars have maintained. Although such children made up a majority of enrollments in the mission schools' first years, full-ancestry children came to account for over two-thirds of the student body. From an original class of fifty-four "scholars" in 1819, enrollment peaked in 1829 when 320 boys and girls attended the eight schools that had been built.[72]

The demanding school regimen and the strict Lancastrian method the teachers employed were not popular with Choctaw parents. Children rose long before the sun to do chores. A breakfast of coffee, cornbread, meat, and potatoes was served half an hour before sunrise. Afterward they sang hymns and recited Scripture until half an hour after sunrise. At 8:45 A.M. their lessons began and continued through the day. All students learned reading and writing, and boys learned mathematics and farming while girls learned how to cook, manage a home, sew, spin, and weave.[73]

Parents, uncles, and aunts were glad their children were learning to read and write, but many resented the missionaries' insistence that their boys become farmers. In the words of one woman who was told she should teach her son to farm: "Would you have me make a woman of my son? He is to be a man and a warrior & he is not going to work like a woman!"[74] Economic change and acculturation had their limits, and when the missionaries pushed the Choctaws' sense of propriety, more often than not they encountered resistance.

The development of the marketplace economy in the early decades of the nineteenth century demonstrated how far culture could both resist and accommodate innovation, for the reciprocity that formerly had linked Choctaws and outsiders and the subsistence production that had characterized the Mississippian economy gave way to notions of sale, profit, and surplus production. Indeed, the innovative marketplace economy restored a measure of prosperity to the Choctaws, much to the surprise of missionaries, who had expected to find savage and impoverished "sons of the forest." As Methodist missionary Alexander Talley wrote of his first sight of a Choctaw town: "I was agreeably disappointed in finding beautiful corn fields attached to most of the houses, having good fences, and every appearance of comfort and plenty."[75] But concerning the cultural meanings that attached to economic production and exchange, neither the market nor the missionaries could break down the gender divisions of the Choctaw economy. Men continued to do men's things and women continued to do women's things.

CHAPTER FIVE

The Creation of a Nation, 1819-28

Your fathers have long possessed this land, notwithstanding their
ignorance. . . . But this you cannot expect to do, unless you become civilized.
Chief Mushulatubbee to a group of Choctaw schoolchildren, *Missionary Herald*

IN SPITE of the federal government's passage of the "civilization act" and
its support of the Choctaw missions, policymakers in the 1820s increasingly came to endorse the removal of Native Americans from the East to
land west of the Mississippi River. Such a move, the federal government
believed, would save the Indians from extinction and, in the hopes of local
politicians and settlers, vacate Indian land for settlement by Americans
and taxation by needy state governments. Choctaws, however, turned to
the mission schools to equip their children to resist the legal and political
pressures to remove them applied by both the federal and Mississippi
state governments. In the late fall of 1822, Chief Mushulatubbee urged a
gathering of schoolchildren to learn their lessons and prepare to defend
their land and their sovereignty. He further promised them an important
role in the nation's future. "I hope," the chief declared, "I shall yet live
to see my council filled with the boys who are now in school and that you
will know much more than we know, and do much better than we do."[1]

While Mushulatubbee uttered these words to the schoolchildren, David
Folsom stood behind him in a demonstration of their unity in support of
the schools and in resistance to the United States. But over time their
common cause broke down as the two leaders disagreed over the extent of
other political reforms and the best way to safeguard their people's future.

86

In the 1820s Mushulatubbee and David Folsom emerged at the heads of rival political factions that articulated distinctly different visions of how the nation should preserve its sovereignty and homeland. Though based on the allegiances of an ancient matrilineal kinship system, the struggles between the two men and their supporters were transformed into a bitter ideological conflict over the nature and structure of chiefly government and civil society.

Many current interpretations of Native American political factionalism, and all studies of Choctaw factionalism, emphasize a division between progressive mixed-bloods and conservative full-bloods. The use of such nineteenth-century racial terms to understand factionalism is problematic because it perpetuates in subtle ways the racist assumptions held by federal policymakers and by popular politicians. To cite one example, Andrew Jackson had served throughout the 1810s as an Indian fighter and as a treaty negotiator, and his experiences led him to see mixed-bloods as exploiters of "real" and "true" Indians. During negotiations with the Cherokees in 1817 he remarked that "half breeds . . . have been and are fattening upon the annuities, the labours, and folly of the native Indians."[2]

Historians have been equally uncharitable in their interpretations of biracial leaders. David Folsom and his ally Greenwood LeFlore have been at various times called members of a "new elite" that "led an assault on Choctaw customs," men who "practiced duplicity," and members of "a small but thriving Choctaw landed aristocracy" that "spoke publicly against removal because of their elected positions, but . . . favored it privately in order to consolidate their political positions."[3] Students of Native American history must abandon the bankrupt notions of blood and genetic ancestry as both interpretative and descriptive devices because they are anachronistic and because they do not work.

The racial paradigm fails to adequately explain Choctaw factionalism because it connotes a false link between race and ideology. In economic matters, for example, "full-blood" leaders like Franchimastabé, Homastubby, and Mushulatubbee endorsed innovative strategies and participated just as enthusiastically in the marketplace economy as did the "mixed-bloods." By the same token, such men were more reluctant to buy into the political reforms proposed by the "mixed-bloods." Moreover, the racial typology cannot explain the sizable number of biracial men who supported the full-ancestry leaders, and full-ancestry men who supported the biracial leaders, all of which begs the question, What can explain Choctaw political factionalism?[4]

Choctaw factionalism cannot be understood as a function of either race or economics. Rather, the struggle was a contest of ideologies held by the chiefs and the commoners who supported them. One side drew its inspiration from post-Mississippian patterns of trade, government, faith, and ethnicity, what one might call a primordialist ideology because it reflected a tendency to cast innovative behavior in terms that were consonant with older customs. The other side was much more influenced by Anglo-American patterns of action and behavior because its leaders, Folsom and LeFlore, had grown up in a commercial and multicultural milieu. They embraced a cosmopolitan ideology that reached to outside rather than inside sources of power and that reflected an abiding need to build a new society poised somewhere between what the primordialists viewed as their ideal and what the Americans held out as "civilization." Despite the two factions' considerable differences, however, neither group abandoned the Mississippian values that coursed through their culture.[5]

The most important primordialist leader was the chief of the Eastern division, Mushulatubbee. He was a prosperous stockman and slaveowner, and he participated comfortably and successfully in the marketplace economy. To this end he supported missionary education and believed that schools were essential to his people's economic prosperity and political survival. But that was the limit of his reformist agenda. As a chief he adhered to an ancient ideology predicated on divisional autonomy and redistribution of prestige goods, and he refused to condone any alteration to these cornerstones of chiefly power. Matrilineal kinship cemented his faction. His relatives, the Pitchlynn family, particularly his nephews James and Peter, provided crucial support, as did the chief of the Southern division, Pushmataha, his nephew Tappenahooma, and his kinfolk by marriage, the Juzon family. Chief Puckshunubbee and his council speaker Robert Cole in the Western division likewise shared Mushulatubbee's thoughts on schools and politics, and they worked together from time to time to thwart the rise of the cosmopolitans.[6]

In opposition to Chiefs Mushulatubbee and Pushmataha and their supporters, Folsom, LeFlore, John Garland, Hwoolatahoomah, and Tunapinchuffa offered a different solution to the Choctaws' political woes. Rather than drawing primarily on indigenous traditions, these leaders were cosmopolitan in their outlook. They sought to graft certain aspects of Anglo-American political culture—namely constitutional government, nationalism, and Christianity—onto a chiefly ideal that would support their independence and satisfy Aba. In particular they tried to demolish the divisional governments, which they viewed as inimical to the Choctaws' long-term interests, and to replace them with a unified national government. In so doing they hoped to replace long-standing ethnic identities and kinship affiliations with a common nationality predicated on civic membership in the Choctaw state.

The primordialists dominated the three divisional chieftainships in the early years of the nineteenth century. Homastubby and then his nephew Mushulatubbee were chiefs of the Eastern division, and Puckshunubbee was chief in the West. After the death of Pooscoos II, "the great French king," the renowned war leader Pushmataha became chief of the Southern towns. But the balance of power began to tilt when David Folsom wrote to the American Board missionaries and asked them to build schools among the Choctaws. The chiefs feared Folsom would use the schools to undermine their authority and augment his own. Some of the chiefs may have even considered removing across the Mississippi River to preserve their authority, for in 1819 James Pitchlynn, John's son and Peter's elder brother, took it upon himself to write a series of letters to Andrew Jackson claiming that the Choctaws wanted to remove. Playing on Jackson's notions of Indian character, Pitchlynn reported to the general that the Choctaws wanted to remove to Arkansas Territory, where "real Indian chiefs" like his maternal uncle Mushulatubbee could govern unchallenged.[7] According to Pitchlynn, Folsom and his party opposed removal and intended to "educate their children" and "defraud . . . the Nation." Folsom, Pitchlynn claimed, had even gone so far as to threaten him with a "knock on the head" should he continue his letter campaign.[8] To counteract Pitchlynn's advocacy of removal, Folsom's supporters spread rumors and Joel Nail circulated a letter reporting that the land west of the Mississippi River "affords neither soil water nor game."[9]

Pitchlynn's letters piqued the interest of Jackson and Secretary of War John C. Calhoun. In 1820 the secretary commissioned Jackson and General Thomas Hinds, a Mississippian who had fought with Jackson in the Creek Civil War, to discuss with the Choctaws a cession of their Mississippi land and their removal to Arkansas Territory. Mushulatubbee, Pushmataha, and Charles Juzon eagerly anticipated the treaty negotiations, but they could not overlook the reluctance of other Choctaws to talk to the commissioners.[10] Federal agent John McKee identified David Folsom as the ringleader of "a few half-breeds, with but little claim to distinction, [who] have . . . alarmed many of the Indians who were disposed to migrate." According to McKee, Folsom was prepared to kill anyone who signed the treaty.[11]

David Folsom's machinations failed to block the treaty talks. After several days of meetings with Jackson and Hinds at Josiah Doak's tavern on the Natchez Trace, the assembled chiefs and captains signed the Treaty of Doak's Stand on 18 October 1820. Puckshunubbee, Pushmataha, Mushulatubbee, James Pitchlynn, and future primordialist leaders Tappenahooma and Robert Cole were among those who endorsed the document with X marks. Even Folsom's future ally Greenwood LeFlore signed the treaty, but Folsom refused to do so.[12]

The treaty brought together both tenets of federal Indian policy. It obtained for the federal government almost half of the Choctaws' Mississippi land in exchange for a larger parcel in Arkansas Territory, and the document provided for a voluntary removal. But few people removed. The treaty further addressed the "civilizing" of the Choctaws. In addition to funding schools, it stipulated that the boundaries between the Choctaws and the United States "shall remain without alteration until the period at which said nation shall become so civilized and enlightened as to be made citizens of the United States."[13] After the federal government granted them citizenship, it would allot land for each family and sell the rest to settlers. The land cession and the provisions for removal and assimilation appalled Folsom. Some time after the treaty's ratification by Congress he remarked, "I see no other way But we must have new Chiefs."[14]

Another incident sharpened the emerging lines of political conflict. During the early 1800s the federal government recognized the authority of the three division chiefs by allowing them to oversee the distribution of the trade goods that were part of the federal annuity payments made to the Choctaws. By the 1820s the chiefs had also come to regard the mission schools as "goods" that could be distributed throughout the nation and that would confer great prestige on the chiefs who sponsored them. Folsom had made his reputation this way, and other chiefs hoped to follow suit.

In the fall of 1822 Pushmataha, chief of the Southern division, complained about the location of a missionary school at the home of Henry Nail, an American settler who had married a Choctaw woman, rather than at his home. He feared that if Nail hosted the school and was associated with its many benefits it would undermine his own prestige and authority. The chief was not without leverage, though, because he controlled the distribution of the annual federal annuity in his division. To persuade the missionaries to build the school at his home, he threatened to withdraw his division's pledge of $2,000 a year to the missionary project.[15] He further refused to share the annuity goods with Nail and his family. To protest the inequitable distribution of the annuity, Nail's son Joel, who had worked with Folsom to oppose the recent treaty, resigned his commission in the district's light horse patrol.[16]

The feud between Pushmataha and the Nails anticipated the emergence of factional divisions in the nation and the use of the new exotic prestige goods like schools to wage the struggle. But the dispute in the Southern division did not signal an opportunity for wholesale political change in the other divisions. Not until the winter of 1824–25, when the Choctaws were invited to Washington to renegotiate certain provisions of the treaty, did factional lines crack each of the three divisions.

After the 1820 Treaty of Doak's Stand, the federal government learned that American citizens inhabited a portion of the Arkansas land it had ceded to the Choctaws. An embarrassed Secretary Calhoun asked the Choctaws to renegotiate the treaty and to retrocede to the United States the occupied portion of the Arkansas parcel. Two of the chiefs eagerly anticipated the upcoming talks. Mushulatubbee and Pushmataha had run up considerable debts at the United States factory to obtain more goods to distribute to their partisans, and they saw the talks as an opportunity to discharge their old accounts. Unlike Mushulatubbee and Pushmataha, Chief Puckshunubbee owed no money to the factory, and he opposed the others' plan to retrocede the Arkansas land. Several other prominent Choctaws shared Puckshunubbee's unease.[17]

A delegation composed of the three chiefs plus Robert Cole, John Pitchlynn, David Folsom, and a few others set out in October 1824 and traveled north by stagecoach for several days. When they arrived in Maysville, Kentucky, late on the night of 10 October, the party was exhausted. David Folsom went into a nearby inn to find rooms, and the lanky Puckshunubbee took the opportunity to walk around and stretch his legs after the long, uncomfortable ride. While walking down a dark street, he slipped and fell down a steep bluff. A number of locals heard him fall and rushed to the scene, and at the commotion Folsom ran outside and peered over the bluff. Below, on a pile of jagged rocks, illuminated by the light of Folsom's lantern, lay Puckshunubbee's broken body. With the help of some of the onlookers who had gathered at the scene, Folsom hauled the chief to the inn and got him into bed. A doctor diagnosed a fractured skull, shoulder blade, and collarbone. After drifting in and out of consciousness for two days, the old chief died. Maysville was abuzz with excitement at the tragic accident and dramatic death, and the townspeople insisted on burying the old chief with full military honors. A throng of six hundred people lined the street to the church and graveyard. Robert Cole, Puckshunubbee's council speaker, led the procession to the cemetery while a fife and drum corps played. After three rounds of musket fire by the local militia, the good citizens of Maysville laid the chief to rest.[18]

The delegation left Maysville and finally arrived in Washington on 27 October 1824. Folsom hated the city: it was, he thought, "a wicked place."[19] While he fretted about sin and God's retribution, Pushmataha, Mushulatubbee, and Robert Cole ran up a bar bill of over $2,000. Causing Folsom further consternation, both Mushulatubbee and Robert Cole contracted syphilis from local prostitutes. Pushmataha was sick as well with a severe cough, and doctors doubted he would survive the talks. No doubt mindful of the honors accorded Puckshunubbee in Maysville, he made arrangements for a grandiose burial at the Congressional Cemetery in his full American military uniform. The funeral went according to plan, and cannons, not muskets, boomed a graveside salute.[20]

The rest of the delegation and John C. Calhoun finally signed a treaty on 22 January 1825. The document extinguished the debts of Pushmataha and Mushulatubbee and retroceded the inhabited Arkansas land to the United States in exchange for financial considerations. More important, the negotiators succeeded in rewriting the provision in the Treaty of Doak's Stand that had permitted the federal government to declare the Choctaws "civilized" when it saw fit and to allot their land. They also obtained a guarantee of Choctaw sovereignty and the right to determine for themselves when they were ready to become citizens of the United States. Although he regretted ceding the Arkansas land, Folsom also obtained from Calhoun more funding for the missionary schools, particularly for the construction of a Choctaw secondary school.[21]

The several months of debauchery, death, and high-pressure negotiations wore heavily on David Folsom, and when he learned that his child had died during his absence, he began to question his religious convictions. "I was not borne again with holly sprite of God," he lamented to a friend, "Now I see what I am."[22] What he had become was a political animal, because the deaths of the two chiefs had a profound influence on his political aspirations. Previously he had confined his activities to supporting mission schools and opposing the chiefs, but when Puckshunubbee and Pushmataha died Folsom became convinced that Aba or God had a plan for the Choctaws. "God is just and write in taking these chiefs," he believed, " . . . so that there may be a better men may rase up in their placez."[23]

Choctaw commoners were of a similar mind, and the Treaty of Washington crippled the public's faith in the primordialist leaders. Mushulatubbee, who was the ranking survivor of the treaty talks, returned home vilified for having agreed to yet another land cession. To recoup the prestige and authority he had lost, he encouraged his subordinate captains to bring whiskey into the Eastern division for a month of drinking and feasting. Many warriors accepted the offer, and reports of the drunkenness that ensued claimed that it exceeded anything ever witnessed in the towns. The alcohol had little effect on his detractors, though, and Mushulatubbee spent several nights hidden in federal agent William Ward's cabin for fear he might be killed.[24]

Ward believed Mushulatubbee had good reason to fear for his life. In February 1825 Creek leader William McIntosh and a rump council packed with his supporters had signed the Treaty of Indian Springs with the federal government. McIntosh's actions violated Creek national law, for the treaty ceded all of their land in Georgia to the United States against the wishes of the Creek national council. In retaliation for McIntosh's treachery, a party of Creeks went to his home in Georgia and poured volley after volley into the disgraced leader's body.[25] Among the Choctaws, Ward had "heard some half breeds exult at the murder of McIntosh," and Mushulatubbee feared that, like him, he would pay for the recent Arkansas cession with his life.[26]

Mushulatubbee had backed himself into a corner, and while he had upset his detractors, more importantly he began to alienate his supporters. Faced with an eroding power base, Mushulatubbee distributed all of his federal annuity goods among his warriors in the Eastern towns to quell discontent on his home turf. But the strategy prevented him from giving goods to his ally Robert Cole in the Western towns as he had done in the past. The imperatives of chiefly politics, in this instance, undermined political cooperation when the primordialists needed it most.[27]

In addition to angering Cole, Mushulatubbee's maladroit handling of the school fund provided in the Treaty of Washington further weakened his precarious political position.[28] Cyrus Kingsbury had suggested that the Choctaws use the money to build a secondary school at Folsom's home, Pigeon Roost, but Mushulatubbee perceived a further augmentation of his rival's authority in the division, and he blocked the plan. Moreover, Mushulatubbee disapproved of the missionaries' willingness to teach in Choctaw. He believed that if the Choctaws were to coexist with their American neighbors and prosper in the marketplace, they had to learn English, the language of the region's commercial economy. Some years later Mushulatubbee complained, "We have never received a Scholar out of their schools that was able to keep a Grog shop book." "When we found we could get nothing from them," he remembered, "we established an academy in Kentucky."[29]

Instead of entrusting the education of future generations of Choctaws to the American Board missionaries, who were reluctant to consult with Mushulatubbee, the chief and his nephew Peter Pitchlynn called for the establishment of a secondary school outside the nation. Unknown to Folsom, Mushulatubbee and Agent Ward appropriated the money set aside by the late treaty and gave it to a Baptist society in Kentucky. David Henderson, a member of the society, agreed to teach the children, and Senator Richard M. Johnson of Kentucky assumed control of the project. That Ward was Johnson's brother-in-law only heightened the sense of scandal among the Choctaws. When the school opened, Mushulatubbee compounded his problems by monopolizing the placement of students in the academy.[30]

Mushulatubbee supported the Choctaw Academy because he wanted some control over the pace of change and over commoners' access to education. Unfortunately for him, the maldistribution of federal annuity goods, education funds, and placements in the school was not enough to restore the popularity he had enjoyed before the Treaty of Washington. His support of the treaty had cost him his moral authority, and the gifts could not recoup it. Having alienated his allies, provoked his opponents, and mismanaged the redistributive prerogatives on which his authority rested, he ruined any chance he might have had to hold his position. When the chief secretly appropriated a further $6,000 from the national annuity to support the Choctaw Academy, David Folsom moved to unseat him.[31]

In April 1826 Folsom called together the Eastern division council to discuss Mushulatubbee's fitness as its leader. The proceedings culminated in an indictment of the chief's conduct. Folsom asserted that "the warriors did positively declare against their chief and were determined that a second McIntosh should not rise up among them and dispose of their lands." But Mushulatubbee's complicity in the 1820 and 1825 cessions was not the only issue. Folsom also charged that Mushulatubbee's warriors had tired of his "intemperence tyrannical disposition ignorance and his manner of disposing of the annuity."[32] Confronted with such overwhelming opposition, Mushulatubbee resigned as chief rather than face the humiliation of being "broken," or voted out of office. The council appointed Folsom chief for four years, and after pledging that he would sell no more land the new chief called on the council to support the mission schools and to turn out Robert Cole and Tappenahooma, who still governed in the Western and Southern divisions, respectively.[33] Folsom closed the council by urging commoners to choose "respectable men to guide their affairs, and [to apply] themselves in earnest to the work of civilization."[34] Such a program was necessary, he argued, for "those Indian tribes which are now in a state of darkness must go through a revolution in some way or other."[35]

The contagion of revolution spread throughout the nation. In the Western division, people agitated for the removal of Chief Robert Cole, who had proved himself a vocal opponent of Folsom and of the mission's program of agricultural education. The American Board operated Bethany mission school in Cole's neighborhood, which the chief supported in principle. But Cole despised the missionaries. He especially resented their insistence on teaching his nephews and the other boys farming rather than trades like blacksmithing or carpentry. Much to the missionaries' surprise, Cole likened their course of instruction to slavery because the children, he complained, "were driven in the fields in the same manner that negros were on the plantations."[36] Cole, who operated a wood yard in Arkansas, instead reiterated Mingo Homastubby's belief that Choctaw men should not farm. In early 1825, after hearing of threats on the life of William Pride, the school's headmaster, Cyrus Kingsbury ordered the school closed. Cole approached a Methodist circuit rider, Wiley Ledbetter, to open a school at his home, but Ledbetter ran into unspecified problems, and he fled the district the same year.[37]

Cole's abuse of the missionaries angered Folsom and his party, and they began to plot to remove him from office. To scotch their schemes, Cole announced that he would hold a feast to discuss whatever complaints the people might have against him. In true chiefly fashion, Cole hoped to use the occasion to distribute food, drink, and probably trade goods to those who attended and thereby restore his authority and the reciprocal ties that bound commoners and chiefs. But the bid for support failed.[38] There was no feast and no discussion of Cole's future as chief. Instead, a number of warriors issued a proclamation that criticized his government as "oppressive" and "ruinous."[39] Furthermore, they complained that he favored American interests and that he had accepted bribes at the treaty negotiations at Doak's Stand and at Washington.[40] Following the lead of the Eastern council, the council of the Western division turned Cole out of office and appointed his nephew Greenwood LeFlore to serve, like Folsom, as chief for four years. In return the chief pledged to the captains and to the commoners never to "turn his coat" on them.[41]

The political upheavals of 1826 fundamentally changed the focus and scope of Choctaw government but not its structure. In place of Mushulatubbee and Robert Cole, the two primordialist leaders who had risen to power through chiefly lineages and maintained it with redistribution, and who only rarely acted in concert with one another, cosmopolitans now governed two of the three divisions on a platform of unified political opposition to the United States, a commitment neither to cede land nor to remove, and a vision to revitalize society through education.

Nevertheless, Folsom and LeFlore retained a traditional intermediate chiefdom hierarchy in their division governments and acted in ways that befitted the office of chief. Beneath Folsom and LeFlore, who had taken to calling themselves colonels, were Talking Warrior, who served as Folsom's war chief, and Hashaushahopiah, who became LeFlore's war chief. Still further down the chain of command were the captains, formerly known as *tascamingoutchy*, whom the colonels appointed to govern individual towns and who wore swords as "marks of distinction." Each colonel and captain in turn had a "pipe lighter" who served the same function as the old *tichou-mingos* who had opened council discussions and passed around the lighted calumet. Also subordinate to the captains were the light horsemen whose duties included carrying news from town to town, summoning people for council meetings, keeping order at public assemblies, and interdicting the alcohol trade.[42] To their commoners the chiefs opened their houses, and the people were not shy about testing their new leaders' generosity. Folsom's and LeFlore's tables, wrote one observer, "must be free to all who visit them, and as they wish to elevate their people, their tables must be well supplyed."[43]

In August 1826, shortly after Folsom and LeFlore had come to power, the division councils of the East and West met together to form a constitutional government to supersede the two divisional governments and unite them into what effectively was a complex chiefdom; only instead of overseeing the distribution of corn or waging war, the new chiefs directed an ambitious school program and tried to keep the federal government at arm's length. The combined councils wrote a constitution and agreed to appoint eight leaders to meet biannually at a council house built in a clearing about two and a half miles from the federal agency. Typical of frontier architecture, the whitewashed building was a simple rectangle, twenty feet wide by thirty feet long, made of split poplar logs. Typical of Choctaw architecture, it was laid out on an east-west axis so that the sun was always over the councilmen's heads. Located near the center of the nation, the new capitol represented the cosmopolitans' goal of overcoming the decentralization and ineffectiveness of the divisional governments, and it symbolized their plan to recenter the Choctaw sacred circle on a new source of power. Not long after its formation, the new government got the chance to fulfill its most important promise, to withstand federal and state pressure to cede land and remove from Mississippi.[44]

On 23 February 1825, Senator Powhatan Ellis of Mississippi introduced a bill to Congress to negotiate a removal treaty with the Choctaws. The measure passed, and a federal commission of William Clark, Thomas Hinds, and John Coffee traveled to Mississippi to negotiate with the new leaders. Although the Southern division was not yet a part of the new nation, Chief Tappenahooma welcomed the commissioners with a calumet ceremony. Following the ritual of hospitality and friendship, the national council refused to consider either removal or a land cession.[45] Weary of the constant demands for more land, LeFlore appealed to Thomas McKenney, director of the Office of Indian Affairs. "Wee are anxious," he wrote, "to be come sivillize Nation if our Father let ous rest few years but wee have been pastured for Land so much wee dout now what to do."[46]

Frustrated by the failure of the federal government to extract further land cessions from the Choctaws, in 1826 Mississippi Governor Gerard Brandon demanded that the Indians be expelled immediately. Brandon claimed that the Choctaws "were depriving us of that territory we had a right to expect when we were admitted into the Union."[47] The governor was wrong, however. The state had no right to expect jurisdiction over the Choctaws because the ordinance that had granted Mississippi statehood in 1817 unquestionably established federal domain over "the waste or unappropriated lands lying within the state of Mississippi" that the Choctaws inhabited. Until the land was acquired by treaty, it remained under federal control.[48]

In spite of the clear-cut assignment of jurisdiction over the Choctaw land, the state legislature agreed with Governor Brandon. The Mississippi House of Representatives formed a committee to examine how the state might acquire title to the Choctaws' land without resorting to a federally negotiated treaty. Like Georgia and Alabama, Mississippi settled on extending state law over lands occupied by Indians. The measure would, if passed, abrogate the sovereignty of the Choctaws as well as revoke the legality of the various federal treaties they had signed, and it would enable the state to survey their land and sell it to prospective immigrants. Doubts over the bill's propriety clouded its future, though, and after passing it in its first reading, the House of Representatives killed it on the second.[49]

Governor Brandon's agitation for extending state law put great pressure on the new nation, but the cosmopolitan chiefs turned their attention to another problem, federal agent William Ward. Believing they were more amenable to removal, Agent Ward supported Cole and Mushulatubbee even after their fall from power, and he became a thorn in the side of the cosmopolitan reformers. To earlier charges that Ward was negligent, incompetent, and alcoholic, Folsom and LeFlore now added corrupt.[50] As early as 1821 Choctaws had complained that Agent Ward embezzled annuity funds and traded whiskey, and his connection with the Choctaw Academy further tarnished his reputation. LeFlore and Folsom accused him of buying shoddy goods with annuity money, overcharging the Choctaws for them, and keeping the profits for himself, his son, and his two sons-in-law, whom he had employed as subagents to purchase and transport the goods. Ward pleaded innocent to all charges.[51]

Thomas McKenney recommended that the matter be forgotten, more to check Folsom and LeFlore than to exonerate Ward. After all, McKenney wrote, the "chiefs are not . . . qualified to administer to their people the wholesome policy which the United States exercises towards them."[52] But McKenney had no satisfactory response to complaints about Ward's incompetence. Ward had often refused to intervene in disputes and was always ready to use his ignorance of the Indians' affairs to justify his inaction, to which one Choctaw replied, "It is his duty *not* to be ignorant."[53]

Federal stonewalling could slow the cosmopolitans' attempt to oust their agent, but it could do little to impede their revolution. In September 1828 Tappenahooma led a party out west to explore the Choctaws' Arkansas land with the expectation of removing there in the near future. One month later the council of the Southern division brought charges against the absent chief similar to those that had toppled Mushulatubbee and Robert Cole.[54] Backed by a war chief named Nittakaichee, John Garland was elected civil chief of the Southern division for a term of four years.[55] Garland could neither read nor write English, and he spoke it only with great difficulty, but he supported the mission schools and Folsom's and LeFlore's reforms. His election made the cosmopolitan revolution final, much to the chagrin of Ward, who complained to Secretary of War Peter Porter, "This nation are now completely governed or under the influence of three men who have a purty good knowledge of the Laws of nations."[56]

Indeed, their "purty good knowledge" had led to the promulgation of a variety of national laws. By 1829, three years after its creation, the Choctaw national government had passed twenty-two laws. With many of these laws the government intended to aid and to regulate the Choctaws' entry into the American market economy. One law, for example, required debts to be paid in a timely fashion and decreed that a deceased's estate be used first to extinguish all outstanding debts. Furthermore, anyone who hired an American was obliged to pay the sum for which the two parties had contracted.[57]

Other laws represented an attempt by the cosmopolitans to bring their culture into conformity with American norms. Estate laws, for example, followed the patterns and practices of American law. Most states accepted the principle of dowry whereby a widow obtained one-third of her husband's estate while the rest was divided among the children. The new government passed such a law, which may have undermined separate ownership of property by men and women.[58] Another law that affected women required that prospective American husbands secure permission from the division chief and a license from the federal agent before proceeding with the marriage. Once permission was secured, the couple could, LeFlore wrote, "mary cordin to white Laws."[59] By asserting such authority the national government prevented Americans from marrying Choctaws simply to establish claims to land and asserted some control over the pace of intercultural interaction.

In an effort to further unite the Choctaws as a nation, the cosmopolitans tackled the complicated rites of Choctaw funerals. Sometime in the early 1800s, many Choctaws abandoned the scaffolding and bone-picking rituals of the eighteenth century for in-ground burials. Why burial became acceptable is unclear. George Gaines, a trader who spent two decades working among the Choctaws, believed they adopted the practice after the Creek Civil War. Seeing the burial of American soldiers convinced them, Gaines thought, "that burying the dead was better than scaffolding."[60] Choctaws may have seen American burial practices as a source of greater power: the interment of Puckshunubbee in Maysville, Kentucky, and Pushmataha's burial in Washington certainly signaled to commoners that burial was acceptable. Burials, however, were accompanied by ceremonies that reflected the continuing importance of the scaffolding rites. Kinfolk buried the deceased in a sitting position either near his or her home or under the bed inside the house, a practice common among the Chickasaws. The bone pickers of each moiety continued to play an important role, but they no longer handled the corpse. Instead, at the beginning of the mourning period they erected around the grave several red poles eight feet long and a fifteen-foot pole topped with a white flag. Female mourners gathered around the grave, shrouded in blankets, and uttered, one missionary commented, "the most piteous lamentations." They despaired of the sundering of their matrilineal lines by death and asked aloud, "O! Why did you leave us. Were you not content with your children? Did you not have corn enough here?"[61] During the time of the pole setting, Choctaws took great care to appease the spirit of the dead. Family members kept a fire burning near the deceased's home lest "their departed friend might be distressed or angry, especially if the nights were cold, dark, or stormy."[62] Though the length of the mourning period depended on the rank of the dceased, once it ended members of

both moieties danced and held a feast that was a "joyous occasion."[63] At
the end of mourning, the bone pickers pulled down the poles to signal
the departure of the spirit.[64] What LeFlore and Folsom sought to end
through law was the pole pulling, because the ceremony perpetuated the
moiety system that divided their society in half. By suppressing moiety
affiliations, the cosmopolitans may have been attempting to uproot the
ancient system while forwarding their own view of a society where one
was Choctaw before one was of the red moiety or of the white one, or
even Imoklasha, Inholahta, or Chickasawhay.[65]

The pole-pulling law threatened a key component of the culture, but
not all cosmopolitan legislation sought to overturn Choctaw traditions.
One law involving witchcraft reflected the striking of a balance between
reform and tradition. In September 1829 the cosmopolitan government
wrote, "In future all persons who shall be accused of being a wizzard or
witch, shall be tried before the chiefs and committees [of the nation], or
by any four captains [in the division]; and if they are found guilty, they
shall be punished at the direction of the court."[66] The law made the state
the arbiter of crime and punishment and not individual Choctaws who
had located witches. But if the law had profound implications for Choctaw
jurisprudence, it also sanctioned popular belief.

Choctaws believed that when witches traveled at night to cast their
spells and shoot their "witch arrows" they removed their skins and their
entrails floated in the air as luminous apparitions. The law continued,
"Be it further enacted, that if any person or persons shall find at any
place the entrails of a wizzard or witch, the said entrails going from or
returning to the body, the said body shall be put to death at the place
where it may be discovered."[67] In this case the "destroyers" of traditional
culture compromised with the object of their destruction.

One of the most popular measures the government passed was a firm
approach to the ongoing problem of black-market whiskey. LeFlore called
a public meeting to discuss matters, and the men who filed into council
formed a ring around a fire LeFlore had set and smoked tobacco and
sumac from a pipe that his pipe lighter passed around. The women who
attended the meeting sat in a circle outside that of the men. A consensus
soon emerged, and the assembled men drew up a national law to ban
the whiskey trade. Any violator of the prohibition, the council declared,
"should be struck a hard lick on the head with a stick and have his
whiskey poured out on the ground." The light horse patrol enforced the

new law enthusiastically—in the summer of 1829 alone they whipped nearly thirty people for importing alcohol.[68]

In the absence of widespread public opposition to the cosmopolitans, how the public received the new government and legislative reform is unknown. The cosmopolitan chiefs' willingness to accommodate and incorporate Choctaw morality, as in the witch law, may have made other measures regarding pole pulling or estates more palatable. To most Choctaws, however, the content of the law may have mattered less than its symbolic and metaphorical power. When LeFlore chaired a national council meeting in 1828 he convened the proceedings at the foot of the Nanih Waiya mound where Aba had handed down the Choctaws' original law. By employing such a sacred symbol to buttress his claims to authority and power, LeFlore fashioned the cosmopolitan ideology into a sacred movement of undeniable appeal. To his audience, the chief would have seemed an imposing figure as he issued the new law in the mound's sanctifying shadow and charted the direction of a new bright path. Wrapped in such deeply felt and shared symbols, the cosmopolitans' innovative and revitalistic program probably resonated on some level with Choctaws of all ideological persuasions.[69]

We can never be sure how commoners perceived the cosmopolitan chiefs and their project, but it is beyond doubt that Folsom, Leflore, and Garland believed their program could revitalize their society and protect their nation's sovereignty from the encroachments of the state of Mississippi and of the federal government. They had gotten the breathing space LeFlore had asked for in 1827 and accomplished much over the course of the following year. Having appropriated certain aspects of Anglo-American political culture, the cosmopolitan chiefs had created a functional Choctaw polity. "Our nation," David Folsom proudly stated, "is beginning to wear a different aspect—As a Nation she is rising and is already high as to look down with contempt upon dissipation."[70]

CHAPTER SIX

The Great Awakening, 1828–30

As you flourished, we decayed. We have been tempted to ask, Why should this be so? Has the Great Spirit frowned upon his red children, that they should have withered in your presence? Mushulatubbee, Robert Cole, Nittakaichee, and James McDonald to the Congress of the United States of America, quoted in Thomas L. McKenney, *Memoirs, Official and Personal*

IN CONTRAST to David Folsom's belief that the Choctaw nation was "rising" and could, in 1828, look down on "dissipation," the primordialist chiefs who had fallen out of power shared none of his optimism.[1] The Choctaws' religion had always existed independent of the chiefs, but religion was also a part of their political arsenal. Having lost their offices, Mushulatubbee and Robert Cole could only conclude that the "Great Spirit" was frowning on them and their people. Indeed, the differing opinions expressed by the two factions as to the state of their nation in 1828 reflected a greater division within the nation that threatened to undermine the most socially integrative structure in Choctaw culture— religion.

As the Choctaws developed out of an amalgamation of remnant groups sometime in the sixteenth century, a religious framework had evolved that contained their latent ethnic, social, and gender divisions. Funeral rituals, marriage ceremonies, and sacred occasions like the green corn ceremony brought together members of rival clans, *iksas*, towns, and divisions as well as both genders under one god and reminded them that they were all the chosen people. Religion, in effect, papered over the deep fissures that divided the society.[2] When there ceased to be a religious consensus, however, religion lost its centripetal force. Not bound by a common conception of the bright path, the constituent parts of the society could go their own ways and search for their own paths. Observers of the bitter political and religious factionalism of the late 1820s concluded that the new nation would fly apart.

At the heart of the conflict were contrasting responses to the pressures on the sacred circle brought by the outside world. In a process common to other societies around the world that also experienced such dislocations as a consequence of contact, Choctaws searched for the sources of instability and disorder in terms specific to their culture. Disorder and its attendant pollution, they believed, reflected a cosmic imbalance, and to reestablish social equipoise they had to repurify their nation. Searching themselves, their towns, homes, and fields for sources of pollution, they scoured the sacred circle, and their eyes fixed not on the new chiefs but on the witches whose malevolent magic had always operated against the community's best interests.[3]

Known as *ishtabe*, man killers, and *hoollabe*, spoilers of things sacred, witches were malevolent beings who in daylight appeared as humans but at night transformed themselves into forest animals or floated about as glowing apparitions.[4] Accidents, sickness, and bad luck encountered by individuals as well as entire communities were all signs of witch activity. We cannot surmise how often witch killings occurred after contact, but beginning in the late 1810s missionaries counted four or five executions a year. In 1823 they reported four in one division alone. The killings terrified many people, and missionaries reported that fearful women were fleeing "into the woods" to avoid being murdered by frightened or angry Choctaws.[5]

From kinship to economic organization to political succession, women provided the basic structures of life and thus threatened social order the most. Accordingly, accusations of witchcraft were not random. Fearful Choctaws singled out for death anomalous women who simultaneously inhabited and polluted their moral space.[6] By striking out at such women, Choctaws purged from their sacred circle individuals whose presence threatened its order. "Numbers are every year butchered in the most inhuman manner," regretted Cyrus Kingsbury, but in executing the witches Choctaws reaffirmed the bonds that defined the "beloved people" and differentiated them from the "accursed people." Far from a last gasp against the threats of cultural dissonance and anomie, the executions were part of a normal and long-standing process of managing change and disorder.

While some Choctaws killed witches in an attempt to order their world from the inside, many others sought to accommodate external sources of power and incorporate them into their indigenous religious system. The magical complex to which witchcraft belonged no longer explained to many Choctaws' satisfaction why bad things were happening, because magic no longer affected all people equally. By the 1820s Choctaws agreed that biracial Choctaws were impervious to the "witch arrows" that afflicted the rest of the population.[7] If certain members of the population were immune to witchcraft, particularly those most associated with the interpenetration of the inside and the outside worlds, then they had to rethink their own cosmology. Such people hoped that the new sacred power would not only reorder life within the circle but also protect it from the external forces that threatened to cave it in.

Like the children who learned to heal from spirits who lived on the edges of their world, the cosmopolitan chiefs who imbibed the religious message of salvation preached by the Protestant missionaries used it to save their chiefdom. The chiefs and the commoners, however, neither converted to nor rejected Christianity wholesale. Rather, they fashioned a syncretic faith that reflected their cultural and intellectual juxtaposition of ancient precedents and more recent innovations.[8]

The new challenge that faced the Choctaws was the extension of state law and a rising clamor calling for their removal from Mississippi. After the failure of the first state law extension bill in 1826, the Mississippi house of representatives drew up similar legislation in 1827 and in 1828. State assemblymen also considered measures that would have prohibited Choctaws from hunting within the state. Such bills flouted federal supremacy in Indian affairs, and the more conservative state senate was less willing to take on the Adams administration, so it refused to pass the provocative legislation.[9]

In answer to the land-grabbing chorus of the Jacksonian politicians, the chiefs took heart from the missionaries' talk of salvation in God, and they encouraged their captains and their commoners to attend church services and speak the "Good Word."[10] Sacred fires soon burned across the nation and promised deliverance from the anomalous beasts prowling in the outside world and planning the sacred circle's destruction.[11] Looking to

the heavens above, Choctaws implored Aba to shine a light on those who
had been so long in the shadows. "We have been very wicked; we have
stood in dark places," admitted Robert Folsom, brother of David, and in
1828 Folsom and thousands of others decided to "embrace the Gospel,
and walk in the straight and bright path."[12]

To find the bright path, the Choctaws turned to the missionaries who
had for so many years been preaching to empty pews and a handful
of slaves. Called *abaonompoolé*, Aba's messengers, by the Choctaws, the
missionaries represented a new and vital link between Aba and the
nation that held great promise for a renewal of the nation's sacred
power.[13] The time had finally come, many believed, when God would
stretch out "his interposing hand" and make the Choctaws strong and
powerful "like white men."[14] Following the light that lit the path involved
abandoning inefficacious forms of religious and magical practice. Robert
Folsom identified drunkenness, ball games, and dances as barriers to
Choctaws' purity and power. Apparently others agreed, because by 1830
missionaries commented proudly on the absence of such pursuits. When
Brother Robert Smith asked one warrior why he no longer went to ball
games, the man replied that "he was afraid to go for fear that he would
lose his good heart."[15] But more than old forms of ritual had fallen into
disuse. The efficacy of the doctors, conjurers, and seers had come under
scrutiny. Missionaries reported that a serious drought had coincided with
the construction of the first missionary station in 1819 and had broken the
public's faith in rainmakers. Unsatisfied with traditional practices, many
Choctaws followed the lead of the biracial chiefs who had proved to be
mightier than magic.[16]

The missionaries initially distrusted both David Folsom and Greenwood LeFlore. Cyrus Kingsbury feared that Folsom was using the missionaries to build schools and that he had little interest in religion. Folsom,
however, proved his piety to Kingsbury with his own tortured attempts
to come to grips with his faith during the Washington treaty talks as
well as with his public pronouncements against drinking and polygamy.[17]
Greenwood LeFlore was under suspicion because in the beginning he had
only feebly supported the missionaries and their proselytizing and they
were unsure of his support. Although LeFlore worked as a translator for
various preachers, as late as August 1828 Methodist missionary Alexander
Talley reported to his superiors in New York that "until he obtains a
clear evidence of justification [LeFlore will not] connect himself with the

Church." But whereas LeFlore tolerated the presence of missionaries, his mother and sister-in-law, like other Choctaw women, bitterly opposed them. One evening his mother stormed into a camp meeting and forcibly pulled his twelve-year-old sister out of the service. After a heated debate with the women about the missionaries, the sister-in-law and daughter subsequently joined the movement in spite of the matriarch's determined opposition.[18]

By the middle of 1829 LeFlore too had become convinced "that no other than the Almighty God, had power to produce . . . a change in the Choctaws," but he still refused baptism.[19] His resistance collapsed on 3 October 1829 when Rosa, the young woman he had fallen in love with during his stay in Nashville, died of complications from childbirth. "In her loss," the Reverend Talley remarked, "the Col learned the vanity of all earthly things, and determined to give himself full to the lord." Eight days later Talley baptized LeFlore in the presence of several hundred of the chief's subjects.[20]

After the new faith's endorsement by two principal chiefs, thousands of people flocked to mission churches and camp meetings, where they discussed among themselves what "*they had been*," and what they might become.[21] Missionary figures for participation in the revitalization movement cannot be accepted without question, for they are uncorroborated, but the proliferation of camp meetings throughout the nation suggests that support was widespread. Building on the 160 converts he had in his church at the end of 1828, Alexander Talley estimated that in April of that year in the Western division, 600 of a total population of 10,000 Choctaws had claimed probationary membership in his church. In August 1829 Talley held a meeting for four or five days and counted 2,000 Choctaws in attendance. Peter Pitchlynn noted that 270 people in the Sixtowns joined the church in September 1829, and in the same month 200 joined at a meeting held at LeFlore's home. By the end of the year the American Board missionaries estimated that one-quarter of the adult population could be counted "anxious inquirers."[22] John Terrell, an Alabama judge and a frequent visitor to the Choctaw towns, captured somewhat cynically the pull that the new faith exerted on the new believers. "What's the doctrine," he explained to one of Andrew Jackson's cronies, "Whisky leads to ruin, we love you—you love your country—come join the church. This is the way to keep your country . . . if you do not get religion your country is gone."[23]

If Terrell understood the basic tenets of the Choctaw Great Awakening, he failed to perceive how far the movement reflected the Choctaws' own long-standing traditions. The new sermons and frequent baptisms were innovations to the Choctaws' ancient Mississippian faith, not wholesale additions made with no regard to what had come before. The camp meetings that proliferated throughout the nation, for example, followed a common pattern that reflected the ceremonial structures of the Mississippian green corn ceremony and other religious celebrations. Though the men and boys dressed in drab homespun suits and the women typically wore frocks of brightly colored calico, they continued to gather at night, to seat themselves around different campfires, and to sing songs throughout the evening. Missionaries rarely preached at the meetings and seem to have had little to do with the course of worship. Instead they stood at the outer edges of the gatherings and genuinely admired the multitude of voices that rose above the flickering campfires and followed the sacred smoke to Aba's home in the sky.[24]

Other informal meetings also brought Choctaw believers together in sacred circles. Following traditional gender rules, on Saturday nights males and females would meet around separate fires "for the purpose of praying for the Holy Spirit."[25] Such meetings may have been a part of Sabbath services, for Cyrus Byington observed that a man he visited on the eve of the Sabbath not only had kindled an impressive fire but had laid aside a sizable pile of firewood cut especially for the Sabbath fire. That the man laid the logs in a cross is a tempting presumption.[26]

Old men were among the first individuals to show an interest in what the missionaries had to say. According to one man's testimony, they participated in Christian services for two reasons—they were overwhelmed by Christianity's emotional appeal and their chiefs had endorsed the new faith. Men like Tahoka, aged fifty, and Hoyopohuma, aged sixty, led the way despite initial ridicule.[27] Younger warriors laughed at the old men who wept in the face of God, but the elders replied, "It is not the hand of man that has made us weep, it is our Maker that has caused it. You never saw us weep for what man could do to us, but we cannot withstand God."[28] Another early believer was the aged uncle of David Folsom, Tunapinchuffa. Likening his attachment to God to "a strong chain of iron," Tunapinchuffa clung tightly as he struggled for stable footing in the uncertain times of the early nineteenth century. "Long time we had been as people in a storm which threatened destruction," he despaired, "until the missionaries came to our land."[29]

Tunapinchuffa rejoiced at God's power and invoked it in his daily life. One day while looking for his horse, he spotted a deer lying in the grass. His gun was at home, so he prayed to God to keep the deer where it lay until he could fetch his firearm. When he returned with the weapon, he saw the deer had not moved. "After lifting up my heart . . . to my father above," he told the missionaries, "I fired and killed it, and returned thanks to my great Benefactor."[30]

Besides the efficacy of the new faith in matters such as hunting, Tunapinchuffa invoked it in a communal sense that revealed the deep roots of his religious beliefs. To David Folsom the old man pledged, "You our brother and chief, found for us a good and bright path, and we would follow you in it." Turning a new religious leaf, Tunapinchuffa had shed what he perceived to be the errors of the past and embraced the hope of the future in language reminiscent of William Bartram's eighteenth-century description of the green corn ceremony: "The black and dirty clothes I used to wear I have taken off and cast away. Clean and good clothes, I now put on. My heart I hope, has been made new."[31]

The parallels Tunapinchuffa drew between old religious meanings and new religious practices were not unique. In fact, based on the conversion experiences of other Choctaws, nothing else brought out more clearly the juxtaposition of Mississippian values and the new practices of the Christian revival. At one "experience meeting" where Alexander Talley had Choctaws witness to one another, Captain Washington discussed his vision at length. He told the crowd that "he had been born and brought up in a dark wilderness where he had no light." "After a long time" he saw, "through the thick undergrowth, a little bright light like a candle." The candle was the "good talk" of Brother Talley, and lest his audience wonder what he did when he saw the light, Captain Washington declared that he "immediately commenced pushing through the bushes and briers to get to that light." Another captain expanded on Washington's use of landscape imagery to explain the process of coming into the new faith. He "had seen his people go down, one after another, into a deep, dark, muddy river and sink out of his sight." If these miscreants had been good, the captain warned, "they would go to the home of the god and be happy forever; but if they continued wicked here, they would go among the wicked in the other world and suffer pain and despair without end."[32] Heaven and hell were new ideas not present in the old Choctaw cosmology, but the belief that marginal areas like forests and muddy rivers where Nalusa Falaya, Kashehotopalo, and other monsters lived were home to darkness and evil had endured in the people's minds. Moreover, the struggle one had to make to find the bright path cast into vivid imagery what was a real and tangible process.

A whole nation was made anew in the preaching and solemnizing that went on in the late 1820s. Choctaws began asking for the "blessing of God" before eating, and excited neophytes looked forward to delivering the "Good Word" to their "old uncles and aunts."[33] Individual acceptance of the bright path and the communal rituals that celebrated it had combined the salvation vocabulary of Christianity and the religious metaphors and structures of Choctaw cosmology into a powerful new "fire." As it emerged under the authority of the cosmopolitan chiefs, the new sacred power legitimated their political reforms and emboldened their opposition to removal and state law extension.

Not surprisingly, the primordialist chiefs regarded the revival suspiciously. Although they had welcomed the mission schools and the education hundreds of children were now getting, the vast upwelling that followed the cosmopolitan chiefs into the church had made their claims to power all the more tenuous. When LeFlore's light horsemen arrested Robert Cole, tied him up, and brought him before a tribunal for judgment, the militant new government challenged Cole and Mushulatubbee to respond, and they waited for an opportunity to strike back.[34]

Although they opposed state law extension and removal, the missionaries feared that the revival had become a political movement. To the Choctaws, however, sacred and political power were inseparable. When LeFlore stood atop Nanih Waiya mound to promulgate his law he assumed the posture of a sun priest. Likewise the camp meetings and the sacred circles he and David Folsom hosted became indistinguishable from their political councils. At one meeting religious services concluded with a debate on removal. Agent Ward reported nervously that Folsom and John Garland had held a council meeting adjacent to a camp meeting hosted by LeFlore to pledge their opposition to removal. As David Folsom argued time and again, Aba had given the Choctaws their land and their sense of self. "Here is our home," he declared, "our dwelling places, our fields, our schools, and all our friends and under us are the dust and bones of our forefathers. This land is dearer to us than any other." He and undoubtedly hundreds of others held out hope that Aba's new fire would defend the sacred circle and protect them from the state and federal governments.[35]

The missionaries, however, refused to participate in the fusion of religion and politics. When some Choctaws at a prayer meeting asked about "the white people" who were threatening to "deprive them of their beloved country," Loring Williams simply reminded them of "the approach of death and the judgement day." As Williams's remark suggests, Choctaws and missionaries rarely saw eye to eye on spiritual matters, and it is little surprise that his unwillingness to preach to their needs precluded him and other missionaries from playing leading roles in the revival. While Williams rigidly admonished Choctaws to "secure an interest in the Lord Jesus Christ," they busily asked God for deliverance.[36] Fearful of Mississippi's threats to extend its state laws over the Choctaws, Robert Folsom prayed that "God won't let them."[37]

CHAPTER SEVEN

The Removal Crisis, 1830

I now feel that the subject of selling our land is like a crakt bowl, I am afraid to
handle it any more, lest it should come to pieces, & we lose it altogether.
A Choctaw captain, as quoted in a letter from Cyrus Kingsbury
to Jeremiah Everts, 24 November 1830

FOR CHOCTAWS, bowls were more than culinary vessels. They were kin
and family and culture. Sitting in a circle around a fire, family members
ate from the same bowl, and when a stranger partook from the bowl
he could count himself a member as well.[1] Bowls also embodied the
larger cosmological order. Pressed by federal and state governments on
the outside and by witches and factionalism on the inside, Choctaws
had to find a way to keep the national family from shattering. Both
the cosmopolitans and the primordialists had presented the public with
ways to hold the "bowl" together, but the two factions' inability to agree
on a common program undermined their ability to counter American
pressures when it mattered most. While chiefs and captains from both
sides attempted to implement their particular visions of a proper society,
the thousands of commoners were left adrift, and the reciprocal ties that
had bound chiefs and subjects frayed as the leaders struggled among
themselves for power.

Just as in earlier times, when the bonds of reciprocity were broken, the
chiefdom collapsed. During the final negotiations for removal Greenwood
LeFlore and David Folsom watched their fragile state fall to pieces while
Mushulatubbee and his allies likewise failed to restore the old order.
In the end no chief was in a position to resist Andrew Jackson and the

federal government, and as the Choctaws bade farewell to the land that surrounded Nanih Waiya mound they could not help bemoaning their inability to maintain the delicate balance between the sun and the moon, between the Upper World and the Underworld, and between the fire of the sky and the water of the earth.

Andrew Jackson's election to the presidency in 1828 signaled to Choctaws and Americans alike that the Choctaws' tenure in Mississippi would no longer be tolerated. To Jackson they were savages, and he would brook no talk of political autonomy from their cosmopolitan chiefs. Lest they fashion a state within a state, Old Hickory dedicated himself to driving them out of Mississippi. Although the first three state law extension bills introduced during the Adams administration had failed to pass the state senate, Governor Gerard Brandon signed the fourth one into law on 4 February 1829, despite some legislators' fears that the measure would prove "awful and dangerous to the peace and welfare of this Union."[2] The act, however, extended state law over the land claimed by the Choctaws, not over the Choctaws themselves.

The Mississippi measure and similar ones passed in Georgia and Alabama sparked heated debates in Congress. National Republican congressmen William Ellsworth of Connecticut, Henry Storrs of New York, and Theodore Frelinghuysen of New Jersey excoriated the "high-handed, heart-breaking legislation" of the southern states.[3] In addition to asserting state sovereignty, the legislators of the Deep South hoped the acts would drive the Indians out of their states. Cyrus Kingsbury feared the law would "coerce the Indians to remove . . . [it is] one of the greatest acts of injustice & oppression that has ever been exercised towards the aborigines of this country."[4] The Methodist Alexander Talley seconded Kingsbury's prophecy: "Mississippi will be the responsible agent, and Heaven will mark and punish the horrid crime."[5]

President Jackson endorsed state law extension for two reasons. First, because the Constitution expressly forbade the erection of sovereign states like the Choctaw, Creek, or Cherokee nation within the chartered boundaries of original sovereign states, the president refused to countenance further Choctaw, Creek, and Cherokee pretensions to political independence. Since he was unable to force the southern Indians to the treaty table, Jackson hoped the climate of hostility that state law extension measures created would induce them to accept removal. Second, in spite of the underlying assimilationist currents of the "civilization" program, the Jacksonians hoped to segregate Native Americans from the Anglo-American society that, the president argued, would otherwise destroy them. "Surrounded by the whites, with their arts of civilization, which, by destroying the resources of the savage, doom him to weakness," he argued, "the fate of the Mohegan, the Narragansett, and the Delaware, is fast overtaking the Choctaw." Rather than await the extinction of the Choctaws, the president believed, the federal government had to remove them to the West, where they could "raise up an interesting commonwealth, destined to perpetuate the race."[6]

After the president's pronouncements in favor of removal, Senator Hugh Lawson White of Tennessee introduced to Congress a bill that, although it did not mandate removal, nonetheless provided funds for the removal of the Indians. The state law extension measures, many believed, would initiate removal itself. Despite the considerable opposition to the proposal in both houses, Jackson garnered enough support in Congress to pass it, and he signed the Indian removal bill into law on 29 May 1830.[7]

The passage of the state law extension bill and the federal removal bill evoked a strong response from the Mississippi press and from the Choctaws. James Cook, editor of the *Natchez*, opposed the agenda of Jackson and his supporters and derided their land grabbing in a series of satirical letters signed by a "Patriot." The unwillingness of the Jacksonians to adhere to the moral precepts of the paternalistic Christianity that had guided earlier Indian policy particularly galled Cook because to his mind the unscrupulous measures passed by the state and federal governments could not be reconciled with more noble ideas of charity and concern for one's fellowman. In the words of the Patriot, Jacksonian Indian policy boiled down to a crude scheme that lacked both principles and rules: "Who cares about the bones of Indians! Shew me an Indian in the street and I could buy the bodies of all his forefathers . . . for a pint of whiskey."[8]

Cook's opposition notwithstanding, the state law extension and removal legislation were popular in Mississippi. Congressman William Haile voiced his approval of the two acts in the *Woodville Republican*. Haile began by assaulting the assignment of jurisdiction over the Choctaws' land to the federal government in the 1817 statehood ordinance. At the time, Haile argued, Mississippi was so weak politically that the federal government had forced the state to surrender certain of its rights. He cited several legal precedents showing that colonies and states had legislated over their Indian populations since the seventeenth century and claimed that to do so now was perfectly legal. Not shy about demagoguery, the ardent Jacksonian further warned that public dissent over state law extension and the removal of the Choctaws would upset Mississippi's political and social order.[9]

Far from silent, the Choctaws contributed several voices to the publicly printed debate over the two measures. An "untutored savage" named Pushemetehaw offered a detailed description of federal laws that ought to have negated Mississippi's state law extension. His self-deprecating tone, however, masked a clever rhetorical strategy. He was particularly worried that the state legislature would tax the Choctaws, so he raised the cry of "no taxation without representation" that his American audience knew so well. Another Choctaw wrote that Jackson, despite Old Hickory's claims to the contrary, cared nothing about justice for the Indians. "He is always talking about his red children," the Choctaw wrote, "and how he loved them, and wished to see them prosper and become a great people, [but] he is at the very same time trying to cheat us out of our lands."[10] Indeed, for all Jackson's claims to have the Choctaws' interest at heart, they regarded him warily. "Verily I do fear," another added, "that the Indian name will become extinct under these mighty *benefits;* and we shall all die with sheer kindness."[11]

That the federal government had finally acknowledged Mississippi's right to exercise sovereignty over the Choctaws spurred the state government to put more pressure on its native population. Governor Brandon demanded that the state's laws be enforced more effectively to punish Choctaws "who may have the hardihood to resist them." Following his recommendations, the state legislature passed a new state law extension act that, unlike the previous one, applied to the Choctaws as well as to their land.[12]

The act's provisions criminalized the exercise of authority by chiefs. Anyone convicted of breaking the law faced a maximum fine of $1,000 and imprisonment for one year. Furthermore, the state abolished all forms of Choctaw custom not recognized by the common law of the state save marriage ceremonies. Having completely undermined the Choctaws' ability to resist removal, the state then extended to them "all the rights, privileges, immunities and franchises, held, and enjoyed by free white persons."[13] Georgia and Alabama did not extend these civil liberties to the Creeks and Cherokees. A few Choctaws took advantage of the clause.

James McDonald, who had studied law under Supreme Court Justice John McLean, hoped to win election to the state legislature in 1831, but he feared that his vocal support of Henry Clay would kill his chances for victory. Mushulatubbee also announced his candidacy for Congress.[14] *Niles' Weekly Register* printed one of his stump speeches in which he pledged to a crowd of onlookers, "If you vote for me I will serve you." But such colorful incidents were exceptions to the rule. No one within the state expected the Choctaws to remain long enough to exercise their new rights.[15]

State law extension caused widespread panic in the Choctaw nation. The churches organized themselves as a first line of defense and bolstered the cosmopolitan chiefs' authority. In September 1829 the congregations passed a law stating "that if any member removed west the church would send after him & kill him." The same law also eliminated Choctaws who removed from participation in councils and from the distribution of the federal annuities.[16] For Greenwood LeFlore the draconian measures were insufficient because neither he nor any of the other chiefs could control the actions of outsiders. LeFlore worried that "bad white men will soon come among us, and settle on our vacant land, and cheat us out of our property," and his fears were realized throughout the nation.[17] At a camp meeting hosted by Alexander Talley, Folsom, LeFlore, and Garland agreed that they could not support removal if it came, but they were at a loss how to resist the state and federal governments.[18] Agent Ward reported to Secretary of War John Eaton that LeFlore had even admitted that "If the Pres. said he would have their lands, [the Choctaws] must yeald to his power as [they] had but few people."[19]

LeFlore left the nation shortly thereafter to travel to Washington so as to get a better sense of the federal government's position. On the way he stopped in the Cherokee nation to consult with Chief John Ross, who was engaged in a similar dispute with Georgia over the extension of its laws. LeFlore consummated an alliance with his counterpart by marrying Ross's niece, Elizabeth Cody. What LeFlore and Ross discussed is unknown, however, and what he learned in Washington—or whether he even got there—is uncertain, but it was only a matter of time before the newlywed chief had to "yeald."[20]

The pessimism of the cosmopolitan camp extended to their primordialist rivals as well. Mushulatubbee too came to see removal as perhaps the best solution to the Choctaws' problems. "I would be glad . . . if the people of Mississippi would adopt us as their children upon equal terms," the chief wrote Secretary of War John Eaton, "but I believe this cannot be expected. Our only chance is to accept your proposition . . . to remove."[21] Mushulatubbee had fought with Jackson against the Red Stick Creeks in the Creek civil war. He kept a portrait of the Old Hero in his home, and he hoped to use his connections to the president to reestablish his political authority in the nation and to oversee removal. In a letter to his fellow warrior, he reminded Jackson that he "has Ever been willing to Do anything that was Reasonable and in the bounds of my power . . . to Vissillitate your views or the views of your government."[22] In December 1829 Mushulatubbee convened a council to discuss Jackson's plans for a Choctaw removal. Rather than "be subject to laws as they did not understand," the council members endorsed their chief's position and wrote to Jackson expressing their desire to negotiate a treaty.[23]

By writing directly to Jackson, Mushulatubbee had outmaneuvered the cosmopolitans, who attempted to regain the upper hand in the increasingly high stakes of the removal game by carrying their political reforms one step further. In February 1830 eight hundred captains and commoners gathered in council to hear the three division chiefs, Folsom, LeFlore, and Garland, discuss the nation's future. All agreed that they had to present a united front against the United States, so at a meeting in March Folsom and Garland resigned their offices and the council unanimously elected LeFlore as chief of the three divisions. The new government, however, retained all the captains who had served the three chiefs at the local level.[24] Missionaries suspected that Folsom and Garland had resigned and deferred to LeFlore because they feared the criminal penalties of the second state law extension act. But LeFlore offered a more persuasive explanation. "We have long seen," the chief wrote, "that to have several chiefs . . . in different parts of the nation was calculated to ruin us."[25] The complex intermediate chiefdom formed by Folsom, LeFlore, and Garland in 1826 had culminated in an integrated chiefdom of which LeFlore was paramount chief.

On 17 March 1830 the new chief asked the council what was to be done in light of the expected passage of the removal bill. The council debated taking up arms but agreed that military resistance was foolhardy. Cyrus Kingsbury proposed that the Choctaws file a Supreme Court case through attorney William Wirt, a strategy the Cherokees employed some years later, but LeFlore refused to consider the tactic. Although the council had "determined that they would not submit to Mississippi law," they would, LeFlore wrote, "move west, if the President would give us a good treaty."[26] The council voted in favor of the decision, and on the eighteenth wrote a treaty that was dispatched to the capital the next day. Alexander Talley applauded the course the council had taken: "By treating we secure the government to the men of information and Christian principles."[27] To President Jackson they wrote, "We love our land but we cannot suffer our council fire to be extinguished by submitting to the laws of our white brothers."[28]

"I have no doubt," affirmed Cyrus Kingsbury, "but Col. LeFlore & Col. Folsom think the course they have marked out, will if carried into effect promote the welfare of the Choctaws."[29] Kingsbury was right. The proposed treaty captured in documentary form the cosmopolitan vision of the society Folsom and LeFlore had hoped to create in Mississippi, a society based on stock raising, cotton cultivation, and a united and autonomous national government. According to the document, all heads of households, male or female, would receive 640 acres each in fee simple to sell or live on as they saw fit. Furthermore, every "young man" who was not the head of a household would receive 320 acres in fee simple. Each man who removed also would receive from the federal government a good rifle and plenty of lead and powder for four years. Once in the West, men would receive an ax, plow, hoe, blanket, and brass kettle, and women would get a spinning wheel and cotton cards. Every fifth family would be given a loom. The nation's herds would be paid for in Mississippi, or else the federal government would supply them with an equivalent number of animals once they had removed. To safeguard the new Choctaw nation in the West, LeFlore demanded that the federal government pledge to defend it from foreign enemies and domestic threats. Finally, LeFlore insisted that the federal government pay the nation $50,000 annually in perpetuity. The president considered the treaty and sent it to the Senate for consideration, but no action was taken. In the meantime Jackson studiously avoided any contact with the envoys who had brought the document to Washington. His ongoing correspondence with Mushulatubbee offered far more pleasing prospects than treating with LeFlore.[30]

News of LeFlore's treaty scandalized the nation because he had risen to power on the promise of opposing removal. Mushulatubbee denounced the document and reminded his fellow Choctaws that he "had always predicted that the Choctaws would be ruined by the introduction of Christianity."[31] Charges of treason filled the air, and one concerned party likened the cosmopolitans to the infamous Aaron Burr.[32] The adverse popular response to LeFlore's treaty led the national government to reconsider its support for removal, but its about-face came too late.[33]

Many Choctaws instead turned to the primordialist chiefs who, they believed, represented the "good old way."[34] Nevertheless, they did not oppose removal; they only hoped to overthrow their rivals in order to set their own terms for the removal treaty. Mushulatubbee, Robert Cole, and Nittakaichee, who had abandoned the cosmopolitans, used the public uproar over LeFlore's treaty to justify a counterrevolution against the Choctaw national government.[35] In April 1830 Mushulatubbee gathered enough support to unseat Folsom in the Eastern division. In hopes of stopping Mushulatubbee, LeFlore sought to conciliate him by inviting him to a council where they might settle their differences. But Mushulatubbee was unwilling to compromise with LeFlore on the issue of religious toleration. When the old chief insisted on barring "Christians" from political office, the "Christian" party broke away from the council and named Folsom as their chief while LeFlore went back to the Western division to plot his next move. Meanwhile Mushulatubbee had received from the federal government a promise that if he persuaded the Choctaws to accept removal, he would be named chief of the nation once it had removed to the West.[36]

While Mushulatubbee set about quietly cultivating support, LeFlore resorted to force of arms. The chief assembled a party of eight hundred men, four hundred armed with rifles, to march on Mushulatubbee's council.[37] When LeFlore's army arrived, "All Mushulatubbee's men broke ground, except a few who laid down their clubs and came up in a submissive manner," wrote eyewitness Robert Jones. "And Mushulatubbee," he continued, "was found in a shuck pen, and draged out and would have been whiped, but he agreed to resign."[38]

The ouster of Mushulatubbee failed to stabilize the situation. With his allies Nittakaichee, who had asserted a claim against John Garland to be chief of the Southern division, and Peter Pitchlynn Mushulatubbee continued to oppose the cosmopolitans, whom he condemned as "yanke Coalitionists."[39] Pitchlynn even organized a party of young men to assassinate LeFlore while his elders deposed several of Leflore's and Folsom's captains who had been "friendly to religion." The two upstart chiefs prohibited any "professor of religion" from holding political office in either the Eastern or the Southern division. They also burned books and seized churchgoers, painting their faces and forcing them to "dance away their religion." Other decrees ended a law requiring the observance of the Sabbath, and they reversed bans on pole pulling, ball games, and dances.[40] A subsequent resolution decreed that ball games, dances, "and all other kinds of sports, should be encouraged."[41]

By enacting such laws the two primordialist leaders hoped to restore old methods of religious propitiation and old forms of power. After all, they had predicted that the Christian revival would be their nation's undoing, and to their minds the events of early 1830 confirmed their worst fears.[42] In language designed to appeal to Jackson's sympathies, Mushulatubbee promised that his "Republican party," and not LeFlore's "Despotic party," would lead the Choctaws to accept removal.[43] Peter Pitchlynn, who considered himself head of the Republicans, oddly enough thanked God for giving him the courage to withstand the threats of the "inequitous and odious proceedings" of the despots.[44] Outside observers believed the Republicans stood only for dumping "Christianity and civilization" and for preserving their "old habits and customs," but Pitchlynn was a churchgoer, and both he and his uncle supported education and economic innovation.[45] The Republicans resented the power of the cosmopolitans and the means by which they had achieved it, and the installation of LeFlore as paramount chief of the nation particularly upset them.[46] The innovation, Mushulatubbee believed, was without precedent. "The extinction of two council fires and the bringing of all the Choctaws under one government and one chief," he charged, "were acts of usurpation not to be endured."[47]

On 15 September 1830 a federal commission comprising John Eaton and John Coffee arrived to discuss removal. The men boarded with Hartwell Hardaway and his Choctaw wife about a quarter mile from a council ground that lay on a wooded patch of land between the two forks of Dancing Rabbit Creek. A flurry of preparation preceded the treaty talks. The commissioners spoke with chiefs and missionaries, and bushels of corn and barrels of coffee, beef, and pork arrived to feed the gathering throng. Between seven and eight thousand Indians and Americans arrived, and temporary saloons and gaming tables sprouted everywhere to tempt onlookers with whiskey and wagers while Choctaws held dances and ball games nearby. In the midst of this hubbub David Folsom and his pious followers "kept up their religious services of preaching, praying and singing every night to a late hour."[48]

Some days after the commissioners arrived the three division chiefs made their way to the treaty ground, and their habits of dress offered a striking example of the cultural continuum of Choctaw history. Greenwood LeFlore showed up in coat, shirt, tie, trousers, and boots, reflecting his cosmopolitan ideology. True to his status as a war chief but also reflecting his ties to the outside world, Mushulatubbee arrived in a spanking new blue military uniform given to him by Jackson. His ally Nittakaichee sported the less audacious ensemble of a hunter. He wore a fringed shirt, buckskin leggings, and silver armbands and gorgets.[49]

Each chief had signaled a willingness to remove, but LeFlore had refused to cooperate with the other two chiefs in the endeavor. Nevertheless the treaty talks hinged on the decision of the rank-and-file captains who would vote on the issue. Negotiations began on the morning of the eighteenth, and John Pitchlynn interpreted Eaton's and Coffee's opening remarks. "It is not your lands," the commissioners implored, "but your happiness that we seek to obtain." Playing on Choctaw fears of state law extension, they continued: "Are you willing to remain here and live as white men? Are you willing to be sued in the courts, there to be tried and punished for any offense you commit? to be subjected to taxes, to work upon roads and attend in musters?"[50]

The Choctaws' reply to the commissioners' queries came on the morning of the twenty-second. Coffee and Eaton returned to the council ground and took their seats on a log that was oriented with the path of the sun. Before them sat the male chiefs and captains in a broad semicircle that stretched southward under the shade of several oak, pine, and mulberry trees. After the fashion of dances and religious ceremonies, seven women, who may have been clan or *iksa* matriarchs, sat within the arc before the commissioners' table.[51]

The councilmen stood before Coffee and Eaton and offered their thoughts on removal, but only one captain, Killihota, advocated it. He urged that "the Choctaws ought to sell everything they owned, land, cattle, horses, and hogs, and all in a body emigrate west." Land, however, lay outside the purview of male authority. "Killihota," snapped one of the women, "I could cut you open with this knife. You have two hearts." "You may hang me," replied the councilman, "and cut my bosom open and you will see that I have only one heart and that for my people." Few were persuaded by Killihota's entreaties, and each subsequent speaker supported the women and denounced removal. The Choctaw women had transformed their ancient influence into authority and for the time being succeeded in defending their land.[52]

The following morning the federal commissioners presented several conditions for a removal treaty, but to no one's surprise the council broke up without agreeing to remove. The various members were, Cyrus Kingsbury noted, "under the full impression that there would be no treaty."[53] Secure in the knowledge that they had thwarted federal ambitions, many of the captains left the council ground for their homes. Eaton, however, refused to concede defeat.

Two days after the negotiations had ended, Eaton and Coffee called together a rump council composed of a handful of leaders who had remained at the treaty ground. Among those included were Greenwood LeFlore, Mushulatubbee, Nittakaichee, and David Folsom. To this small gathering Eaton delivered a "very sharp and angry" talk warning the leaders that he would remove the federal agent and close the inns and shops that Choctaws had opened along the Natchez Trace. After all, the secretary of war argued, the federal government had a right to be angry with its "Choctaw children." LeFlore, Mushulatubbee, and Nittakaichee had written to him and proposed to remove, and, if they failed to live up to their end of the bargain, he threatened, he would repossess their land west of the Mississippi River, charge them for the treaty negotiations, and leave them to the mercy of the state of Mississippi.[54]

Of Eaton's tirade, one observer remarked, "The Choctaws knew not what to do. The government had broken all their treaties, & they supposed they could & would put all their threats into execution."[55] None of the chiefs favored military resistance, and under LeFlore's lead they grudgingly accepted that a removal treaty was their best chance to have some say in the final dispossession of the nation. The treaty proposed by the council bore a strong resemblance to LeFlore's first removal treaty, for it sought through its various provisions to confirm the cosmopolitans' revitalistic program. The federal government, the treaty promised, would support schools as well as female academies for twenty years. For students interested in education beyond the secondary level, the treaty provided for fifty youths to be educated at federal expense at institutions of higher learning. Missionary funding was to continue for three more years, and one article extended toleration to all religious denominations. To give the new nation a voice in the federal government, the chiefs asked that they receive a territorial delegation in Congress. Most important, the document provided for individuals who wished to remain in Mississippi; if they registered with the federal agent, they would receive a parcel of land determined by the size of the family, and after a set term of years they would acquire title to it.[56]

The final treaty signed by the federal commissioners and the Choctaw leaders differed substantially from the draft they had proposed. The federal government agreed to guarantee the nation's western land in fee simple, defend it from invasion, provide individuals with certain specific land reservations, and pay for the nation's removal, but the federal commissioners rejected several proposals that would have furthered the cosmopolitan agenda. To the leaders' request that the nation be allowed to petition to have disagreeable agents removed, the commissioners gave final authority on the decision to the president. The federal government agreed to provide only a fraction of the money the Choctaws requested for the support of their schools: Eaton and Coffee whittled the original demand for $10,000 a year for twenty years for schools and $5,000 a year for twenty years for female academies down to $2,500 for three teachers for twenty years. Most important, the commissioners granted neither an extension of Choctaw sovereignty in Mississippi for three more years— the period of removal—nor a territorial delegation in Congress. But in the fourteenth article the federal government did provide for people who did not want to remove. If they registered with the federal agent they would receive a parcel of land and, if they occupied it for ten consecutive years they would receive a fee simple title.[57]

While most of the captains sat comfortably in their homes unaware of the continuing talks at the council ground, at 1:00 P.M. on the twenty-seventh the councilors who had remained reluctantly signed the Treaty of Dancing Rabbit Creek and ceded the Choctaws' last ten million acres of land in Mississippi to the United States.[58] Many of the leaders received generous allotments of land in the treaty, which they could sell for a considerable profit. Cyrus Kingsbury expected LeFlore would realize nearly $50,000 from his reservations alone. David Folsom, Mushulatubbee, and others could also expect to profit handsomely, but such were the prerogatives of chiefly leadership. The financial remuneration, however, was a poor salve for the deep wounds caused by the cession. "The treaty was a bad one & the reason he acceded to it was," Cyrus Kingsbury wrote of David Folsom, "he had lost all confidence in the government of the U. States."[59]

While Folsom despaired of his misplaced faith, the commoners reacted angrily to what they believed were misguided leaders, and the fragile chiefdom and nation built by the cosmopolitans collapsed completely. In the Southern towns, where only one captain had endorsed the treaty, Israel Folsom, David's brother, urged the captains and warriors to depose Nittakaichee, which they did. In his stead the Southern council named Joel Nail, who five years earlier had argued with Pushmataha over the disbursement of the district annuity and the location of a mission school and who ten years before had aided Folsom in opposing the Doak's Stand cession.[60] In the Eastern division Folsom again challenged Mushulatubbee, but he failed to unseat the chief. Nevertheless, even Mushulatubbee came under fire for the treaty from younger Choctaws who had had little say in the politics of removal. Having lost support "amongst his own friends," Mushulatubbee resigned and his nephew Peter Pitchlynn succeeded him as chief of the East.[61]

LeFlore had earned the greatest scorn. In mid-October the Western council charged that their chief was "totally unfit to rule a free people" because he had broken his pledge to never "turn his coat" on the nation. Not surprisingly, Robert Cole was the first to sign the proclamation that formally deposed him.[62] But LeFlore believed he was following the best course possible. He knew Eaton would make good on his promises to punish the nation, and he knew Jackson would not tolerate any resistance. In spite of threats of death against any chief who ceded land, LeFlore "determined to risk my life in what I believed a good cause."[63] His belief, however, was based on his assumption that the federal government would uphold the crucial fourteenth article, which enabled Choctaws to remain in Mississippi with land. Agent Ward, however, refused to enroll the Choctaw claimants because he believed they were put up to it by "designing men."[64] The federal agent's malfeasance in the matter completely undermined LeFlore's reason for including the provision. Many years later LeFlore admitted he was "sorry to say that the benefits realized from [the fourteenth article] by my people were by no means equal to what I had a right to expect, nor to what they were justly entitled."[65] For the time being, however, commoners resented the chief's conduct, and in his stead the Western council named as chief LeFlore's nephew George Washington Harkins, who pledged "not to do what my uncle did."[66] The new chief urged Choctaws to resist removal for four more years, in expectation of Andrew Jackson's leaving the White House, but he eventually came to accept removal.[67]

The ouster of Nittakaichee, Mushulatubbee, and LeFlore overshadowed innumerable incidents of violence directed primarily at the cosmopolitans. All who had opposed removal attributed "the loss of their country, and all their present calamities, to the introduction of the gospel and the change of their customs."[68] Those who resented the influence of the missionaries harassed, beat, and humiliated those who had participated in the revival. But the bruises the believers took paled in comparison with the greater blow that removal delivered to their Great Awakening.

As Choctaws came to realize that God had not protected the beloved people's sacred circle from the accursed people of the outside world, the churches emptied. "There is a great falling off," missionary Loring Williams noted, "since the treaty was concluded."[69] Just as Tunapinchuffa had put on clean new clothes, thousands of other Choctaws stripped off their metaphorical garments and abandoned the new faith. When asked why he had forsaken the revival, one Choctaw responded that he was "so distressed with the loss of my beloved country [that] . . . I can neither sing nor pray, and why should I pretend to do so when my heart is not in it."[70] Among the few Choctaws who held to the new faith, Tunapinchuffa remained a steadfast devotee. To Loring Williams he cried as his people prepared for the long trek west, "O my brother, I hold you fast. I am a poor distressed man. Do help me. The Secretary of War came and took my country. I am in great distress. O that my father above would help me, is my desire."[71]

No help from Aba was forthcoming, and the first removal party left the Choctaw nation in December 1830. Though they had "said it was not their wish to go," Cyrus Kingsbury wrote, " . . . their chief said they must go, & so they went."[72] In the meantime American settlers poured into the nation stealing livestock, confiscating homes and improvements, and abusing Choctaws who refused to leave. "It is a bad time," wrote an elderly and nearly incapacitated John Pitchlynn to his son Peter, "This country is settled with the [most] Damed peple in the world[;] the[y] can out s[t]eal out lye out swar" anyone Pitchlynn had ever met.[73] Over the next three years nearly eighteen thousand Choctaws worked their way west carrying with them what they could to build new homes and a new circle in an unfamiliar land. Meanwhile Andrew Jackson lauded the treaty and removal as the "happy consummation" of thirty years of benevolent federal Indian policy. The Mississippi House of Representatives likewise celebrated the "dawn of an era . . . when . . . this state would emerge from obscurity, and justifiably assume an equal character with her sister states of the Union."[74]

As he departed his homeland on a steamer bound for Fort Smith, Arkansas, George Washington Harkins reflected on what had happened over the past few years, and he composed a letter to the state of Mississippi to be published in James Cook's *Natchez*. Against the rhythmic splashing of the ship's paddle wheel, the chief outlined on paper numerous grievances, mourned the inability of LeFlore and Folsom to resist removal, and despaired of his people's plight. And though he could have blamed Mississippi's expansionism and the president's politics for removal, Harkins ultimately attributed it to his own people's inability to walk the straight bright path. "We found ourselves," he wrote, "like a benighted stranger, following false guides until [we were] surrounded by fire and water—the fire was certain destruction, and a feeble hope was left [to us] of escaping by water."[75]

Like the captain's "crakt bowl" metaphor, Harkins's images of fire and water cast the Choctaws' attempts to explain and to understand removal in their own terms. Burned by a sun that now blazed for the United States, Harkins and thousands of Choctaws escaped by water on board crowded and filthy steamers bound for Arkansas. And along the way they could not help but wonder what lay at the end of the watery road to the west, the direction that for centuries had been associated with darkness and an absence of light.

CONCLUSION

The Return of Oakatibbé

But [Oakatibbé] could not withstand the reproaches of a conscience formed upon principles which his own genius was not equal to overthrow. His thoughts, during his flight, must have been of a very humbling character. . . . By his flight and subsequent return, he had in fact, exhibited a more lively spectacle of moral firmness, than would have been displayed by his simple submission in remaining. . . . He leaped from his horse, exclaiming, while he slapped his breast with his open palm: "Oakatibbé is come!"
William Gilmore Simms, *The Wigwam and the Cabin*

MUCH TO Colonel Harris's and William Gilmore Simms's sorrow and surprise, Oakatibbé had returned. A cry of relief escaped the crowd that had gathered by the grave Loblolly Jack's kin had dug for the condemned man earlier that morning. Before the many faces—some sad, some glad— he began, Simms wrote, "a low chant, slow, measured, and composed."[1] This was the guilty man's death song, his personal "narrative of the past, in proper form for the acceptance of the future."[2] When the last note had been sung and the last syllable pronounced, he bared his chest and faced his executioners. Three rifle shots broke the stillness that had settled on the proceeding, and Oakatibbé's lifeless body tumbled into the fresh grave. Simms peered one last time at Slim Sampson's face and reflected wistfully on "the noble form of one, who, under more favoring circumstances, might have been a father to his nation."[3]

The reconciliation of past and future that constituted Oakatibbé's death song expressed the central problem of the Choctaws—how to adapt to the exigencies of the present without sacrificing what had defined them as Choctaws in the past. Oakatibbé had advocated innovation as a means to adjust to life in Jacksonian America. But he could not repudiate the deepest layers of the culture he sought to change. To him culture was not the disconnected jumble of attributes, traits, and beliefs that anthropologists and ethnohistorians sort through in search of patterns. It was an internalized moral code through which he understood the world in terms of what was right and what was wrong. And he chose to do what he thought was right: he returned to accept his comeuppance.

In the tenth century A.D. a culture scholars call the Mississippian tradition arose in the American South. Inspired by innovative ideas about government, society, and economy, the region's indigenous societies planted fields of corn, squash, and beans, built clusters of towns and mound centers, and created chiefdom organizations. New people, new goods, and new ideas invaded the region in force in the mid-sixteenth century, and like other remnant Mississippian populations the Choctaws constructed with the interlopers a new world. Their ability to weave the weft of change into the warp of their own value system not only shaped their responses to the problems of European contact and colonization in the eighteenth century and American expansion in the nineteenth century but framed their understanding of the process as well.

Europeans had encountered among the Choctaws not a nation but three loosely connected ethnic groups that were organized as intermediate chiefdoms. Differentiated from commoners by birth and by status, chiefs used their authority to place themselves between colonists and their people. As distributors of exotic prestige goods like guns, cloth, and alcohol, chiefs bolstered their own authority and incorporated the Europeans into patterns of interaction and exchange that had characterized life in the prehistoric period. Men like Alibamon Mingo and Red Shoe built careers on manipulating French and English officials, extracting gifts from all but pledging allegiance to none.

The play-off policy, however, was not without its drawbacks. In the 1740s Red Shoe I chafed at Alibamon Mingo's authority, and he led the Western towns into an alliance with the Chickasaws and their English traders. Although both chiefs avoided killing other Choctaws for as long as they could, Red Shoe's involvement in the murder of three Frenchmen forced Alibamon Mingo's hand. To maintain the French supplies his authority depended on, the francophile chief waged war on the Western towns, and over a thousand Choctaws died before peace could be reestablished.

Open warfare between the divisions did not recur, but the next generation of chiefs, Franchimastabé, Taboca, and Pooscoos II encountered many of the same problems. Playing off Spanish and American interests was a difficult game, and when a latter-day Red Shoe, Chief Thloupouye Nantla, arose in the Eastern towns to challenge their authority, the Choctaws reached a point where the conflicts of the civil war might have been repeated.

The displacement of the English and Spanish by the United States, however, ended the play-off system before chiefly conflict could develop into civil strife. Forced to cede land for debts incurred by the play-off, chiefs found that the fractious politics of the eighteenth century were incapable of resisting American expansion. New leaders like Mushulatubbee and Pushmataha and the next generation of chiefs, David Folsom and Greenwood LeFlore, came to accept that American hegemony had dramatically changed the nature of chiefly leadership. And though the chiefs retained their redistributive and diplomatic responsibilities, they added to their list of duties instigating economic, cultural, and political changes.

The new chiefs agreed, for example, that education had to be the nation's priority, but they differed over the unification of the three divisions into one complex constitutional chiefdom. Religious change only exacerbated political tensions, and on the eve of removal the nation's leaders were divided into two well-defined factions. David Folsom, Greenwood LeFlore, and John Garland led the cosmopolitans, and Mushulatubbee, Robert Cole, and the Pitchlynns stood in defiant opposition at the head of the primordialists. Contrary to what many historians have described as a struggle between progressive mixed-bloods and conservative full-bloods, the factionalism embodied two groups each composed of both "mixed-bloods" and "full-bloods" who held different visions of how Choctaws should respond to the United States. The deep kinship divisions within the society as well as the indigenous social structure militated against the formation of the sort of racial classes that some scholars have argued existed among the Choctaws before removal. Kinship, not genotype, organized the factions because matriliny remained a persuasive and powerful institution throughout the period.

The vitality of matrilineal institutions helped perpetuate the gender divisions that had characterized the economy of the prehistoric Mississippians. Many products like cotton and horses fit well into the female and male economies. For others, like cattle, it required linguistic ingenuity to construct them so as to enable men and women to participate in the opportunities that cattle created in the Old Southwest. In spite of scant evidence, Choctaw women appear also to have maintained their traditional control of the distribution and use of land. The seven women at the Dancing Rabbit Creek treaty talks revealed as much when they refused to give the men permission to cede *their* land.

The growth of the marketplace economy paralleled the development of the American market economy, but whereas the market revolution differentiated the responsibilities and roles of Anglo-American men and women more sharply and undermined the women's power, Choctaws survived its impact with their premarket institutions intact. Men continued to oversee the animal world, and women remained in control of the plant world. For those men who did become involved in agriculture, field slaves guarded them against the criticism that otherwise would have been lodged against such "womanly" men.

In spite of the many moral and cultural persistences that characterized the Choctaws' history, a substantial and undeniable revolution had occurred. The land had changed, triggering a crisis in cosmology. Before the arrival of Europeans, Choctaws had envisioned the world about them as a circle. Above them lived the sun, whose light brought order and prosperity to This World. Below them swirled the watery powers of fertility and chaos. When the two forces existed in harmony, good things happened, the women's corn grew, the men were successful in the hunt and in war, and the community enjoyed health and prosperity. But when discord arose, sickness and misfortune spread throughout the land and witches reveled in their ability to destroy all that was moral and good. Beyond the circle sat the anomalous monsters that combined animal and human forms and juxtaposed gender into terrifying combinations. The creatures reminded Choctaws of the need to keep Aba's law and to maintain not only the boundaries between their world and the outside world but those that separated women from men, plants from animals, and the sacred from the profane.

Initially, Choctaws incorporated Europeans into their traditional cosmology. They carried Frenchmen across their sacred squares to avoid pollution, and they were on constant guard against the magic of the English. But Europeans, unlike their Mississippian analogues, refused to confine their activities to out-of-the-way paths, dark corners of the forests, and gurgling springs and swamps. Their forts, towns, and farms pressed on the sacred circle and began to break down the boundary that separated the orderly inside from the disorderly outside. Warriors lashed out at frontier farmers, killing their cattle, stealing their horses, and burning their cabins, but they could not stem the tide. The "plague of locusts" was too great, and as the regional market economy grew to incorporate the Choctaws the two worlds swirled together, one indistinguishable from the other.

The resulting dissolution of boundaries caused serious problems. Unwilling to tolerate an alien government within its chartered limits, the state of Mississippi agitated for the Choctaws' removal, and the federal government slowly came to agree. The last years of the Choctaw nation's occupation of its ancestral homeland centered on an attempt to reestablish its boundaries and to redefine its sovereignty. To recreate the sacred circle in the early nineteenth century, the cosmopolitan chiefs drew on the prerogatives of their offices and marshaled new powers to buttress their cause. By outfitting their government in indigenous religious trappings, they grafted the missionaries' message of salvation onto an existing body of ritual belief and action. The Great Awakening that followed did not pit Christians against pagans, nor did it represent a wholesale conversion to American Christianity. The leaders of the movement had garnered great wealth from the American economy, had drawn political inspiration from the American model, and consequently looked outside for sources of sacred power as well.

The external focus of the cosmopolitans did not sit well with the primordialists who repudiated the revival. Jealous of the power the cosmopolitans had taken from them, they plotted a counterrevolution predicated on the reestablishment of divisional government and the repudiation of Christianity. When the Mississippi government passed a state law extension measure and the federal government approved the removal bill, the cosmopolitans accepted removal as inevitable, and their proposed removal treaty revealed them to the public as chiefly charlatans. The primordialists stepped into the power vacuum, reclaiming their chiefly authority, and the two factions squabbled about who would finally negotiate the Choctaws' removal from the land that surrounded Nanih Waiya mound.

When the Choctaws left Mississippi they carried with them a culture that bore a remarkable yet superficial resemblance to that of their Anglo-American antagonists. They farmed cotton, owned slaves, raised livestock, wore American clothes, lived in square cabins, and furnished their homes with American furniture. But for all these appearances, they remained at heart Choctaw. In spite of epidemic diseases, the shattering of Mississippian societies, and the amalgamation of disparate remnant groups, the moral imperatives that defined each individual's experiences in Mississippian times had persisted through the nearly 130 years that had followed their first contact with the French.

But culture can go only so far toward explaining why things happened the way they did. If we look at Choctaw history from the tenth century to the nineteenth, certain seemingly immutable features of Choctaw life emerge in a consistent pattern. Only when we fix our gaze on the unfolding of the generations of Choctaws who lived in the eighteenth century (the short duration) and those who struggled to cope with life in the early decades of the 1800s (event time) can we begin to appreciate how individuals shaped their own fates. From Red Shoe's careful calculations and Franchimastabé's diplomacy on the fly to David Folsom's fear of sin and one young woman's decision to sell her cow so she could go to school, the contingencies of particular personalities and experiences must be given a weight equal to that of culture in interpreting a people's past. The history of the Choctaws involved a complex interaction between received culture and personal choice. After all, Red Shoe I had chosen to alienate Alibamon Mingo, Franchimastabé had chosen to abandon the Spanish, David Folsom had chosen to invite missionaries to build schools, and the young woman had chosen to raise and sell her cow, just as Oakatibbé had chosen to return.

In many ways the story of the Choctaws is incomplete and only half told. Many histories of Native American peoples end with some sort of dramatic tragedy or with the author's admiration for the remarkable ability of the subject Indians to retain their identities and cultures in spite of a history of population collapse, cultural anomie, dispossession, and marginalization. Certainly the Choctaw removal was a tragedy. To Choctaws like George Harkins, though, removal was to a large extent his fault, his neighbor's fault, and his chief's fault. He and thousands of others had followed what they thought was a bright path only to find that it led nowhere. The new chiefdom and its sacred ideology had not prevented removal. Harkins and his people had strayed from the true path, angered Aba, and paid a terrible price for their heresy.

But they were not finished yet. When the Choctaws landed in Indian Territory, they quickly reestablished the three divisions, and they named their new towns after those they had left behind in Mississippi. The nephews of the old chiefs took the place of their uncles, and men and women rebuilt their herds and planted new fields. In many ways removal is not the final chapter in this drama, for the reconstruction of the nation and of the sacred circle in the West represented yet another attempt to find the bright path. But that is a story for another day.

Abbreviations for Document Collections

ABCFM   Papers of the American Board of Commissioners for Foreign Missions (Woodbridge CT: Research Publications, 1985), Indian Archives, Oklahoma State Historical Society, Oklahoma City.

Allen Papers   James and Charles B. Allen Papers, Southern Historical Collection, Manuscript Division, Wilson Library, University of North Carolina at Chapel Hill.

C13A   Series C13A, vol. 16, Archives Nationales, France, Library of Congress, Washington DC.

C05   British Public Record Office, Colonial Office 5: America and West Indies, Library of Congress, Washington DC.

Claiborne Papers   John F. H. Claiborne Papers, Southern Historical Collection, Manuscript Division, Wilson Library, University of North Carolina at Chapel Hill.

Coffee Papers   John Coffee Papers, Alabama Department of Archives and History, Montgomery.

Draper Collection   Lyman Draper Collections, Western History Collections, University of Oklahoma, Norman.

Halbert Papers   Henry S. Halbert Papers, microfilm, Mississippi Department of Archives and History, Jackson.

Hargrett Papers   Jay L. Hargrett Papers, Western History Collections, University of Oklahoma, Norman.

Jesuit Relations   *The Jesuit Relations and Allied Documents,* ed. Reuben Gold Thwaites (Cleveland: Burrows, 1900).

M15   Microfilm series M15, Letters Sent by the Secretary of War relating to Indian Affairs: 1800–1824, Office of Indian Affairs, Record Group 75, Records of the Bureau of Indian Affairs, National Archives, Washington DC.

M234   Microfilm series M234, Choctaw Agency, Letters Received: 1824–81, Correspondence of the Office of Indian Affairs and Related Records, Record Group 75, Records of the Bureau of Indian Affairs, National Archives, Washington DC.

M271   Microfilm series M271, Letters Received by the Secretary of
War relating to Indian Affairs: 1800–1823, Office of the Secretary
of War, Record Group 75, Records of the Bureau of Indian Affairs,
National Archives, Washington DC.

M668   Microfilm series M668, Ratified Indian Treaties: 1722–1869,
Record Group 75, Records of the Bureau of Indian Affairs, National
Archives, Washington DC.

MPA:ED   "Mississippi Provincial Archives: English Dominion"
(microfilm), Record Group 25, Mississippi Department of Archives
and History, Jackson.

MPA:FD   *Mississippi Provincial Archives: French Dominion*, ed. and
trans. Dunbar Rowland and A. G. Sanders (Jackson: Press of the
Mississippi Department of Archives and History, 1927, 1929, 1932).

MPA:SD   "Mississippi Provincial Archives: Spanish Dominion"
(microfilm) (Jackson: Mississippi Writers' Project, 1942), Record
Group 26, Mississippi Department of Archives and History, Jackson.

T494   Microfilm series T494, Documents relating to the Negotiation
of Ratified and Unratified Treaties with Various Indian Tribes:
1801–1869, Record Group 75, Records of the Bureau of Indian Affairs,
National Archives, Washington DC.

T500   Microfilm series T500, Records of the Choctaw Trading House:
1803–1824, Record Group 75, Records of the Bureau of Indian Affairs,
National Archives, Washington DC.

Vaudreuil Letterbooks   *Letterbooks of Marquis de Pierre de Rigaud de
Vaudreuil* (San Marino CA: Huntington Library, 1994), M. I. King
Library, University of Kentucky, Lexington.

Westward Expansion   *British Public Record Office: Colonial Office, Class
Five File–Westward Expansion, 1700–1783* (University Publications of
America, 1983), Western History Collections, University of Oklahoma,
Norman.

Winans Papers   William Winans Papers, J. B. Cain Archives, Manuscript
Collection, Millsaps College, Jackson MS.

Notes

THE FLIGHT OF OAKATIBBÉ

1. William Gilmore Simms, "Oakatibbé, or The Choctaw Sampson," in *The Wigwam and the Cabin* (New York: Redfield, 1856), 200. The incident involving Oakatibbé occurred during the 1820s.

2. Simms, "Oakatibbé," 202.

3. *Missionary Herald* 26 (May 1830): 156.

4. Marshall Sahlins, *Islands of History* (Chicago: University of Chicago Press, 1985), 144.

5. Clifford Geertz, ed., "Thick Description: Toward an Interpretive Theory of Culture," in *The Interpretation of Cultures* (New, York: Basic Books, 1973), 89, 27.

6. Alfred L. Kroeber, "The Superorganic," *American Anthropologist* 19 (April–June 1917): 202.

7. William Simmons, "Culture Theory in Contemporary Ethnohistory," *Ethnohistory* 35 (winter 1988): 9.

8. E. P. Thompson, "The Moral Economy of the English Crowd in the Eighteenth Century," in *Customs in Common: Studies in Traditional Popular Culture* (New York: New Press, 1993), 185–258.

9. For the concept of morality I drew upon E. P. Thompson, "The Moral Economy Reviewed," in Thompson, *Customs in Common,* 259, and on Norma Haan, "An Interactional Morality of Everyday Life," in *Social Science as Moral Inquiry,* ed. Norma Haan, Robert Bellah, Paul Rabinow, and William Sullivan (New York: Columbia University Press, 1983), 218–50.

10. Lesser, quoted in Melville Herskovits, *Acculturation: The Study of Culture Contact* (New York: J. J. Augustin, 1938), 3.

11. Louise Spindler, *Culture Change and Modernization: Mini-Models and Case Studies* (New York: Holt, Rinehart and Winston, 1977), 31.

12. Hope Landarine and Elizabeth A. Klonoff, *African American Acculturation: Reconstructing Race and Reviving Culture* (Thousand Oaks CA: Sage, 1996), 1.

13. See, for example, Morris W. Foster, *Being Comanche: A Social History of an American Indian Community* (Tucson: University of Arizona Press, 1991), 7–9.

14. Anthony Giddens, *The Constitution of Society: Outline of the Theory of Structuration* (Berkeley: University of California Press, 1986), 257.

15. Anthony Giddens, *A Contemporary Critique of Historical Materialism* (London: Macmillan, 1995), 54.

16. Anthony Giddens, *Central Problems in Social Theory: Action, Structure, and Contradiction in Social Analysis* (Berkeley: University of California Press, 1979), and Christopher G. A. Bryant and David Jary, eds., *Giddens' Theory of Structuration: A Critical Appreciation* (London: Routledge, 1991).

1. MISSISSIPPIAN FOUNDATIONS

1. Vernon James Knight Jr., "Symbolism of Mississippian Mounds," in *Powhatan's Mantle: Indians in the Colonial Southeast*, ed. Peter H. Wood, Gregory A. Waselkov, and M. Thomas Hatley (Lincoln: University of Nebraska Press, 1989), 282; Henry S. Halbert, "A Choctaw Migration Legend," *American Antiquarian and Oriental Journal* 16 (July 1894): 215–16; Henry S. Halbert, "Nanih Waiya, the Sacred Mound of the Choctaws," *Publications of the Mississippi Historical Society* 2 (1899; rpt. 1919): 223–34; David I. Bushnell Jr., *The Choctaw of Bayou Lacomb, St. Tammany Parish, Louisiana*, Bureau of American Ethnology Bulletin 48 (Washington DC: United States Government Printing Office, 1909), 30; David I. Bushnell Jr., "Myths of the Louisiana Choctaw," *American Anthropologist* 12 (1910): 527; Gideon Lincecum, "History of the Chahta Nation," microfilm, Gideon Lincecum Papers, Center for American History at the University of Texas at Austin, 79, 472; Alfred Wright, "Choctaws: Religious Opinions, Traditions, etc.," *Missionary Herald* 24 (June 1828): 179; and *Monthly Paper of the American Board of Commissioners for Foreign Missions*, no. 3 (June 1832): 10.

2. Three recent investigations of the Choctaw archaeological record are Patricia Galloway, *Choctaw Genesis, 1500–1700* (Lincoln: University of Nebraska Press, 1995); Timothy P. Mooney, "Many Choctaw Standing: An Archaeological Study of Culture Change in the Early Historic Period" (M.A. thesis, University of North Carolina at Chapel Hill, 1994); and John H. Blitz, *An Archaeological Study of the Mississippi Choctaw Indians*, Archaeological Report 16 (Jackson: Mississippi Department of Archives and History, 1985).

3. See, for example, Vernon J. Knight Jr., "The Formation of the Creeks," in *The Forgotten Centuries: Indians and Europeans in the American South, 1521–1704*, ed. Charles Hudson and Carmen Chaves Tesser (Athens: University of Georgia Press, 1994), 373–92; Marvin T. Smith, *Archaeology of Aboriginal Culture Change in the Interior Southeast: Depopulation during the Early Historic Period* (Gainesville: University Press of Florida, 1987), 134–37; and James Merrell, *The Indians' New World: Catawbas and Their Neighbors from European Contact through the Era of Removal* (Chapel Hill: University of North Carolina Press, 1989).

4. Charles Hudson, *The Southeastern Indians* (Knoxville: University of Tennessee Press, 1976), 206.

5. Alfred W. Crosby, "Virgin Soil Epidemics," *William and Mary Quarterly,* 3d ser., 33 (April 1976): 289–99, and Henry Dobyns, *Their Number Become Thinned: Native American Population Dynamics in Eastern North America* (Knoxville: University of Tennessee Press, 1983), 131, 187, 292. Several scholars have characterized Dobyns's figures as grossly inflated, particularly because he bases them on estimates of the land's maximum carrying capacity rather than its minimum carrying capacity. See William Cronon, review of *Their Number Become Thinned, Journal of American History* 71 (September 1984): 374–75, and Douglas H. Ubelaker's review of the same in *Ethnohistory* 31 (1983): 304–5.

6. Smith, *Archaeology of Aboriginal Culture Change;* Ann F. Ramenofsky, *Vectors of Death: The Archaeology of European Contact* (Albuquerque: University of New Mexico Press, 1987); and Charles Hudson, "A Spanish-Coosa Alliance in Sixteenth-Century North Georgia," *Georgia Historical Quarterly* 72 (winter 1988): 599–626. Patricia Galloway has raised doubts about the veracity of Hudson's account of the chief's attempt to use the Spanish to subdue the formerly tributary Napochies. See Galloway, *Choctaw Genesis,* 147.

7. Dobyns, *Their Number Become Thinned,* 328–34; Smith, *Archaeology of Aboriginal Culture Change,* chap. 6; and Galloway, *Choctaw Genesis,* chap. 3, 352.

8. Dobyns, *Their Number Become Thinned,* 303–4; Smith, *Archaeology of Aboriginal Culture Change,* chap. 7; Knight, "Formation of the Creeks," 373–91; and Merrell, *Indians' New World.*

9. Galloway, *Choctaw Genesis,* chaps. 7–9; Christopher S. Peebles, "The Rise and Fall of the Mississippian in Western Alabama: The Moundville and Summerville Phases, A.D. 1000 to 1600," *Mississippi Archaeology* 22 (June 1987): 1–31; Henry T. Wright, "Prestate Political Formations," in *On the Evolution of Complex Societies: Essays in Honor of Harry Hoijer, 1982,* ed. Timothy K. Earle (Malibu CA: Udena, 1984), 41–78; John F. Scarry, "The Rise, Transformation, and Fall of Apalachee: A Case Study of Political Change in a Chiefly Society," in *Lamar Archaeology: Mississippian Chiefdoms in the Deep South,* ed. Mark Williams and Gary Shapiro (Tuscaloosa: University of Alabama Press, 1990), 175- 86; and Craig Sheldon, "The Mississippian-Historic Transition in Central Alabama" (Ph.D. diss., University of Oregon, 1974), 12–13, 23–25, 39, 48–54, 59, 66, 79, 97–98.

10. Galloway, *Choctaw Genesis,* 46–52, 197, 352–57, and Jeffrey P. Brain, *Winterville: Late Prehistoric Culture Contact in the Lower Mississippi Valley,* Archaeological Report 23 (Jackson: Mississippi Department of Archives and History, 1989), 114–33.

11. "The Historical Journal of Sauvole, First Royal Governor of Louisiana," in *Historical Collections of Louisiana,* part 3, comp. B. F. French (New York: D. Appleton, 1851), 230, and Pierre Le Moyne d'Iberville, *Iberville's Gulf Journals,* trans. and ed. Richebourg Gaillard McWilliams, intro. Tennant S. McWilliams (Tuscaloosa: University of Alabama Press, 1981), 143.

12. Scarry, "Rise, Transformation, and Fall of Apalachee," 177; Galloway, *Choctaw Genesis,* 94; and Randolph J. Widmer, "The Structure of Southeastern Chiefdoms," in *The Forgotten Centuries: Indians and Europeans in the American South, 1521–1704,* ed. Charles Hudson and Carmen Chaves Tesser (Athens: University of Georgia Press, 1994), 373–92, 126–27.

13. Wright, "Prestate Political Formations," 41, and Timothy R. Pauketat, *The Ascent of Chiefs: Cahokia and Mississippian Politics in Native North America* (Tuscaloosa: University of Alabama Press, 1994), 19–20.

14. Widmer, "Structure of Southeastern Chiefdoms," 139.

15. Peter Peregrine, "Networks of Power: The Mississippian World-System," in *Native American Interactions: Multiscalar Analyses and Interpretations in the Eastern Woodlands,* ed. Michael S. Nassaney and Kenneth E. Sassaman (Knoxville: University of Tennessee Press, 1995), 249; John H. Blitz, *Ancient Chiefdoms of the Tombigbee* (Tuscaloosa: University of Alabama Press, 1993), 16, 126, 178–81; Marion Johnson Mochon, "Language, History, and Prehistory: Mississippian Lexico-reconstruction," *American Antiquity* 37 (October 1972): 480, 499, 501; Scarry, "Rise, Transformation, and Fall of Apalachee," 178; and Wright, "Prestate Political Formations," 45.

16. Christopher S. Peebles and Susan M. Kus, "Some Archaeological Correlates of Ranked Societies," *American Antiquity* 42 (July 1977): 421–24, and Blitz, *Ancient Chiefdoms,* 98.

17. Peebles and Kus, "Some Archaeological Correlates," 15, 98; Chester B. DePratter, *Late Prehistoric and Early Historic Chiefdoms in the Southeastern United States* (New York: Garland, 1991), 47; Timothy Earle, "The Evolution of Chiefdoms," in *Chiefdoms: Power, Economy, and Ideology,* ed. Timothy Earle (New York: Cambridge University Press, 1991), 1–15; Scarry, "Rise, Transformation, and Fall of Apalachee," 175–77; Peebles and Kus, "Some Archaeological Correlates," 431–33; John A. Walthall, *Prehistoric Indians of the Southeast: Archaeology of Alabama and the Middle South* (Tuscaloosa: University of Alabama Press, 1980) 191; Wright, "Prestate Political Formations," 41; and Thomas E. Emerson, "Cahokian Elite Ideology and the Mississippian Cosmos," in *Cahokia: Domination and Ideology in the Mississippian World,* ed. Timothy R. Pauketat and Thomas E. Emerson (Lincoln: University of Nebraska Press, 1997), 190–228.

18. David A. McKivergan Jr., "Balanced Reciprocity and Peer Polity Interaction in the Late Prehistoric Southeastern United States," in *Native American Interactions: Multiscalar Analyses and Interpretations in the Eastern Woodlands,* ed. Michael S. Nassaney and Kenneth E. Sassaman (Knoxville: University of Tennessee Press, 1995), 235.

19. John R. Swanton, "An Early Account of the Choctaw Indians," in *Memoirs of the American Anthropological Association,* vol. 5, no. 2 (Lancaster PA: American

Anthropological Association, 1918), 54–55, and Mochon, "Language, History, and Prehistory," 480.

20. Widmer, "Structure of Southeastern Chiefdoms," 127.

21. See Duane Champagne, *Social Order and Political Change: Constitutional Governments among the Cherokee, the Choctaw, the Chickasaw, and the Creek* (Stanford: Stanford University Press, 1992), 26–27, 40 and n.73, 269–72.

22. Blitz, *Ancient Chiefdoms*, 11–12, and folder 53, microfilm reel 3, Henry S. Halbert Papers, Mississippi Department of Archives and History, Jackson. For a discussion of Choctaw kinship see Fred Eggan, "Historical Changes in the Choctaw Kinship System," *American Anthropologist* 39 (January–March 1937): 34–52.

23. Blitz, *Ancient Chiefdoms*, 11–12, 125, and Hudson, *Southeastern Indians*, 132.

24. Richard Huntington and Peter Metcalf, *Celebrations of Death: The Anthropology of Mortuary Ritual* (Cambridge: Cambridge University Press, 1979), 14, 63.

25. James Adair, *Adair's History of the American Indians*, ed. Samuel Cole Williams (Johnson City TN: Watauga Press, 1930; rpt. Nashville: National Society of the Colonial Dames of America, in Tennessee, 1953), 192; Jean-Bernard Bossu, *Travels in the Interior of North America, 1751–1762*, trans. and ed. Seymour Feiler (Norman: University of Oklahoma Press, 1962), 166–67; Bernard Romans, *A Concise Natural History of East and West Florida; A Facsimile Reproduction of the 1775 Edition* (Gainesville: University of Florida Press, 1962), 89–90; William Bartram, *The Travels of William Bartram*, ed. Mark Van Doren (New York: Barnes and Noble, 1940), 403; and John A. Watkins, "A Contribution to Chacta History," *American Antiquarian* 16 (September 1894): 262–63. The Lincecum manuscript asserts that Choctaws buried the remains in the small mounds in imitation of the great mound Nanih Waiya. Lincecum, "History," 481–82, 492.

26. Galloway, *Choctaw Genesis*, 276–79.

27. Michelle Zimbalist Rosaldo, "Women, Culture, and Society: A Theoretical Overview," in *Women, Culture, and Society*, ed. Michelle Zimbalist Rosaldo and Louise Lamphere (Stanford: Stanford University Press, 1974). See also Jane Fishburne Collier and Sylvia Junko Yamagisako, "Toward a Unified Analysis of Gender and Kinship," in *Gender and Kinship: Essays toward a Unified Analysis*, ed. Jane Fishburne Collier and Sylvia Junko Yamagisako (Stanford: Stanford University Press, 1987), 14–52.

28. Diane Rothenberg, "The Mothers of the Nation: Seneca Resistance to Quaker Intervention," in *Women and Colonization: Anthropological Perspectives*, ed. Mona Etienne and Eleanor Laycock (New York: Praeger, 1980), 68, and Joy Bilharz, "First among Equals? The Changing Status of Seneca Women," in *Women and Power in Native North America*, ed. Laura F. Klein and Lillian A. Ackerman (Norman: University of Oklahoma Press, 1995), 103.

29. Daniel Maltz and JoAllyn Archambault, "Gender and Power in Native North

America," in *Women and Power in Native North America,* ed. Laura F. Klein and Lillian A. Ackerman (Norman: University of Oklahoma Press, 1995), 234.

30. Guy Prentice, "An Analysis of the Symbolism Expressed by the Birger Figurine," *American Antiquity* 51 (April 1986): 239–66; Thomas E. Emerson, "Water, Serpents, and the Underworld: An Exploration into Cahokian Symbolism," in *The Southeastern Ceremonial Complex: Artifacts and Analysis, the Cottonlandia Conference,* ed. Patricia Galloway (Lincoln: University of Nebraska Press, 1984), 50–55; Bruce D. Smith, "Mississippian Patterns of Subsistence and Settlement," in *Alabama and the Borderlands: From Prehistory to Statehood,* ed. R. Reid Badger and Lawrence A. Clayton (Tuscaloosa: University of Alabama Press, 1984), 64–65; Malcolm C. Webb, "Prehistoric Settlement, Subsistence and Social Formation in the Lower Mississippi Valley," in *Culture, Form, and Place: Essays in Cultural and Historical Geography,* ed. Kent Mathewson (Baton Rouge: Geoscience Publications, Department of Geography and Anthropology, Louisiana State University, 1993), 1–32; R. Douglas Hurt, *Indian Agriculture in America: Prehistory to the Present* (Lawrence: University Press of Kansas, 1987), 13–15; Mochon, "Language, History, and Prehistory," 499; Walthall, *Prehistoric Indians,* 190–91; and Blitz, *Ancient Chiefdoms,* 124.

31. Folder 42, microfilm reel 2, Halbert Papers.

32. Patricia Galloway, "Henri de Tonti du Village des Chacta, 1702: Beginnings of the French Alliance," in *La Salle and His Legacy: Frenchmen and Indians in the Lower Mississippi Valley,* ed. Patricia Galloway (Jackson: University Press of Mississippi, 1982), 167.

33. Richard White, *The Roots of Dependency: Subsistence, Environment, and Social Change among the Choctaws, Pawnees, and Navajos* (Lincoln: University of Nebraska Press, 1983), 26; Hudson, *Southeastern Indians,* 259, 266–67; Swanton, "Early Account," 59, 67–68; Romans, *Concise Natural History,* 71.

34. Dumont de Montigny, *Mémoires historiques sur la Louisiane,* . . . (Paris: C. J. B. Bauche, 1753), 1:203–4; Bossu, *Travels in the Interior,* 169–70; Romans, *Concise Natural History,* 77; Bartram, *Travels,* 396; and Mary Haas, "Creek Inter-town Relations," *American Anthropologist* 42 (July–September 1940): 483.

35. Romans, *Concise Natural History,* 75–76, and Bossu, *Travels in the Interior,* 165.

36. Pauketat and Emerson, "Cahokian Elite Ideology," 195; Widmer, "Structure of Southeastern Chiefdoms," 140–52; and Mochon, "Language, History, and Prehistory," 501–2.

37. Hudson, *Southeastern Indians,* chap. 3. Hudson's model was derived mostly from Cherokee sources, but in the absence of an equivalent body of Choctaw source materials, it will have to suffice.

38. The idea of moral space comes from Robert Thornton, *Space, Time, and Culture among the Iraqw of Tanzania* (New York: Academic Press, 1980), 19.

39. Adair, *Adair's History*, 185.

40. Romans, *Concise Natural History*, 85, 88; Bossu, *Travels in the Interior*, 167; Louis LeClerc de Milford, *Memoir, or A Cursory Glance at My Different Travels and My Sojourn in the Creek Nation*, ed. John Francis McDermott, trans. Geraldine de Courcy (Chicago: R. R. Donelley, 1956), 205; and Lincecum, "History," 291.

41. Robin Horton, "A Hundred Years of Change in Kalabari Religion," in *Black Africa: Its People and Their Cultures Today*, ed. John Middleton (London: Macmillan, 1970), 199.

42. DePratter, *Late Prehistoric and Early Historic Chiefdoms*, 57; Wright, "Choctaws," 179–80; Dumont de Montigny, *Mémoires historiques*, 1:183–84; Lincecum, "History," 68, 80, 311, 356; and Adair, *Adair's History*, 122.

43. Patricia Galloway, "Where Have All the Menstrual Huts Gone? The Invisibility of Menstrual Seclusion in the Late Prehistoric Southeast," paper presented at the Southeastern Archaeological Conference, 1991.

44. Adair, *Adair's History*, 121–23, 130, 141, and 185; Bossu, *Travels in the Interior*, 171; Jean-Bernard Bossu, *Travels through That Part of North America Formerly Called Louisiana* (London: T. Davies, 1771), 1:307; Lincecum, "History," 377–78; and Swanton, "Early Account," 59–60. My discussion of taboos and boundaries has been greatly influenced by Mary Douglas, *Purity and Danger: An Analysis of Concepts of Pollution and Taboo* (Harmondsworth UK: Penguin Books, 1970), and Arnold van Gennep, *The Rites of Passage*, trans. Monika B. Vizedom and Gabrielle L. Caffee (London: Routledge and Kegan Paul, 1960).

45. Walthall, *Prehistoric Indians*, 194; Lincecum, "History," 282 and Swanton, "Early Account," 58.

46. Adair, *Adair's History*, 325; Antoine Simon Le Page du Pratz, *The History of Louisiana Translated from the French of M. Le Page du Pratz*, ed. Joseph G. Tregle Jr. (Baton Rouge: Louisiana State University for the Louisiana American Revolution Bicentennial Commission, 1975), 351; Bartram, *Travels*, 396, 398–99; and Wright, "Choctaws," 178–80; emphasis in the original.

47. Lincecum, "History," 250. Lincecum claimed to have taken down his history of the Choctaws as it was dictated by a Choctaw informant. Lincecum no doubt took liberties with the document, as its flowery language and romantic stylizing indicate. But I think Patricia Galloway goes too far in dismissing Lincecum as a "con-man," his interest in native medicine as "claptrap," and the "History" as "not reliable." Much of the tale he transcribed fits well with the features of Mississippian culture as discussed above. See Galloway, *Choctaw Genesis*, 332.

48. Bossu, *Travels in the Interior*, 169–70; Dumont de Montigny, *Mémoires*

historiques, 1:203–4; Romans, *Concise Natural History,* 77; and Bartram, *Travels,* 396.

49. Lincecum, "History," 117–18, 159, 163, 367.

50. Hudson, *Southeastern Indians,* 122–31; Antonio J. Waring Jr., "The Southern Cult and Muskogean Ceremonial," in *The Waring Papers: The Collected Works of Antonio J. Waring, Jr.,* ed. Stephen Williams (Athens: University of Georgia Press, 1968), 33; Choctaw Indian Claims, folder 79, series 4, Fisher Family Papers, Southern Historical Collection, Manuscripts Department, Wilson Library, University of North Carolina at Chapel Hill; folder 41, microfilm reel 2, Halbert Papers; William S. Simmons, "Culture Theory in Contemporary Ethnohistory," *Ethnohistory* 35 (winter 1988): 1; Robert L. Hall, "Ghosts, Water Barriers, Corn and Sacred Enclosures in the Eastern Woodlands," *American Antiquity* 41 (July 1976): 360; and John R. Swanton, "Sun Worship in the Southeast," *American Anthropologist* 30 (April–June 1928): 206–13. My discussion of the Choctaw sacred circle owes much to a theory put forth by anthropologist Robin Horton in "African Conversion," *Africa* 41 (April 1971): 85–108.

51. Romans, *Concise Natural History,* 85; Lincecum, "History," 336- 37; and Jon Muller, "The Southern Cult," in *The Southeastern Ceremonial Complex: Artifacts and Analysis, the Cottonlandia Conference,* ed. Patricia Galloway (Lincoln: University of Nebraska Press, 1984), 13.

52. Eron Opha Dunbar, ed., "Peter Chester, Third Governor of the Province of West Florida under British Dominion, 1770–1781," *Publications of the Mississippi Historical Society, Centenary Series* 5 (1925): 83–84, and George S. Gaines, "Gaines' Reminiscences," *Alabama Historical Quarterly* 26 (fall–winter 1964): 145.

53. Journal of Joseph de Lusser, 14 March 1730, in *Mississippi Provincial Archives: French Dominion,* ed. and trans. Dunbar Rowland and A. G. Sanders (Jackson: Press of the Mississippi Department of Archives and History, 1927, 1929, 1932), 1:104— hereafter cited as MPA:FD; Journal of Régis du Roulet, April 1732, MPA:FD, 1:137; Bossu, *Travels in the Interior,* 168; Romans, *Concise Natural History,* 77–78; and Douglas, *Purity and Danger,* 117.

54. Louis Narcisse Baudry des Lozieres, *Voyage . . . la Louisiane, et sur le continent de l'Amérique Septentrionale, fait dans les années 1794 . . . 1798; Contenant un tableau historique de la Louisiane . . . Par B*** D***.* (Paris: Dentu, 1802), 193, and Adair, *Adair's History,* 35.

55. John Gregory Keyes, "Water Roads and Burned Forests: Nineteenth-Century Ethnoecology of the Mississippi Choctaw," paper presented at the American Society for Ethnohistory conference, 1993.

56. Bushnell, "Myths of the Louisiana Choctaw," 532, and Bushnell, *Choctaw of Bayou Lacomb,* 31.

57. Bushnell, *Choctaw of Bayou Lacomb,* 30–31.

58. Neal Salisbury, "The Indians' Old World: Native Americans and the Coming of Europeans," *William and Mary Quarterly*, 3d ser., 53 (July 1996): 435–58.

59. Amoroleck, quoted in Merrell, *Indians' New World*, 8.

60. Adair, *Adair's History*, 310.

2. EMERGENCE OF A CHOCTAW POLITY

1. Patricia Galloway, " 'So Many Little Republics': British Negotiations with the Choctaw Confederacy, 1765," *Ethnohistory* 41 (fall 1994): 531 n.2; Pierre Le Moyne d'Iberville, *Iberville's Gulf Journals*, trans. and ed. Richebourg Gaillard McWilliams, intro. Tennant S. McWilliams (Tuscaloosa: University of Alabama Press, 1981), 170–72; Alexander Moore, ed., *Nairne's Muskhogean Journals: The 1708 Expedition to the Mississippi River* (Jackson: University Press of Mississippi, 1988), 37; and Patricia Galloway, "Henri de Tonti du Village des Chacta, 1702: Beginnings of the French Alliance," in *La Salle and His Legacy: Frenchmen and Indians in the Lower Mississippi Valley*, ed. Patricia Galloway (Jackson: University Press of Mississippi, 1982), 157.

2. Iberville, *Gulf Journals*, 170–72; Galloway, "Henri de Tonti," 167–72; Jean-Baptiste Bénard de la Harpe, *Journal historique du l'établissement des Français . . . la Louisiane* (New Orleans: A. L. Boimare, 1831), 35–36; and Marcel Giraud, *A History of French Louisiana*, vol. 1, *The Reign of Louis XIV, 1698–1715*, trans. Joseph C. Lambert (Baton Rouge: Louisiana State University Press, 1974; rpt. 1990), 82–66.

3. Cyrus Byington, *A Dictionary of the Choctaw Language*, ed. John R. Swanton and Henry S. Halbert, Bureau of American Ethnology Bulletin 46 (Washington DC: United States Government Printing Office, 1915), 341.

4. Richard White, *The Roots of Dependency: Subsistence, Environment, and Social Change among the Choctaws, Pawnees, and Navajos* (Lincoln: University of Nebraska Press, 1983), 64–65.

5. Memoir on Louisiana, Jean-Baptiste Le Moyne, Sieur de Bienville, 1726, MPA:FD, 3:538.

6. Patricia Galloway, " 'The Chief Who Is Your Father': Choctaw and French Views of the Diplomatic Relation," in *Powhatan's Mantle: Indians in the Colonial Southeast*, ed. Peter Wood, Gregory A. Waselkov, and M. Thomas Hatley (Lincoln: University of Nebraska Press, 1989), 254–78.

7. Letter by Jean-Baptiste Le Moyne, Sieur de Bienville, 25 August 1733, MPA:FD, 1:193.

8. Galloway, " 'So Many Little Republics,' " 517; Pierre Le Moyne, Sieur de Bienville, "La Loüisianne, sur les Sauvages," 11 May 1733, ser. C13A, vol. 16, Archives Nationales, France, Library of Congress, Washington DC—hereafter cited as C13A followed by volume number; Galloway, " 'Chief Who Is Your Father,' " 254–78; Richard White, "Red Shoes: Warrior and Diplomat," in *Struggle and Survival in*

Colonial America, ed. David G. Sweet and Gary B. Nash (Berkeley: University of California Press, 1981), 51; Patricia Galloway, *Choctaw Genesis, 1500–1700* (Lincoln: University of Nebraska Press, 1995), 314; and John R. Swanton, "An Early Account of the Choctaw Indians," in *Memoirs of the American Anthropological Association*, vol. 5, no. 2 (Lancaster PA: American Anthropological Association, 1918), 60.

9. Swanton, "Early Account," 56–57, 60; Memoire from the Council of Louisiana to the Council of the Company of the Indies, 23 April 1725, MPA:FD, 2:461; and Galloway, "Henri de Tonti," 170.

10. Jean Baptiste Le Moyne, Sieur de Bienville to Jean-Frédéric Phélypeaux, Comte de Maurepas, 28 April 1738, MPA:FD, 3:714.

11. Galloway, " 'So Many Little Republics,' " 517–18, and Pierre de Rigaud, Marquis de Vaudreuil to Jean-Frédéric Phélypeaux, Comte de Maurepas, 12 February 1744, LO 9, vol. 1, microfilm reel 1, *Letterbooks of Marquis de Pierre de Rigaud de Vaudreuil* (San Marino CA: Huntington Library, 1994), M. I. King Library, University of Kentucky, Lexington—hereafter cited as *Vaudreuil Letterbooks*.

12. Jean-Baptiste Le Moyne, Sieur de Bienville to Edmen Gatien Salmon and Jean-Frédéric Phélypeaux, Comte de Maurepas, 13 September 1736, MPA:FD, 3:691–92.

13. White, *Roots of Dependency*, 49–55, and Extract from the Register of the Minutes of the Council of Louisiana, 8 February 1721, MPA:FD, 3:375.

14. Mary Musgrove to James Oglethorpe, 17 July 1734, and Isaac Chardon to Oglethorpe, 1 August 1734, *Colonial Records of the State of Georgia*, ed. Kenneth Coleman and Milton Ready (Athens: University of Georgia Press, 1982), 20:64; Letter of Jean-Baptiste Le Moyne, Sieur de Bienville, 30 September 1734, C13A, 18; Letter of Le Chevalier de Noyen, 8 November 1734, C13A, 18; Thomas Jones to Harman Verelst, 17 February 1738, *Colonial Records of the State of Georgia*, comp. Allen D. Candler, ed. William J. Northen (Atlanta: Chas. P. Byrd, 1913), vol. 22, part 2, p. 79; Letter of Jean- Baptiste Le Moyne, Sieur de Bienville, 10 February 1736, C13A, 21; Henri Chevalier de Loüboey to Jean- Frédéric Phélypeaux, Comte de Maurepas, 21 November 1738, C13A, 23; Edmen Gatien de Salmon to Maurepas, 30 August 1739, C13A, 24; Maurepas to Pierre Rigaud, Marquis de Vaudreuil, 27 October 1742, *Vaudreuil Letterbooks*, LO 9, vol. 1, microfilm reel 1; and Edmund Atkin, "Historical Account of the Revolt of the Choctaw Indians, 20 January 1753," microfilm copy, Mississippi Department of Archives and History, Jackson.

15. Jean-Frédéric Phélypeaux, Comte de Maurepas to Pierre Rigaud, Marquis de Vaudreuil, 27 October 1742, *Vaudreuil Letterbooks*, LO 9, vol. 1, microfilm reel 1.

16. White, "Red Shoes," 61–62.

17. Pierre de Rigaud, Marquis de Vaudreuil to Jean-Frédéric Phélypeaux, Comte de Maurepas, 18 July 1743, Vaudreuil to Henri Chevalier de Loüboey, 23 September 1744, Vaudreuil to Father Michel Baudouin, 23 September 1744, Vaudreuil to Captain

Derneville, 27 October 1744, all *Vaudreuil Letterbooks*, LO 9, vol. 1, microfilm reel 1; Vaudreuil to Henri Chevalier de Loüboey, 29 February 1744, Vaudreuil to Captain Derneville, 10 September 1744, Vaudreuil to Loüboey, 20 December 1745, Vaudreuil to Loüboey, 10 June 1746, all *Vaudreuil Letterbooks*, LO 9, vol. 3, microfilm reel 1; Letter of Jean-Baptiste Le Moyne, Sieur de Bienville, 25 March 1739, C13A, 24; and "La Loüisianne: Sauvages Chactas et Chicachas," 25 March 1739, C13A, 24.

18. Pierre de Rigaud, Marquis de Vaudreuil to Henri Chevalier de Loüboey, 4 September 1745, Vaudreuil to Father Michel Baudouin, 19 December 1745, Vaudreuil to Henri Chevalier de Loüboey, 5 July 1746, and Vaudreuil to Captain Le Sueur, 4 August 1746, all *Vaudreuil Letterbooks*, LO 9, vol. 3, microfilm reel 1.

19. "Parole a porté . . . la nation chactas touchant l'attentat qui vieut d'être commis sur les 3 françois que le Soulier Rouge a fait," 28 August 1746, and Pierre Rigaud, Marquis de Vaudreuil, to Captain Hazeur, 28 October 1746, both *Vaudreuil Letterbooks*, LO 9, vol. 3, microfilm reel 1; and "Journal du Voyage de Monsieur de Beauchamps," 20 November 1746, C13A, 30.

20. Pierre Rigaud, Marquis de Vaudreuil, to Jean-Frédéric Phélypeaux, Comte de Maurepas, 20 November 1746, *Vaudreuil Letterbooks*, LO 9, vol. 1, microfilm reel 1.

21. Letter by James Glen, 3 February 1748, British Public Record Office, Colonial Office 5: America and West Indies, vol. 13, Library of Congress, Washington DC. Hereafter cited as CO5 followed by volume number.

22. Pierre de Rigaud, Marquis de Vaudreuil, to Henri Chevalier de Loüboey, 1 December 1746, Vaudreuil to Captain Hazeur, 1 December 1746, and Vaudreuil to Loüboey, 7 April 1747, all in *Vaudreuil Letterbooks*, LO 9, vol. 3, microfilm reel 1; Vaudreuil to the Court, 20 March 1748 and 19 September 1747, *Vaudreuil Letterbooks*, LO 9, vol. 2, microfilm reel 1; Atkin, "Historical Account"; and White, "Red Shoes," 49.

23. Pierre de Rigaud, Marquis de Vaudreuil, to the Court, 6 March 1749, *Vaudreuil Letterbooks*, LO 9, vol. 2, microfilm reel 1.

24. Atkin, "Historical Account," and Letter by James Glen, 3 February 1748, CO5, 13.

25. Quoted in Galloway, " 'The Chief Who Is Your Father,' " 264.

26. Beauchamps to Pierre de Rigaud, Marquis de Vaudreuil, 15 January 1753, *Vaudreuil Letterbooks*, LO 433, microfilm reel 3; John Buckles to James Glen, 26 June 1754, Journal of John Buckles, *Colonial Records of South Carolina: Documents relating to Indian Affairs*, ed. William L. McDowell (Columbia: South Carolina Archives Department, 1958), 1:510.

27. Charles Gayarré, *Louisiana: Its History as a French Colony* (New York: John Wiley, 1852), 2:83–89; quotation on 84.

28. Edmund Atkin to William Pitt, 27 March 1760, CO5, 64.

29. Minutes of a meeting between English traders and Choctaw chiefs at Okfuskee, 27 March 1760, CO5, 64.

30. Cecil Johnson, *British West Florida, 1763–1783* (New Haven: Yale University Press, 1943), 1–2.

31. James Colbert's Journal, Journal of the Congress to Augusta in Georgia 1763, vol. 65, microfilm reel 4, *British Public Record Office: Colonial Office, Class Five File—Westward Expansion, 1700- 1783* (University Publications of America, 1983), Western History Collections, University of Oklahoma, Norman—hereafter cited as *Westward Expansion* followed by volume number; and Galloway, " 'So Many Little Republics,' " 519.

32. 5 November 1763, Journal of the Congress to Augusta in Georgia 1763, *Westward Expansion*, 65, microfilm reel 4.

33. 10 November 1763, Journal of the Congress to Augusta in Georgia 1763, and letter by James Wright, Arthur Dobbs, Thomas Boone, Francis Fauquier, and John Stuart, 10 November 1763, both *Westward Expansion*, 65, microfilm reel 4.

34. George Johnstone to John Pownall, 31 October 1764, "Mississippi Provincial Archives: English Dominion," 1:576, microfilm reel 1, Mississippi Department of Archives and History, Jackson.Hereafter cited as MPA:ED.

35. John Stuart, Speech delivered to Choctaw and Chickasaw chiefs, 27 March 1765, *Westward Expansion*, 66, microfilm reel 4.

36. Minutes of a conference of the English, Choctaws, and Chickasaws, March and April 1765, *Mississippi Provincial Archives: English Dominion, 1763–1766*, ed. and comp. Dunbar Rowland (Nashville: Brandon, 1911), 239–40, 244, 694.

37. Galloway, " 'So Many Little Republics,' " 519–21.

38. Charles Stuart to Peter Chester, 10 April 1771, part 1, Correspondence of General Haldimand and Brigadier-General Taylor, 21672, Additional Manuscripts, British Museum, Library of Congress, Washington DC.

39. "Record of a congress held at Mobile with the Chickasaws and Choctaws," 2 January 1772, *Westward Expansion*, 73, microfilm reel 6.

40. Charles Stuart to John Stuart, 1 July 1778, CO5, 79.

41. "Record of a Congress Held at Mobile with the Chickasaws and Choctaws," 2 January 1772, *Westward Expansion*, 73, microfilm reel 6.

42. John Stuart to John Pownall, 16 April 1765, CO5, 66; "Regulations Settled as Necessary for the Better Carrying on the Trade with the Indian Nations Surrounding the Province of West Florida," 10 April 1765, *Westward Expansion*, 66, microfilm reel 4, and John Stuart to the Earl of Hillsborough, 7 January 1772, *Westward Expansion*, 73, microfilm reel 6.

43. "Memorial of the Council of His Majesty's Province of West Florida," 24 August 1768, MPA:ED, 3:178–78, microfilm reel 2, and Montfort Browne to Earl of Hillsborough, 20 August 1768, MPA:ED, 3:183.

44. Government Expenses, 1767, "Spain in the Mississippi Valley, 1765–1794," ed. Lawrence Kinnaird, in *Annual Report of the American Historical Association* (Washington DC, 1946–49), 2:18.

45. John Stuart to lord George Germain, 2 May 1778, *Westward Expansion*, 76, microfilm reel 7; Charles Stuart to Alexander Cameron, 20 December 1779, and Alexander Cameron to Sir Henry Clinton, 20 December 1779, both *Westward Expansion*, 81, microfilm reel 8.

46. A talk from the Six Towns to Capt. James Colbert, 19 November 1779, *Westward Expansion*, 81, microfilm reel 8.

47. Farquhar Bethune to Alexander Cameron, 27 August 1780, *Westward Expansion*, 82, microfilm reel 8.

48. John Stuart to the Choctaws and Chickasaws, 14 May 1777, *Westward Expansion*, 76, microfilm reel 7.

49. Lord George Germain to John Campbell, 4 April 1780, MPA:ED, 9:188, microfilm reel 5, and James H. O'Donnell III, "Hamstrung by Penury: Alexander Cameron's Failure at Pensacola," in *Anglo-Spanish Confrontation on the Gulf Coast during the American Revolution*, ed. William S. Coker and Robert R. Rea (Pensacola FL: Gulf Coast History and Humanities Conference, 1982), 79–80.

50. Alexander Cameron to Lord George Germain, 30 November 1780, *Westward Expansion*, 82, microfilm reel 8.

51. Alexander Cameron to Major General Campbell, 8 November 1780, *Westward Expansion*, 82, microfilm reel 8.

52. Farquhar Bethune to Alexander Cameron, 27 August 1780, *Westward Expansion*, 82, microfilm reel 8.

53. Charles Stuart to Alexander Cameron, 24 December 1779, *Westward Expansion*, 81, microfilm reel 8.

54. Ferquhar Bethune to John Stuart, 16 June 1778, CO5, 79; Farquhar Bethune to Alexander Cameron, 4 September 1780, *Westward Expansion* 82, microfilm reel 8; Alexander Cameron to Lord George Germain, 10 February 1781 and 30 November 1781, *Westward Expansion*, 82, microfilm reel 8; General John Campbell to Sir Henry Clinton, 9 April 1781, Orwin Rush, *Spain's Final Triumph over Great Britain in the Gulf of Mexico: The Battle of Pensacola, March 9 to May 8, 1781* (Tallahassee: Florida State University Press, 1966), 93; Simon Favre to Francisco Bouligny, 8 November 1785, "Spain in the Mississippi Valley," 3:154; Jack D. L. Holmes, "Juan de la Villebeuvre and Spanish Indian Policy in West Florida, 1784–1797," *Florida Historical Quarterly* 58 (April 1980): 388–89; Ethan A. Grant, "The Natchez Revolt of 1781: A Reconsideration," *Journal of Mississippi History* 56 (November 1994): 310–12; and O'Donnell, "Hamstrung by Penury," 87.

55. Pierre Juzon to Josef de Ezpeleta, 19 February 1781, "Spain in the Mississippi

Valley," 2:419, and Simon Favre to Tugean, 25 November 1783, "Spain in the Mississippi Valley," 3:92.

56. Treaty of Mobile, 13 and 14 July 1784, "Mississippi Provincial Archives: Spanish Dominion " (Jackson: Mississippi Writers' Project, 1942), Record Group 26, Mississippi Department of Archives and History, Jackson—hereafter cited as MPA:SD—2:59–66, microfilm reel 32; Holmes, "Juan de la Villebeuvre," 388–89, 392; and Jack D. L. Holmes, "Spanish Treaties with West Florida Indians, 1784–1802," *Florida Historical Quarterly* 48 (October 1969): 143–44.

57. Thomas Watson, "Continuity in Commerce: Development of the Panton, Leslie and Company Trade Monopoly," *Florida Historical Quarterly* 54 (April 1976): 549–62; Francisco Bouligny to Estevan Miró, 24 July 1785 and 4 August 1785, "Papers from the Spanish Archives relating to Tennessee and the Old Southwest, 1783–1800," ed. D. C. and Roberta Corbitt, *East Tennessee Historical Society Publications* 9 (1937): 126 and 128; and Alexander McGillivray to Miró, 1 May 1786, "Papers from the Spanish Archives," 10 (1938): 134–35.

58. *American State Papers: Documents, Legislative and Executive of the Congress of the United States. Class II. Indian Affairs,* ed. Walter Lowrie and Matthew St. Clair Clarke (Washington DC: Gales and Seaton, 1832), 1:49–50, and Letter by Estevan Miró, 28 June 1786, MPA:SD, 2:311–14, microfilm reel 32.

59. Treaty of Hopewell, 3 January 1786, reel 2, microfilm series M668, Ratified Indian Treaties: 1722–1869, Record Group 75, Records of the Bureau of Indian Affairs, National Archives, Washington DC—hereafter cited as M668 followed by reel number.

60. "Original Papers concerning the Hopewell Treaties, 1785–86," 3 and 5 January 1786, 14U82, 87, 90, Lyman Draper Collections, Western History Collections, University of Oklahoma, Norman.

61. William Blount and Andrew Pickens to the Secretary of War, 1 August 1793, *The Territorial Papers of the United States: The Territory South of the Ohio River, 1790–1796,* comp. and ed. Clarence Carter (Washington DC: United States Government Printing Office, 1936), 4:291.

62. "Original Papers concerning the Hopewell Treaties, 1785–86," 3 and 5 January 1786, 14U82, 87, 90, Draper Collection.

63. Marios de Villiers to Estevan Miró, 30 August 1787, "Spain in the Mississippi Valley," 3:233.

64. Philip Hay to Estevan Miró, 30 July 1788, "Spain in the Mississippi Valley," 3:258.

65. Carlos de Grand-Pré to Estevan Miró, 4 January 1790, "Spain in the Mississippi Valley," 3:291.

66. Estevan Miró to Josef de Ezpeleta, 20 February 1788, MPA:SD, 3:107–11, microfilm reel 33.

67. Article 3, Treaty of Mobile, 13 and 14 July 1784, MPA:SD 2:63, microfilm reel 32.

68. Juan de la Villebeuvre to Francisco Luis Héctor, Baron de Carondelet, 22 July 1794, "Spain in the Mississippi Valley," 4:328.

69. Juan de la Villebeuvre to Manuel Gayoso de Lemos, 10 September 1792, "Spain in the Mississippi Valley," 4:79.

70. Estevan Miró to Marquis de Sonora, 1 June 1787, Arturo O'Neill to Miró, 8 June 1787, and Benjamin James to James Mather and Arthur Strother, 23 July 1787, all "Papers from the Spanish Archives," 11 (1939): 76, 81, 86.

71. Estevan Miró and Martin Navarro to Antonio Valdes, 1 April 1787, and Vincente Folch to Miró, 26 April 1787, both "Papers from the Spanish Archives," 14 (1942): 97, 100; Manuel Gayoso de Lemos to Francisco Luis Héctor, Baron de Carondelet, 21 July 1792, "Papers from the Spanish Archives," 27 (1955): 87; and Miró to Joseph Espeleta, 1 April 1788 and 20 February 1788, MPS:SD, 3:113 and 106, microfilm reel 33.

72. Watson, "Continuity in Commerce," 549–62; J. A. Brown, "Panton, Leslie and Company: Indian Traders of Pensacola and St. Augustine," *Florida Historical Quarterly* 37 (January–April 1953): 329–31; Ulrich Bonnell Phillips, *Georgia and State Rights: A Study of the Political History of Georgia from the Revolution to the Civil War, with Particular Regard to Federal Relations* (Washington DC: United States Government Printing Office, 1902), 29- 30; and Estevan Miró to Antonio Valdes, 10 August 1790, MPA:SD, 3:222, microfilm reel 33.

73. Manuel Gayoso de Lemos to Estevan Miró, 10 May 1791, MPA:SD, 3:302–8.

74. Franchimastabé and Taboca to Manuel Gayoso de Lemos, 14 May 1791, MPA:SD, 3:310.

75. Christopher J. Malloy and Charles A. Weeks, eds. and trans., "Shuttle Diplomacy Eighteenth Century Style: Stephen Minor's First Mission to the Choctaws and Journal, May–June 1791," *Journal of Mississippi History* 55 (February 1993): 31–36.

76. Manuel Gayoso de Lemos to Francisco Luis Héctor, Baron de Carondelet, 14 April 1792, microfilm reel 7, *Papers of Panton, Leslie and Co.* (Woodbridge CT: Research Publications, 1986), Newberry Library, Chicago; Holmes, "Juan de la Villebeuvre," 395; Holmes, "Spanish Treaties, with West Florida Indians," 140, 144–45, 148, 151; Lawrence Kinnaird and Lucia B. Kinnaird, "Nogales: Strategic Post on the Spanish Frontier," *Journal of Mississippi History* 42 (February 1980): 1–2; and Malloy and Weeks, "Shuttle Diplomacy," 31–47.

77. Francisco Luis Héctor, Baron de Carondelet to Conde de Floridablanca, 29 May 1792, MPA:SD, 4:107–53, microfilm reel 33; Natchez Treaty, 14 May 1792, Thomas Gilcrease Institute of American History and Art, Tulsa OK; Holmes, "Juan de la Villebeuvre," 395; Holmes, "Spanish Treaties with West Florida Indians," 140, 144–45, 148, 151; Kinnaird and Kinnaird, "Nogales," 1–2; and Deborah Hay, "Fort St.

Stephens and Fort Confederation: Two U.S. Factories for the Choctaws, 1802–1822" (M.A. thesis, Auburn University, 1979), 33–34.

78. Franchimastabé to Manuel de Lanzo, 22 April 1793, "Spain in the Mississippi Valley," 4:151, and Gayoso de Lemos to Francisco Luis Héctor, Baron de Carondelet, 14 April 1792, *Papers of Panton, Leslie and Co.*, microfilm reel 7.

79. Franchimastabé to Manuel Gayoso de Lemos, June 1794, "Spain in the Mississippi Valley," 4:309.

80. "List of Debts Due by the Traders and Half Breed Indian Factors of the Choctaw Nation to the House of Panton Leslie & Co. of Mobille the 31st day of December 1799," *Papers of Panton, Leslie and Co.*, microfilm reel 12.

81. Memoir of Nathaniel Folsom (1829), box H57, folder 59, Jay L. Hargrett Papers, Western History Collections, University of Oklahoma, Norman; Horatio B. Cushman, *A History of the Choctaw, Chickasaw, and Natchez Indians* (Greenville TX: Headlight, 1899), 387, 399–400; Allene Smith, *Greenwood LeFlore and the Choctaw Indians of the Mississippi Valley* (Memphis: C. A. Davis, 1951), 19–39; W. David Baird, *Peter Pitchlynn: Chief of the Choctaws* (Norman: University of Oklahoma Press, 1972), 6; William A. Love, "Lowndes County, Its Antiquities and Pioneer Settlers," *Publications of the Mississippi Historical Society* 7 (1903): 42; and Peter James Hudson, "A Story of Choctaw Chiefs," *Chronicles of Oklahoma* 17 (March 1939): 8.

82. "Letter from the Secretary of War . . . ," Executive Document 109, *Executive Documents*, 26th Cong., 2d sess., 1840–42 (Washington DC: Blair and Rives, 1840), 40.

83. John D. W. Guice, "Face to Face in Mississippi Territory, 1798–1817," in *The Choctaw before Removal*, ed. Carolyn Keller Reeves (Jackson: University Press of Mississippi, 1985), 159.

84. Manuel Gayoso de Lemos to Francisco Luis Héctor, Baron de Carondelet, 21 July 1792, "Papers from the Spanish Archives," 27 (1955): 87.

85. Alexander McGillivray to Estevan Miró, 1 May 1786, MPA:SD, 2:304, microfilm reel 32.

86. Simon Favre to Francisco Luis Héctor, Baron de Carondelet, 29 June 1792, "Spain in the Mississippi Valley," 4:57; Manuel Gayoso de Lemos to Carondelet, 13 September 1797, MPA:SD, 4:202- 6, microfilm reel 33; Henry Knox to the Chiefs and Warriors of the Choctaw Nation, 1792, MPA:SD, 4:5, microfilm reel 33; Juan de la Villebeuvre to Carondelet, 5 September 1792, MPA:SD, 4:75–76, microfilm reel 33; Anthony Foster to William Blount, 29 July 1792, *American State Papers, Indian Affairs*, 1:283; William Blount to the Secretary of War, 20 September 1792, and Blount to Henry Knox, 20 September 1792, both *Territorial Papers of the United States*, 4:172–73. Foster's name appears as Forster in these documents.

87. William Blount to the Chiefs and Warriors of the Choctaw Nation, 10 May 1792, "Spain in the Mississippi Valley," 4:7.

88. Minutes of a Conference Held at Nashville, 7, 8, and 10 August 1782, *American State Papers, Indian Affairs*, 1:283–87.

89. Juan de la Villebeuvre to Manuel Gayoso de Lemos, 10 September 1792, *American State Papers, Indian Affairs*, 1:79.

90. Treaty of Boucfouca, 10 May 1793, MPA:SD, 4:370–71, microfilm reel 33, and Jack D. L. Holmes, "Up the Tombigbee with the Spaniards: Juan de la Villebeuvre and the Treaty of Boucfouca (1793)," *Alabama Historical Quarterly* 40 (spring–summer 1978): 151–61.

91. Francisco Luis Héctor, Baron de Carondelet, Proposals for an Indian Congress, 26 February 1793, "Spain in the Mississippi Valley," 4:141–43; Manuel Gayoso de Lemos to Juan de la Villebeuvre, 31 July 1792, MPA:SD, 4:180, microfilm reel 33; Treaty of Friendship between Indians and Spaniards, 28 October 1793, *Papers of Panton, Leslie and Co.*, microfilm reel 23; and Holmes, "Up the Tombigbee with the Spanish," 51–60.

92. Juan de la Villebeuvre, quoted in James P. Pate, "The Fort of the Confederation: The Spanish on the Upper Tombigbee," *Alabama Historical Quarterly* 44 (fall–winter 1982): 174–75.

93. Ougoulayacabé to Manuel Gayoso de Lemos, 2 July 1794, "Papers from the Spanish Archives," 40 (1968): 110.

94. Juan de la Villebeuvre to Francisco Luis Héctor, Baron de Carondelet, 16 June 1795, "Papers from the Spanish Archives," 49 (1977): 149.

95. Juan de la Villebeuvre to Francisco Luis Héctor, Baron de Carondelet, 7 February 1793, "Papers from the Spanish Archives," 29 (1957): 152; Manuel Lanzos to Carondelet, 29 April 1795, "Papers from the Spanish Archives," 47 (1975): 139; and Villebeuvre to Carondelet, 16 June 1795, "Papers from the Spanish Archives," 49 (1977): 149–50.

96. Franklin L. Riley, "Spanish Policy in Mississippi after the Treaty of San Lorenzo," *Publications of the Mississippi Historical Society* 1 (1898): 50–66.

97. Andrew Ellicott, *The Journal of Andrew Ellicott . . .* (Philadelphia: W. Fry, 1814), 45–46, 50, 85, and Holmes, "Up the Tombigbee," 60.

98. "An Act for the Government of the Mississippi Territory . . . ," *Territorial Papers of the United States*, 5:16–18.

99. William McLiesh to David Henley, 16 December 1797, David Henley Papers, Special Collections, William R. Perkins Library, Duke University, Durham NC.

100. Treaty of Fort Adams, 1 December 1801, M668, 1.

101. William Simpson, Abstract of Debts Owed to Panton, Leslie and Company, 20 August 1803, reel 1, microfilm series M271, Office of the Secretary of War, Letters Received by the Secretary of War relating to Indian Affairs, 1800–1822, Records of

the Bureau of Indian Affairs, Record Group 75, National Archives, Washington DC—hereafter cited as M271 followed by reel number; and William Panton to Benjamin Hawkins, 11 June 1799, *Papers of Panton, Leslie and Co.*, microfilm reel 12.

102. Article 2, Treaty of Mount Dexter, 16 November 1805, M668, 1.

103. Folder 9, microfilm reel 1, Halbert Papers.

3. CHANGE AND PERSISTENCE IN CHOCTAW CULTURE

1. Richard White, *The Roots of Dependency: Subsistence, Environment, and Social Change among the Choctaws, Pawnees, and Navajos* (Lincoln: University of Nebraska Press, 1983), and Wilma A. Dunaway, *The First American Frontier: Transition to Capitalism in Southern Appalachia, 1700–1860* (Chapel Hill: University of North Carolina Press, 1996).

2. Record of a congress held at Mobile with the Chickasaws and Choctaws, 1 January 1772, *Westward Expansion*, 63, microfilm reel 6.

3. Timothy P. Mooney, "Many Choctaw Standing: An Archaeological Study of Culture Change in the Early Historic Period" (M.A. thesis, University of North Carolina, Chapel Hill, 1994), 82, 94.

4. James Merrell, *The Indians' New World: Catawbas and Their Neighbors from European Contact through the Era of Removal* (Chapel Hill: University of North Carolina Press, 1989).

5. Antoine Le Page du Pratz, *The History of Louisiana Translated from the French of M. Le Page du Pratz*, ed. Joseph G. Tregle Jr. (Baton Rouge: Louisiana State University for the Louisiana American Revolution Bicentennial Commission, 1975), 71–72, 166; John R. Swanton, ed., "An Early Account of the Choctaw Indians," in *Memoirs of the American Anthropological Association*, vol. 5, no. 2 (Lancaster PA: American Anthropological Association, 1918), 70; Governor Périer to Jean-Frédéric Phélypeaux, Compte de Maurepas, 1 April 1730, MPA:FD, 4:32; William Bartram, *The Travels of William Bartram*, ed. Mark Van Doren (New York: Barnes and Noble, 1940), 185; Timothy K. Perttula, *The Caddo Nation: Archaeological and Ethnohistoric Perspectives* (Austin: University of Texas Press, 1992), 11, 29; and Marc de Villiers du Terrage, "Notes sur les Chactas d'après les journaux de voyage de Régis du Roullet (1729–1732)," *Journal de la Société des Américanistes de Paris* 15 (1923): 234.

6. Cyrus Byington, *A Dictionary of the Choctaw Language*, ed. John R. Swanton and Henry S. Halbert, Bureau of American Ethnology Bulletin 46 (Washington DC: United States Government Printing Office, 1915), 74; David S. Rood, *Wichita Grammar* (New York: Garland, 1976), 295; John Owen Dorsey and John R. Swanton, eds., *A Dictionary of the Biloxi and Ofo Languages*, Bureau of American Ethnology Bulletin 47 (Washington DC: United States Government Printing Office, 1912), 301; Durbin Feeling, *Cherokee-English Dictionary* (Talequah: Cherokee Nation

of Oklahoma, 1975), 187; Henry Frieland Buckner, *A Grammar of the Masjwke [Muskogee], or Creek Language: To Which Are Prefixed Lessons in Spelling, Reading, and Defining* (Marion AL: Domestic and Indian Mission Board of the Southern Baptist Convention, 1869), 35; and James Crawford, *The Mobilian Trade Language* (Knoxville: University of Tennessee Press, 1978), 4, 76, 83.

7. Horatio B. Cushman, *A History of the Choctaw, Chickasaw and Natchez Indians* (Greenville TX: Headlight, 1899), 389–90.

8. Villiers du Terrage, "Notes sur les Chactas," 234–35.

9. David I. Bushnell Jr., "Drawings by A. DeBatz in Louisiana, 1732–1735," in *Smithsonian Miscellaneous Collections*, vol. 80, no. 5 (Washington DC: Smithsonian Institution, 1927); Swanton, "Early Account," 71; and Dumont de Montigny, *Mémoires historiques sur la Louisiane . . .* (Paris: C. J. B. Bauche, 1753), 1:74–75.

10. James Adair, *Adair's History of the American Indians*, ed. Samuel Cole Williams (Johnson City TN: Watauga Press, 1930; rpt. Nashville: National Society of the Colonial Dames of America, in Tennessee, 1953), 139; Byington, *Dictionary*, 197; Francis Haines, "The Northward Spread of Horses among the Plains Indians," *American Anthropologist* 40 (July–September 1938): 429- 31; and Villiers du Terrage, "Notes sur les Chactas," 234. Father Gravier transcribed the term as *su'ba.*

11. Adair, *Adair's History*, 139, 142, 242, 340, 457; Diron d'Artaguette to Jean-Frédéric Phélypeaux, Comte de Maurepas, 24 October 1737, MPA:FD, 4:151; Cushman, *History*, 180, 235; and log of His Majesty's Galiot, *La Fleche*, 23 January 1793, "Spain in the Mississippi Valley, 1765–1794," ed. Lawrence Kinnaird, *Annual Report of the American Historical Association* (Washington DC: 1946–49), 4:114.

12. Villiers du Terrage, "Notes sur les Chactas," 236–37, and Percy L. Rainwater, ed., "The Autobiography of Benjamin Grubb Humphreys, August 26, 1808–December 20, 1882," *Mississippi Valley Historical Review* 21 (June 1934): 232.

13. Sauvole de la Villantray to Pontchartrain [?], 4 August 1701, MPA:FD, 2:10; Census of Louisiana by Nicolas de La Salle, 31 August 1704, MPA:FD, 2:20; Census of Louisiana by de La Salle, 12 August 1708, MPA:FD, 2:32; Dumont de Montigny, *Mémoires historiques*, 1:85; Le Page du Pratz, *History of Louisiana*, 19; David J. Weber, *The Spanish Frontier in North America* (New Haven: Yale University Press, 1992), 151; Adair, *Adair's History*, 17; "Relation or Journal of the Voyage of Father Gravier, of the Society of Jesus, in 1700, from the Country of the Illinois to the Mouth of the Mississippi River," in *The Jesuit Relations and Allied Documents, 1610–1791*, ed. Reuben Gold Thwaites, 73 vols. (Cleveland: Burrows Brothers, 1896–1901), 65:151—hereafter cited as *Jesuit Relations;* Garret Rapalje Notebook, 10, microfilm 1697, James and Charles B. Allen Papers, Southern Historical Collection, Manuscript Division, Wilson Library, University of North Carolina at Chapel Hill; Byington, *Dictionary*, 334.

14. Swanton, "Early Account," 67.

15. Bernard Romans, *A Concise Natural History of East and West Florida; a Facsimile Reproduction of the 1775 Edition* (Gainesville: University of Florida Press, 1962), 84.

16. "Relation or Journal of the Voyage of Father Gravier, of the Society of Jesus, in 1700, from the Country of the Illinois to the Mouth of the Mississippi River," in *Jesuit Relations,* 65:151.

17. Romans, *Concise Natural History,* 84.

18. Daniel H. Usner Jr., *Indians, Settlers, and Slaves in a Frontier Exchange Economy: The Lower Mississippi Valley before 1763* (Chapel Hill: University of North Carolina Press, 1992), 211, and Eron Opha Rowland, ed., "Peter Chester, Third Governor of the Province of West Florida under British Dominion, 1770–1781," *Publications of the Mississippi Historical Society, Centenary Series* 5 (1925): 83–84.

19. Usner, *Indians, Settlers, and Slaves.*

20. Journal and Field Notes of Levin Wailes, 1809, box 2, folder 16, p. 26, John F. H. Claiborne Papers, Southern Historical Collection, Manuscript Division, Wilson Library, University of North Carolina at Chapel Hill.

21. Gregory A. Waselkov, "Indian Maps of the Colonial Southeast," in *Powhatan's Mantle: Indians in the Colonial Southeast,* ed. Peter Wood, Gregory A. Waselkov, and M. Thomas Hatley (Lincoln: University of Nebraska Press, 1989), 292–342, and Marc de Villiers du Terrage, "Note sur deux cartes dessinées par les Chikachas en 1737," *Journal de la Société des Américanistes de Paris* 13 (1921): 7–9.

22. Richard White, "Red Shoes: Warrior and Diplomat," in *Struggle and Survival in Colonial America,* ed. David G. Sweet and Gary B. Nash (Berkeley: University of California Press, 1981), 54–55, and Governor Périer to Jean-Frédéric Phélypeaux, Comte de Maurepas, 18 March 1730, MPA:FD, 1:72.

23. "Introduction," in *Jesuit Relations,* 1:36–37; Father Le Petit to Father d'Avaugour, 12 July 1730, in *Jesuit Relations,* 68:195; and "Catalogue of the Persons and Officers in the Society of Jesus, for the Provinces of France, at the End of the Year 1749: Missions of North America in New France," in *Jesuit Relations,* 69:79.

24. Jean-Bernard Bossu, *Travels in the Interior of North America, 1751–1762,* trans. and ed. Seymour Feiler (Norman: University of Oklahoma Press, 1962), 168–69.

25. Régis du Roullet to Governor Périer, 21 February 1732, MPA:FD, 4:58–62.

26. Adair, *Adair's History,* 35; emphasis in the original.

27. Minutes of a Conference at Mobile between the English, the Choctaws, and the Chickasaws, 1 April 1765, *Mississippi Provincial Archives: English Dominion,* ed. Dunbar Rowland (Nashville: Brandon, 1911), 241.

28. Adair, *Adair's History,* 38.

29. Cecil Johnson, *British West Florida, 1763–1783* (New Haven: Yale University Press, 1943), 133–36; Peter J. Hamilton, *Colonial Mobile,* ed. Charles G. Summersell

(1919; rpt. Tuscaloosa: University of Alabama Press, 1976), 153, 333; and Manuel Gayoso de Lemos, "Instructions for the Admission of Settlers into the District of Nogales," 1 April 1791, "Mississippi Provincial Archives: Spanish Dominion," 3:373–75, microfilm reel 33 (Jackson: Mississippi Writers' Project, 1942), Mississippi Department of Archives and History, Jackson; Jean-Baptiste Le Moyne, Sieur de Bienville, Memoire on Louisiana, 1726, MPA:FD, 3:522; Bienville to Salmon and Jean-Frédéric Phélypeaux, Comte de Maurepas, 20 March 1734, MPA:FD, 3:638; Jack D. L. Holmes, "Law and Order in Spanish Natchez, 1781–1798," *Journal of Mississippi History* 25 (July 1963): 192–95; and D. Clayton James, *Antebellum Natchez* (Baton Rouge: Louisiana State University Press, 1968), 5–46.

30. Francis DuBose Richardson Memoirs, 15, microfilm 3010, Southern Historical Collection, Manuscript Division, Wilson Library, University of North Carolina at Chapel Hill.

31. Autobiography of John Hutchins, 60, microfilm 1311, Breckinridge Family Reminiscences, Manuscript Division, Wilson Library, University of North Carolina at Chapel Hill.

32. Antonio Maxent to Estevan Miró, 5 December 1782, "Spain in the Mississippi Valley," 3:67.

33. Francisco Cruzat to Estevan Miró, 23 August 1784, "Spain in the Mississippi Valley," 3:117.

34. James P. Pate, "Fort of the Confederation: The Spanish on the Upper Tombigbee," *Alabama Historical Quarterly* 44 (fall and winter 1982): 178; Juan de la Villebeuvre to Francisco Luis Héctor, Baron de Carondelet, 5 September 1792, "Spain in the Mississippi Valley," 4:77; and White, *Roots of Dependency*, 28, 101.

35. Record of a congress held in Mobile with the Chickasaws and Choctaws, 31 December 1771, *Westward Expansion*, 73, microfilm reel 6; John Stuart to George Germain, 13 April 1778, CO5, 78; John Stuart to Governor Lord Botetourt, 13 January 1770, *Documents of the American Revolution, 1770–1783*, ed. K. G. Davies (Shannon: Irish University Press, 1972), 2:28, and Nancy Foner, *Ages in Conflict: A Cross-Cultural Perspective on Inequality between Old and Young* (New York: Columbia University Press, 1984), 39–48, 145–46.

36. White, *Roots of Dependency*, 83–85, 91.

37. Peter C. Mancall, *Deadly Medicine: Indians and Alcohol in Early America* (Ithaca: Cornell University Press, 1995), 7.

38. Cushman, *History*, 171, and Garret Rapalje Notebook, Allen Papers.

39. Rowland, "Peter Chester," 48.

40. René Roi to John Stuart, 11 August 1769, *Westward Expansion*, 70, microfilm reel 5; Record of a congress held at Mobile with the Chickasaws and Choctaws, 31 December 1771 and 2 January 1772, *Westward Expansion*, 73, microfilm reel 6; Section 4, "An Act to Prevent Stealing of Horses and Neat Cattle and for the More

Effectual Discovery and Punishment of Such Persons as Shall Unlawfully Brand, Mark or Kill the Same (28 June 1769)," *The Minutes Journals, and Acts of the General Assembly of British West Florida,* comp. Robert R. Rea (Tuscaloosa: University Press of Alabama, 1979), 363; 19 March 1770, "Journal of the Common House of Assembly of the Province of West Florida . . . ," *Minutes Journals,* 230; "Edward Mease Narrative, 1770–1771," Rowland, "Peter Chester," 84; James White, Rapides District, Sworn Statement, 28 December 1798, microfilm reel 11, *Papers of Panton, Leslie and Co.* (Woodbridge CT: Research Publications, 1986), Newberry Library, Chicago; Romans, *Concise Natural History,* 83, and Bartholemew Tardiveau, Mémoire concernant le commerce avec différentes nations sauvages, écrit . . . la chute de l'Ohio en mars 1784, Tardiveau Collection, Chicago Historical Society, Chicago.

41. Article 4, Treaty of Hopewell, 3 January 1786, M668, 2.

42. Ephraim Kirby to Thomas Jefferson, 1 May 1804, Ephraim Kirby Papers, Special Collections, William R. Perkins Library, Duke University, Durham NC.

43. Carlos de Grand-Pré to Estevan Miró, 2 October 1790, "Spain in the Mississippi Valley," 3:38.

44. William C. C. Claiborne to Daniel Burnet, 3 October 1802, *Official Letter Books of W. C. C. Claiborne, 1801–1816,* ed. Dunbar Rowland (Jackson MS, 1917), 1:193.

45. John Q. Anderson, ed., "The Narrative of John Hutchinson," *Journal of Mississippi History* 20 (January 1958): 6.

46. William Panton to Estevan Miró, 9 June 1789, Miró to Don Domingo Cabello, 15 July 1789, and Alexander McGillivray to Estevan Miró, 10 and 12 August 1789, all *Papers of Panton, Leslie and Co.,* microfilm reel 5.

47. Romans, *Concise Natural History,* 86.

48. Winthrop Sargent to Timothy Pickering, 26 May 1799, *Mississippi Territorial Archives, 1798–1803,* ed. Dunbar Rowland (Nashville: Brandon, 1905), 148.

49. William G. Mcloughlin, *The Cherokee Ghost Dance* (Macon GA: Mercer University Press, 1984), 30–36.

50. The names come from a roster of Choctaws who claimed to have lost property during removal, 8 October 1837, reel 184, microfilm series M234, Choctaw Agency West, Letters Received by the Office of Indian Affairs, 1824–1880, Record Group 75, Records of the Bureau of Indian Affairs, National Archives, Washington DC— hereafter cited as M234 followed by reel number; and *1830 Choctaw Roll: "Armstrong Roll,"* introduction and index by Larry S. Watson (Laguna Hills CA: Histree, 1988), 60, 35, 104, 122, 139.

51. "A Proclamation by His Excellency William C. C. Claiborne Governor and Commander in Chief in and over the Mississippi Territory," 14 December 1801, *Official Letter Books,* 1:25, and Henry Dearborn to William Davie, James Wilkinson, and Benjamin Hawkins, 24 June 1801, reel 1, microfilm series M15, Letters Sent by

the Secretary of War relating to Indian Affairs: 1800–1824, Office of Indian Affairs, Record Group 75, Records of the Bureau of Indian Affairs, National Archives, Washington DC—hereafter cited as M15 followed by reel number.

52. *The Statistical History of the United States from Colonial Times to the Present* (New York: Basic Books, 1976), 30, and James Taylor Carson, "Frontier Development and Indian Removal: Mississippi and the Choctaws, 1788–1833" (M.A. thesis, Tulane University, 1992), chap. 2.

53. Henry Knox to George Washington, 7 July 1789, *American State Papers: Documents, Legislative and Executive of the Congress of the United States. Class II. Indian Affairs,* ed. Walter Lowrie and Matthew St. Clair Clarke (Washington DC, 1832–61), 1:53, and Francis Paul Prucha, *The Great Father: The United States Government and the American Indians,* unabridged version (Lincoln: University of Nebraska Press, 1984), chap. 1.

54. Bernard Sheehan, *Seeds of Extinction: Jeffersonian Philanthropy and the American Indian* (Chapel Hill: University of North Carolina Press, 1973), 6–24, 96, 119, 169, and Prucha, *Great Father,* chap. 1.

55. Sheehan, *Seeds of Extinction,* 135–41.

56. "Federal Laws relating to the Mississippi Territory," *Digest of the Statutes of the Mississippi Territory . . . . ,* comp. Harry Toulmin (Natchez: Territorial Printer, 1807), 590–92, and Prucha, *Great Father,* chap. 3.

57. Henry Dearborn to John McKee, 25 March 1801, M15, 1.

58. William Claiborne to Silas Dinsmoor, 28 January 1803, The Proceedings of the Governor of the Mississippi Territory as Superintendent of Indian Affairs, Territorial Governors' Papers, Alabama Department of Archives and History, Montgomery.

59. Deborah Hay, "Fort St. Stephens and Fort Confederation: Two U.S. Factories for the Choctaw, 1802–1822" (M.A. thesis, Auburn University, 1979), 26–51; Henry Dearborn to Joseph Chambers, 25 July 1803, M15, 1; "Letter from the Secretary of War . . . ," House Document 110, *Executive Documents, Printed by Order of the House of Representatives,* 16th Cong., 1st sess., 1819–20 (Washington DC: Gales and Seaton, 1820); and *American State Papers, Indian Affairs,* 2:208, 352.

60. Indent books, 14 December 1805, reel 1, indent books, 24 January 1809 and 6 February 1809, reel 2, and miscellaneous accounts, 3 April 1816, reel 3, all microfilm series T500, Records of the Choctaw Trading House: 1803–24, Record Group 75, Records of the Bureau of Indian Affairs, National Archives, Washington DC—hereafter cited as T500 followed by reel number; and Hay, "Fort St. Stephens," 39–43, 88–93, 112.

61. Edward Hunter Ross and Dawson A. Phelps, "A Journey on the Natchez Trace in 1792: A Document from the Archives of Spain," *Journal of Mississippi History* 15 (July 1953): 271.

62. Minutes of the Fort Adams Treaty Conference, 12 December 1801, reel 1,

microfilm series T494, Documents relating to the Negotiation of Ratified and Unratified Treaties with Various Indian Tribes: 1801–1869, Record Group 75, Records of the Bureau of Indian Affairs, National Archives, Washington DC— hereafter cited as T494 followed by reel number.

4. MARKET REVOLUTION

1. Horatio B. Cushman, *A History of the Choctaw, Chickasaw, and Natchez Indians* (Greenville TX: Headlight, 1899), 387; Allene Smith, *Greenwood LeFlore and the Choctaw Indians of the Mississippi Valley* (Memphis: C. A. Davis, 1951), 19–39; W. David Baird, *Peter Pitchlynn: Chief of the Choctaws* (Norman: University of Oklahoma Press, 1972), 6; and Peter Pitchlynn to John Coffee [no date], box 2, folder 6, John Coffee Papers, Alabama Department of Archives and History, Montgomery.

2. Mushulatubbee is usually mentioned as Homastubby's son, but given Choctaw matrilineality and rules of succession, he was probably Homastubby's nephew. Folder 89, reel 4, Halbert Papers.

3. *Panoplist and Missionary Herald* 16 (August 1820): 379.

4. Gavin Wright, *The Political Economy of the Cotton South: Households, Markets, and Wealth in the Nineteenth Century* (New York: Norton, 1978), chap. 3.

5. Kathryn Holland Braund, Joel Martin, and Richard White argue that the deer-skin trade fostered socioeconomic differentiation among the Creeks and Choctaws that produced a class-based society. Theda Perdue sees a similar process in the Cherokees' adoption of plantation slavery. See Kathryn Holland Braund, *Deerskins and Duffels: Creek Indian Trade with Anglo-America, 1685–1815* (Lincoln: University of Nebraska Press, 1993); Joel W. Martin, *Sacred Revolt: The Muskogees' Struggle for a New World* (Boston: Beacon Press, 1991); Richard White, *The Roots of Dependency: Subsistence, Environment, and Social Change among the Choctaws, Pawnees, and Navajos* (Lincoln: University of Nebraska Press, 1983); Theda Perdue, *Slavery and the Evolution of Cherokee Society, 1540–1866* (Knoxville: University of Tennessee Press, 1979); as well as Duane Champagne, *Social Order and Political Change: Constitutional Governments among the Cherokee, the Choctaw, the Chickasaw, and the Creek* (Stanford: Stanford University Press, 1992), for a comparison of the rise of class divisions among the four largest southeastern Indian groups.

6. Winifred Barr Rothenberg, *From Market-Places to a Market Economy: The Transformation of Rural Massachusetts, 1750–1850* (Chicago: University of Chicago Press, 1992), 5–23.

7. Karl Polyani, *The Great Transformation* (New York: Farrar and Rinehart, 1944), 43–71.

8. Marc Bloch, quoted in Rothenberg, *From Market-Places to a Market Economy,* 23.

9. Benjamin Henry Boneval Latrobe, *Impressions respecting New Orleans: Diary and Sketches, 1818–1820*, ed. Samuel Wilson Jr. (New York: Columbia University Press, 1951), 21–22, 76; Fortescue Cuming, *Sketches of a Tour to the Western Country* . . . (Pittsburgh: Palmer, Spear and Eichbaum, 1810), 335–36; Berquin-Duvallon, *Travels in Louisiana and the Floridas, in the Year 1802, Giving a Correct Picture of Those Countries. Tr. from the French, with Notes, &c. by John Davis* (New York: I. Riley, 1806), 96; Paul Wilhelm, Duke of Württemberg, *Travels in North America, 1822–1824*, trans. W. Robert Nitske, ed. Savoie Lottinville (Norman: University of Oklahoma Press, 1973), 33; Gideon Lincecum, "Life of Apushimataha," *Publications of the Mississippi Historical Society*, 9 (1906): 480; and "Papers of George S. Gaines, Copied from the Original Now on File in the Mississippi State Department of Archives and History in a Collection of Letters Once Owned by J. F. H. Claiborne," 1, Indian Archives, Oklahoma Historical Society, Oklahoma City.

10. "A Partial Biography of the James Ware Davis Family," 3–4, William Penn Davis Papers, Special Collections, William R. Perkins Library, Duke University, Durham NC.

11. Cuming, *Sketches*, 336.

12. Berquin-Duvallon, *Travels in Louisiana*, 96.

13. Latrobe, *Impressions*, 76; Lincecum, "Life of Apushimataha," 480; Juan de la Villebeuvre to Francisco Luis Héctor, Baron de Carondelet, February 1793, "Papers from the Spanish Archives relating to Tennessee and the Old Southwest, 1783–1800," ed. D. C. and Roberta Corbitt, *East Tennessee Historical Society Publications* 29 (1957): 158; and Extract from John McKee's Journal, 2 November 1817, M271, 2.

14. Treaty of Fort Adams, 12 December 1801, T494, 1.

15. Harriet Owsley, ed., "Travels through the Indian Country in the Early 1800s: Memoirs of Martha Philips Martin," *Tennessee Historical Quarterly* 21 (March 1962): 75.

16. Latrobe, *Impressions*, 80.

17. Jacob Young, *Autobiography of a Pioneer* . . . (Cincinnati: L. Swormstedt, 1857), 213–14.

18. Young, *Autobiography of a Pioneer*, 213–14.

19. Henry S. Halbert, "Origin of Mashulaville," *Publications of the Mississippi Historical Society* 7 (1903): 394.

20. Gideon Lincecum, "Adenda," 1, Gideon Lincecum Papers, microfilm, Center for American History, University of Texas at Austin.

21. William A. Love, "Moshulitubbee's Prairie Village," *Publications of the Mississippi Historical Society* 7 (1903): 375, and *Niles' Weekly Register* 38 (31 July 1830): 345.

22. Cushman, *History*, 153, 389.

23. *Panoplist and Missionary Herald* 15 (October 1819): 460, 463; *Missionary*

Herald 18 (May 1822): 150; Adam Hodgson, *Letters from North America Written during a Tour in the United States and Canada* (London: Hurst, Robinson, 1824), 1:23, 241, 253; Francis Baily, *Journal of a Tour in Unsettled Parts of North America in 1796 and 1797* (London: Baily, 1856), 373; Kenneth D. Israel, "A Geographical Analysis of the Cattle Industry in Southeastern Mississippi from Its Beginnings to 1860" (Ph.D. diss., University of Southern Mississippi, 1970), 26, 65; Harry Toulmin, comp., *Digest of the Statutes of the Mississippi Territory* (Port Gibson MS: Territorial Printer, 1807), 403; Terry Jordan, *North American Cattle-Ranching Frontiers: Origins, Diffusion, and Differentiation* (Albuquerque: University of New Mexico Press, 1993), 150–55, 183; Gary Dunbar, "Colonial Cowpens," *Agricultural History* 35 (July 1961): 125–30; John D. W. Guice, "Cattle Raisers of the Old Southwest: A Reinterpretation," *Western Historical Quarterly* 8 (April 1977): 167–87; Forrest McDonald and Grady McWhiney, "The Antebellum Southern Herdsmen: A Reinterpretation," *Journal of Southern History* 41 (May 1975): 147–66; Daybook Entries, 18 August 1808, 16 September 1808, 22 May 1809, 13 July 1809, 9 October 1809, 18 April 1810, 8 March 1811, and 19 February 1813, T500, 4; Halbert, "Origins of Mashulaville," 393; Andre Michaux, "Travels to the West of the Allegheny Mountains in the States of Ohio, Kentucky, and Tennessee . . . ," in *Early Western Travels, 1748–1846*, ed. Reuben Gold Thwaites (Cleveland: Arthur H. Clarke, 1904), 246; 18 June 1820, Elliot Journal, microfilm reel 755, *Papers of the American Board of Commissioners for Foreign Missions* (Woodbridge CT: Research Publications, 1985), Indian Archives, Oklahoma State Historical Society, Oklahoma City—hereaftr cited as ABCFM followed by reel number; Sam Bowers Hilliard, *Hog* Meat and Hoecake; Food Supply in the Old South, 1840–1860 (Carbondale: Southern Illinois Press, 1972), 22–27; and Daniel H. Usner Jr., "American Indians on the Cotton Frontier: Changing Economic Relations with Citizens and Slaves in the Mississippi Territory," *Journal of American History* 72 (September 1985): 297.

24. *Missionary Herald* 17 (April 1821): 110; "Milley Yates," House Report 447, *Reports of Committees—House of Representatives*, 24th Cong., 1st sess., 1835–36 (Washington DC: Blair and Rives, 1836), 1; and Charles Lanman, "Peter Pitchlynn, Chief of the Choctaws," *Atlantic Monthly* 25 (April 1870): 486.

25. *Niles' Weekly Register* 38 (5 July 1830): 345; emphasis in the original.

26. William Ward to John C. Calhoun, 7 June 1822, *Papers*, ed. Robert L. Meriwether (Columbia: University of South Carolina Press for the South Caroliniana Society, 1959), 7:150; Deposition by William Doak, James Thompson, William Swain, and Josiah Doak, 12 April 1823, M234, 169; Ward to Calhoun, 18 April 1823, George Gaines to Ward, 24 January 1824, Middleton Mackey Deposition, 4 July 1826, Ward to James Barbour, 11 July 1826, Ward to Thomas L. McKenney, 4 November 1825, Ward to Thomas L. McKenney, 14 September 1826, Iahocautubbee and Tishohuabbee Testimony, 14 September 1826, and Ward to the Secretary of War,

17 February 1829, all in M234, 169; *1830 Choctaw Roll: "Armstrong Roll,"* introduction and index by Larry S. Watson (Laguna Hills CA: Histree, 1988), 70.

27. David Folsom and James McDonald to John C. Calhoun, 1 December 1824, Treaty of Washington Talks, T494, 1.

28. James L. McDonald to John C. Calhoun, 9 November 1824, M234, 169.

29. *Missionary Herald* 25 (December 1829): 378.

30. November 1822, Mayhew Journal, 755.

31. Cyrus Kingsbury to Thomas L. McKenney, 11 October 1825, "Letter from the Secretary of War . . . ," Executive Document 109, *Executive Documents,* 26th Cong., 2d sess., 1840–41 (Washington DC: Blair and Rives, 1840), 17.

32. *Missionary Herald* 19 (January 1823): 9–10.

33. 15 August 1822, Mayhew Journal, ABCFM, 755.

34. 28 August 1822, Mayhew Journal, ABCFM, and Joel Wood to Cyrus Kingsbury, 13 November 1828, ABCFM, 757.

35. Article 13, Treaty of Doak's Stand, 18 October 1820, M668, 5; Cushman, *History,* 393; *Missionary Herald* 19 (January 1823): 8; William Ward to Thomas L. McKenney, 26 March 1825, M234, 169; and Mushulatubbee to Peter Pitchlynn, 25 September 1824, box 1, folder 3, Peter Perkins Pitchlynn Papers, Western History Collections, University of Oklahoma, Norman.

36. Hodgson, *Letters from North America,* 1:224, 241, 253. Hodgson did not record that women milked the cows and cooked the steaks, but according to the conventions of Choctaw culture they must have done both of these things, much as a Cherokee woman served William Bartram cream from one of her cows. Gregory A. Waselkov and Kathryn E. Holland Braund, eds., *William Bartram on the Southeastern Indians* (Lincoln: University of Nebraska Press, 1995), 77.

37. Mary Haas, "Men's and Women's Speech in Koasati," in *Language in Culture and Society,* ed. Dell Hymes (New York: Harper and Row, 1964), 228–33, and Amelia Rector Bell, "Separate People: Speaking of Creek Men and Women," *American Anthropologist* 92 (June 1992): 332–45.

38. Bell, "Separate People," 332–35, and Charles Hudson, *The Southeastern Indians* (Knoxville: University of Tennessee Press, 1976), 368–68. The Choctaw names come from a roster of Choctaws claiming to have lost possessions during removal, 8 October 1837, M234, 184.

39. Antoine Simon Le Page du Pratz, *The History of Louisiana Translated from the French of M. Le Page du Pratz,* ed. Joseph Tregle Jr. (Baton Rouge: Louisiana State University for the Louisiana American Revolution Bicentennial Commission, 1975), 234; Lauren C. Post, "The Domestic Animals and Plants of French Louisiana as Mentioned in the Literature with References to Sources, Varieties, and Uses," *Louisiana Historical Quarterly* 16 (October 1933): 560, and U. P. Hedrick, *The Peaches of New York* (Albany NY: J. B. Lynn, 1917), 44–45.

40. White, *Roots of Dependency*, 103–5, 130–37; *Missionary Herald* 25 (November 1829): 350; and Hedrick, *Peaches of New York*, 44–45.

41. *Panoplist and Missionary Herald* 16 (July 1820): 320.

42. See, for example, Mary C. Wright, "Economic Development and Native American Women in the Early Nineteenth Century," *American Quarterly* 33 (1981): 525–36; Carol Devens, "Separate Confrontations: Gender as a Factor in Indian Adaptation to European Colonization in New France," *American Quarterly* 38 (1986): 461–80; Karen Anderson, "Commodity Exchange and Subordination: Montagnais- Naskapi and Huron Women, 1600–1650," *Signs* 11 (autumn 1985): 48–62.

43. Minutes of the Fort Adams Treaty Talks, 12 December 1801, T494, 1; John Forbes to Juan Ventura Morales, 11 February 1802, microfilm reel 14, *Papers of Panton, Leslie and Co.* (Woodbridge CT: Research Publications, 1986), Newberry Library, Chicago; James Wilkinson, Benjamin Hawkins, and Andrew Pickens to Henry Dearborn, 18 December 1802, M271, 1; Samuel Mitchell to David Henley, 17 January 1800, David Henley Papers, Special Collections, William R. Perkins Library, Duke University, Durham NC; Jesse D. Jennings, "Nutt's Trip to the Chickasaw Country," *Journal of Mississippi History* 9 (January 1947): 40; and William Crawford to John McKee, 13 September 1816, M15, 3.

44. John McKee to Winthrop Sargent, 21 March 1801, microfilm reel 5, *Winthrop Sargent Papers: Massachusetts Historical Society Microfilm Publication Number 1*, ed. Frederick S. Allis Jr. (Boston: Massachusetts Historical Society, 1965), Mississippi Department of Archives and History, Jackson.

45. Elias Cornelius, 2 December 1817, part 1, Indian Missionary Journals, Elias Cornelius Papers, Special Collections, William R. Perkins Library, Duke University.

46. Jedidiah Morse, *A Report to the Secretary of War of the United States . . .* (New Haven: Howe and Spalding, 1822), 182.

47. *Niles' Weekly Register* 38 (3 July 1830): 345.

48. L. R. Bakewell to James Barbour, 2 September 1825, M234, 169.

49. John McKee to William Crawford, Claims against the Choctaw Agency, 11 April 1816, M271, 1. I have used two figures to calculate the numbers of acres required for Choctaw cotton cultivation. Fortescu Cuming reported that upland land, the kind the Choctaws inhabited, yielded one thousand pounds of cotton in seed per acre. I have also used Forrest McDonald's and Grady McWhiney's more conservative figure of 530 pounds per acre, which was the average yield throughout the South. Cuming, *Sketches*, 323, and Forrest McDonald, "The South from Self-Sufficiency to Peonage: An Interpretation," *American Historical Review* 85 (December 1980): 1096–97. For other estimates of cotton production in Mississippi see Jennings, "Nutt's Trip," and James Hall, "A Brief History of the Mississippi Territory (1801)," *Publications of the Mississippi Historical Society* 9 (1903): 534.

50. See Perdue, *Slavery and the Evolution of Cherokee Society,* and Gregory Evans Dowd, "North American Indian Slaveholding and the Colonization of Gender: The Southeast before Removal," *Critical Matrix* 3 (fall 18): 16.

51. Arthur DeRosier Jr., "Pioneers with Conflicting Ideals: Christianity and Slavery in the Choctaw Nation," *Journal of Mississippi History* 21 (April 1959): 188.

52. Love, "Mingo Moshulitubbee's Prairie Village," 375, and *1830 Choctaw Roll: "Armstrong Roll,"* passim.

53. 21 November 1817, part 1, Elias Cornelius's Missionary Journal, Elias Cornelius Papers, Special Collections, William R. Perkins Library, Duke University.

54. *1830 Choctaw Roll: "Armstrong Roll,"* passim.

55. John Pitchlynn to Peter Pitchlynn, 19 July 1824, folder 4, 1824 file, Pitchlynn Papers, Thomas L. Gilcrease Institute of American History and Art, Tulsa OK.

56. *American State Papers: Documents, Legislative and Executive of the Congress of the United States. Class VIII. Public Lands,* ed. Walter Lowrie and Matthew St. Clair Clarke (Washington DC: Gales and Seaton, 1832–61), 7:14.

57. James L. McDonald to John C. Calhoun, 9 November 1824, M234, 169.

58. *Missionary Herald* 20 (February 1824): 47, and Loring Williams to Jeremiah Everts, 30 June 1823, ABCFM, 755.

59. John Pitchlynn to Peter Pitchlynn, 29 September 1824, box 1, folder 4, Pitchlynn Papers, Western History Collections, University of Oklahoma, Norman.

60. McDonald, "South from Self-Sufficiency to Peonage," 1096; *Missionary Herald* 18 (March 1822): 81; Loring Williams to Jeremiah Everts, 3 January 1822, ABCFM, 755; and Report of the Station at Elliot, February 1828, ABCFM, 757.

61. Francis DuBose Richardson Memoirs, 27, 33, microfilm 3010, Southern Historical Collection, Manuscript Division, Wilson Library, University of North Carolina at Chapel Hill; George S. Gaines, "Gaines' Reminiscences," *Alabama Historical Quarterly* 26 (fall–winter, 1964): 184; Horace Smith Fulkerson, *Random Recollections of Early Days in Mississippi* (Vicksburg MS: Vicksburg Printing and Publishing, 1885), 12; Mary J. Welsh, "Recollections of Pioneer Life in Mississippi," *Publications of the Mississippi Historical Society* 4 (1906): 350; H. G. Hawkins, "History of Port Gibson," *Publications of the Mississippi Historical Society* 10 (1909): 283; Sarah Tuttle, *Conversations on the Choctaw Mission* (Boston: T. R. Marvin, 1830), 2:47–48; James R. Creecy, *Scenes in the South, and Other Miscellaneous Pieces, by the Late James R. Creecy* (Washington DC: Thomas McGill, 1860), 121; Cuming, *Sketches,* 322; and folder 28, reel 2, Halbert Papers.

62. David Folsom to David W. Haley, 14 December 1829, ABCFM, 755.

63. Cyrus Kingsbury to Thomas McKenney, 8 February 1830, "Report from the Secretary of War . . . ," Senate Document 110, in *Public Documents, Printed by*

Order of the United States Senate, 21st Cong., 1st sess., 1829–30 (Washington DC: Duff Green, 1830), 12.

64. Jennings, "Nutt's Trip," 41; Halbert, "Origins of Mashulaville," 392–93; and Charles Hillman Brough, "Historic Clinton," *Publications of the Mississippi Historical Society* 7 (1903): 283.

65. "Papers of George S. Gaines," 10; F. B. Young, "Notices of the Chactaw or Choktah Tribe," *Edinburgh Journal of Natural and Geographical Science* 2 (1830): 14; and Willard H. Rollings, *The Osage: An Ethnohistorical Study of Hegemony on the Prairie-Plains* (Columbia: University of Missouri Press, 1992), 18.

66. David Folsom to Elias Cornelius, 13 September 1819, box H57, folder 17, Jay L. Hargrett Papers.

67. *The Debates and Proceedings in the Congress of the United States, . . . ,* 15th Cong., 2d sess., 1819 (Washington DC: Gales and Seaton, 1855), 34, appendix, 2527, and Arthur DeRosier Jr., "Cyrus Kingsbury—Missionary to the Choctaws," *Journal of Presbyterian History* 50 (winter 1972): 272.

68. *Missionary Herald* 15 (August 1819): 589, 16 (February 1820): 79, and 16 (July 1820): 320.

69. Resolutions of a Choctaw Council, 3 June 1820 ABCFM, 755; Cyrus Kingsbury to Jeremiah Everts, 14 May 1821, ABCFM; *Panoplist and Missionary Herald* 15 (December 1819): 535, and 16 (February 1820): 81; Eden Brashears to Thomas McKenney, 26 April 1820, reel 1, microfilm series T58, Letters Received: 1816–24, Records of the Superintendent of the Indian Trade, Record Group 75, Records of the Bureau of Indian Affairs, National Archives, Washington DC; and "Memorial of the Prudential Committee of the American Board of Commissioners for Foreign Missions . . . ," House Document 194, *Executive Documents, Printed by Order of the House of Representatives,* 22d Cong., 1st sess., 1831–32 (Washington DC: Duff Green, 1832), 11.

70. *Missionary Herald* 16 (August 1820): 366, 16 (December 1820): 565, and 17 (March 1821): 74; 17–28 May and 14 June 1820, Elliot Journal, ABCFM, 755.

71. Cyrus Kingsbury, Moses Jewell, Loring Williams, A. Williams, and J. G. Vanouse to Samuel Worcester, 12 April 1819, ABCFM; 11 September 1819, Elliot Journal, ABCFM; Cyrus Kingsbury, Isaac Fisk, William Pride, and Loring Williams to Samuel Worcester, 21 September 1819, ABCFM; Cyrus Kingsbury to Samuel Worcester, 5 May 1820, ABCFM; 9 December 1821 and 29 November 1822, Mayhew Journal, ABCFM; 14 January 1823, Elliot Mission Journal, ABCFM; 13 October 1823, Elliot Journal, ABCFM; Mayhew Mission Accounts, 1822, ABCFM, 763; 1 September–31 December 1828, Aiikhunna Accounts, ABCFM; and March 1828, Accounts of Aiikhunna, ABCFM, 757.

72. Champagne, *Social Order,* 149; *Missionary Herald* 26 (November 1830): 346;

and Scholars in the Choctaw Schools, from 1818 to August, 1831, "Memorial of the Prudential Committee," 14.

73. Cyrus Kingsbury to John C. Calhoun, 15 January 1823, M271, 4.

74. "Papers of George S. Gaines," 1.

75. *Christian Advocate and Journal, and Zion's Herald* 3 (24 October 1828): 30.

5. CREATION OF A NATION

1. *Missionary Herald* 18 (December 1822): 377–78.

2. Andrew Jackson to Robert Butler, 21 June 1817, John Spencer Bassett, ed., *Correspondence of Andrew Jackson*, 5 vols. (Washington DC: Carnegie Institution of Washington, 1927), 2:299.

3. Richard White, *The Roots of Dependency: Subsistence, Environment, and Social Change among the Choctaws, Pawnees, and Navajos* (Lincoln: University of Nebraska Press, 1983), 127–28; Samuel J. Wells, "Federal Indian Policy: From Accommodation to Removal," in *The Choctaw before Removal*, ed. Carolyn Keller Reeves (Jackson: University Press of Mississippi, 1985), 206; and Clara Sue Kidwell, *Choctaws and Missionaries in Mississippi, 1818–1918* (Norman: University of Oklahoma Press, 1995), 135, 106, 141.

4. Maurice Bloch, "The Long Term and the Short Term: The Economic and Political Significance of the Morality of Kinship," in *The Character of Kinship*, ed. Jack Goody (Cambridge: Cambridge University Press, 1973), 75–88.

5. Edward Shils, "Primordial, Personal, Sacred and Civil Ties," *British Journal of Sociology* 8 (1957): 130–45; Konstantin Symmons-Symonolewicz, "Nationalist Movements: An Attempt at a Comparative Typology," *Comparative Studies in Society and History* 7 (January 1965): 221–30; and Clifford Geertz, "The Integrative Revolution: Primordial Sentiments and Civil Politics in the New States," in *The Interpretation of Cultures: Selected Essays by Clifford Geertz*, ed. Clifford Geertz (New York: Basic Books, 1973), 261–63.

6. Mushulatubbee to John Eaton, 16 January 1832, and James McDonald to Thomas McKenney, 27 April 1826, both M234, 169.

7. Andrew Jackson to John C. Calhoun, 30 December 1818, *Correspondence of Andrew Jackson*, 2:405–6; James Pitchlynn to Jackson, 7 December 1818, *Correspondence of Andrew Jackson*, 2:406- 7; and John McKee to Jackson, 31 July 1819, Andrew Jackson Collection, Chicago Historical Society, Chicago.

8. James Pitchlynn to Andrew Jackson, 13 September 1819, *Correspondence of Andrew Jackson*, 2:429, and Pitchlynn to Jackson, 18 March 1819, *American State Papers: Documents, Legislative and Executive of the Congress of the United States. Class II. Indian Affairs*, ed. Walter Lowrie and Matthew St. Clair Clarke (Washington DC: Gales and Seaton, 1832–34), 2:229.

9. John McKee to Andrew Jackson, 13 August 1819, microfilm reel 7, *The Papers of Andrew Jackson* (Washington: Library of Congress, 1967), William R. Perkins Library, Duke University, Durham NC, and Edmund Folsom to Andrew Jackson, 13 September 1820, *Papers of Andrew Jackson,* microfilm reel 7.

10. John McKee to Andrew Jackson, 31 July 1819, Andrew Jackson Collection; James Pitchlynn to Jackson, 22 June 1819, M271, 2; and folder 89, microfilm reel 4, Halbert Papers.

11. John McKee to Andrew Jackson, 13 August 1819, *American State Papers, Indian Affairs,* 2:230, and Address by Jackson and Thomas Hinds to the Choctaw council, 30 October 1820, *American State Papers, Indian Affairs,* 2:234.

12. Treaty of Doak's Stand, 18 October 1820, M668, 5.

13. Article 4, Treaty of Doak's Stand, 18 October 1820, M668, 5.

14. David Folsom to Israel Folsom, 29 March 1822, microfilm reel 757, ABCFM.

15. *Missionary Herald* 19 (August 1823): 252.

16. 7 November 1822, Mayhew Journal, ABCFM, 755, and L. R. Bakewell to John Barbour, 2 September 1825, M234, 169.

17. D. W. Wright to James Monroe, 1 October 1826, M234, 169.

18. Gideon Lincecum, "Adenda," 5, microfilm, Gideon Lincecum Papers, Center for American History, University of Texas at Austin; John Pitchlynn to Peter Pitchlynn, 17 October 1824, box 1, folder 7, Peter Perkins Pitchlynn Papers, Western History Collections, University of Oklahoma, Norman; and David Folsom to Cyrus Byington, 13 October 1824, box H57, folder 22, Hargrett Papers.

19. David Folsom to Cyrus Byington, 7 December 1824, box H57, folder 23, Hargrett Papers.

20. "Expenses of Choctaw Delegation While in Washington, Dec 24–Jan 25," M234, 169; David Folsom to Cyrus Byington, 24 December 1824, box H57, folder 31, Hargrett Papers; and David Folsom to Cyrus Byington, 14 January 1825, box H57, folder 56, Hargrett Papers.

21. Articles 2, 3, 4, 6, and 10, Treaty of Washington, 20 January 1825, M668, 5; Choctaw Delegation to John C. Calhoun, 20 February 1825, T494, 1; and David Folsom to Jeremiah Everts, 19 January 1825, ABCFM, 757.

22. David Folsom to Ann Burnham, 4 November 1824, David Folsom Letter, Mississippi Department of Archives and History, Jackson.

23. David Folsom to Cyrus Kingsbury, 24 December 1824, box H57, folder 31, Hargrett Papers.

24. Cyrus Kingsbury to Thomas L. McKenney, 11 October 1825, "Letter from the Secretary of War . . . ," Executive Document 109, *Executive Documents,* 26th Cong., 2d sess., 1840–41 (Washington DC: Blair and Rives, 1840), 17.

25. Michael D. Green, *The Politics of Indian Removal: Creek Government and Society in Crisis* (Lincoln: University of Nebraska Press, 1982), 78–97.

26. William Ward to Thomas McKenney, 12 December 1825, M234, 169.

27. James L. McDonald to Thomas L. McKenney, 27 April 1826, M234, 169.

28. Cyrus Kingsbury to Jeremiah Everts, 8 August 1825, ABCFM, 756.

29. Cyrus Kingsbury to Jeremiah Everts, 8 August 1825, ABCFM, 765, and Mushulatubbee to Andrew Jackson, 10 December 1830, *Papers of Andrew Jackson*, microfilm reel 16.

30. Richard M. Johnson to John C. Calhoun, 19 February 1821, *Papers,* ed. Robert L. Meriwether (Columbia: University of South Carolina Press for the South Caroliniana Society, 1959–95), 5:637; Mushulatubbee to John Eaton, 28 September 1829, M234, 185; Cyrus Kingsbury to James Barbour, 6 July 1825, "Letter from the Secretary of War," Executive Document 109, 5–6; *American Baptist Magazine* 7 (August 1827): 250; Evelyn Cindy Adams, "Kentucky's Choctaw Academy, 1819–1842: A Commercial Enterprise," *Filson Club Historical Quarterly* 26 (January 1952): 28–30; Ella Wells Drake, "Choctaw Academy: Richard M. Johnson and the Business of Indian Education," *Register of the Kentucky Historical Society* 91 (summer 1991): 260–97; and John R. Goss, comp. and ed., *The Choctaw Academy: Official Correspondence, 1825–1841* (Conway AR: Oldbuck Press, 1992), i–ii.

31. James McDonald to Thomas McKenney, 27 April 1826, and David Folsom to Thomas McKenney, 27 June 1826, both M234, 169; and Resolution of the Choctaw Council, 27 August 1825, "Letter from the Secretary of War," Executive Document 109, 9.

32. David Folsom to Thomas McKenney, 27 June 1826, M234, 169.

33. William Ward to James Barbour, 15 April 1826, M234, 169, and *Missionary Herald* 26 (August 1830): 252.

34. David Folsom to Thomas McKenney, 27 June 1826, M234, 169, and *Missionary Herald* 26 (August 1830): 252.

35. David Folsom to Thomas McKenney, 27 June 1826, M234, 169.

36. Cyrus Kingsbury to Jeremiah Everts, 8 August 1825, ABCFM, 765.

37. 7 June 1821, Elliot Journal, ABCFM, 755; Cyrus Kingsbury to Jeremiah Everts, 10 February 1825, ABCFM, 755; 8 August 1825, ABCFM, 756; 18 October 1824 and 13 May 1825, ABCFM, 756; Francis Armstrong to Elbert Herring, 21 January 1834, M234, 184; Kingsbury to John C. Calhoun, 15 January 1823, 14 February 1823, and 30 October 1823, all in M271, 4.

38. An interview between the United States commissioners and the two deposed Choctaw chiefs Mushulatubbee and Bob Cole, 17 November 1826, M234, 169.

39. Proclamation, 1826, United States, M234, 169, and W. David Baird, *Peter Pitchlynn: Chief of the Choctaws* (Norman: University of Oklahoma Press, 1972), 25.

40. Communication from Robert Cole and Mushulatubbee to the War Department, 17 November 1826, M234, 169.

41. Choctaw Proclamation, 22 June 1826, David Folsom to Thomas McKenney, 27

June 1826, and Thomas McKenney to James Barbour, 21 October 1827, all in M234, 169.

42. List of Choctaw names and ranks at a council held 16 October 1827, M234, 169; C. M. Thayer to William Winans, 25 September 1830, box 2, folder 12, William Winans Papers, J. B. Cain Archives, Manuscript Collection, Millsaps College, Jackson MS; folder 10, microfilm reel 1, Halbert Papers; and folder 25, microfilm reel 2, Halbert Papers.

43. Alexander Talley to William Winans, 5 July 1830, box 2, folder 12, Winans Papers.

44. William Ward to James Barbour, 9 August 1826, M234, 169, and Henry S. Halbert, "The Last Indian Council on Noxubbee River," *Publications of the Mississippi Historical Society* 4 (1901): 275–76.

45. James Taylor Carson, "State Rights and Indian Removal in Mississippi, 1817–1835," *Journal of Mississippi History* 57 (February 1995): 27–30, and *Journal of the Senate of the United States,* 19th Cong., 1st sess., 1826–27 (Washington DC: Gales and Seaton, 1855), 159, 387.

46. Greenwood LeFlore to Thomas L. McKenney, 15 December 1827, M234, 169.

47. *Journal of the Senate of the State of Mississippi at Their Ninth Session, Held in the Town of Jackson* (Jackson: Peter Isler, 1826), 13.

48. *[1817] Constitution and Form of Government* (Port Gibson MS: State Printer, 1831), 35.

49. Carson, "State Rights and Indian Removal," 28–30.

50. Petition, 17 September 1828, M234, 169.

51. Edward Mitchell to [John C. Calhoun], 24 January 1824, and Petition to John Quincy Adams, 17 September 1828, both M234, 169.

52. Thomas McKenney to Peter Porter, 3 November 1828, M234, 169.

53. Edward Mitchell to [John C. Calhoun], 24 January 1824, Petition to John Quincy Adams, 17 September 1828, Thomas McKenney to Peter Porter, 3 November 1828, and quoted, James L. McDonald to Thomas McKenney [emphasis in the original], 27 April 1826, all M234, 169.

54. Benjamin Johnson to Thomas L. McKenney, 30 September 1828, M234, 185; Middleton Mackey to John Eaton, 27 November 1829, M234, 185; and David Folsom to Thomas McKenney, 14 October 1828, M234, 169.

55. Proclamation by the Captains of the Southeastern District, 6 October 1828, M234, 169.

56. William Ward to Peter Porter, 11 October 1828, M234, 169.

57. *Missionary Herald* 25 (May 1829): 153, and Allene Smith, *Greenwood LeFlore and the Choctaw Indians of the Mississippi Valley* (Memphis: C. A. Davis, 1951), 50–53.

58. *Missionary Herald* 25 (May 1829): 153, and Smith, *LeFlore,* 50–53.

59. Greenwood LeFlore to Thomas McKenney, 3 May 1828, M234, 169.

60. George S. Gaines, "Gaines' Reminiscences," *Alabama Historical Quarterly* 26 (fall–winter 1964): 182.

61. *Christian Advocate and Journal* 2 (16 May 1828): 146; Henry Frieland Buckner, "Burial among the Choctaws," *American Antiquarian and Oriental Journal* 2 (July–September 1879): 58; and Richard Huntington and Peter Metcalf, *Celebrations of Death: The Anthropology of Mortuary Ritual* (Cambridge: Cambridge University Press, 1979), 25–27.

62. Buckner, "Burial among the Choctaws," 58.

63. Buckner, "Burial among the Choctaws, 56, and Gideon Lincecum, "History of the Chahta Nation," 150, Gideon Lincecum Papers, Center for American History at the University of Texas at Austin.

64. Buckner, "Burial among the Choctaws," 56, and Sarah Tuttle, *Conversations on the Choctaw Mission* (Boston: T. R. Marvin, 1830), 2:86.

65. *Missionary Herald* 24 (December 1828): 380, 25 (May 1829): 153, 25 (December 1829): 377, and 25 (May 1829): 152–53; *Christian Advocate and Journal, and Zion's Herald* 3 (24 October 1828): 30.

66. *Niles' Weekly Register* 37 (14 November 1829): 181.

67. *Niles' Weekly Register* 37 (14 November 1829): 181.

68. John G. Jones, *A Complete History of Methodism as Connected with the Mississippi Conference of the Methodist Episcopal Church, South,* vol. 2 (Nashville: Methodist Episcopal Church, South, 1908), 182–83, and Alexander Talley to William Winans, 1 June 1829, box 1, folder 11, Winans Papers, 69. Henry S. Halbert, "Nanih Waiya, the Sacred Mound of the Choctaws," *Publications of the Mississippi Historical Society* 2 (1899; rpt. 1919): 233.

69. Halbert, "Nanih Waiya," 233.

70. David Folsom to Thomas McKenney, 14 October 1828, M234, 169.

6. THE GREAT AWAKENING

1. David Folsom to Thomas L. McKenney, 14 October 1828, M234, 169.

2. Clifford Geertz, "Religion as a Cultural System," in *The Interpretation of Cultures,* ed. Clifford Geertz (New York: Basic Books, 1973), 87–125.

3. Ralph A. Austen, "The Moral Economy of Witchcraft: An Essay in Comparative History," in *Modernity and Its Malcontents: Ritual and Power in Postcolonial Africa,* ed. Jean Comaroff and John Comaroff (Chicago: University of Chicago Press, 1993), 98; Nancy Foner, *Ages in Conflict: A Cross-Cultural Perspective on Inequality between Old and Young* (New York: Columbia University Press, 1984), 157–60; and Raoul Naroll, "A Tentative Index of Culture-Stress," *International Journal of Social Psychiatry* 5 (autumn 1959): 108–14.

4. James Adair, *Adair's History of the American Indians,* ed. Samuel Cole Williams (Johnson City TN: Watauga Press, 1930; rpt. Nashville: National Society of the Colonial Dames of America, in Tennessee, 1953), 185.

5. *Panoplist and Missionary Herald* 15 (October 1819): 462; 21 April 1819, Elliot Journal, ABCFM; George S. Gaines, "Gaines' Reminiscences," *Alabama Historical Quarterly* 26 (fall–winter 1964): 182; and L. R. Bakewell to James Barbour, 2 September 1815, M234, 169.

6. L. R. Bakewell to James Barbour, 2 September 1825, M234, 169; *Panoplist and Missionary Herald* 15 (October 1819): 460; Clyde Kluckhohn, *Navaho Witchcraft,* Papers of the Peabody Museum, vol. 22, no. 2 (Cambridge: Peabody Museum, 1944), 56; Lewis A. Coser, *The Functions of Social Conflict* (New York: Free Press, 1956), 46; Robert F. Murphy, "Intergroup Hostility and Social Cohesion," *American Anthropologist* 59 (December 1957): 1028; Naroll, "Tentative Index of Culture-Stress," 109; Robert Bales, "Cultural Differences in Rates of Alcoholism," *Quarterly Journal of Studies on Alcohol* 6 (March 1946): 483; and Anthony F. C. Wallace, "Revitalization Movements: Some Theoretical Considerations for Their Comparative Study," *American Anthropologist* 58 (April 1956): 268–69.

7. Calvin Cushman to David Green, 23 June 1829, ABCFM, 756; *Panoplist and Missionary Herald* 15 (October 1819): 463; *Missionary Herald* (January 1830): 21; Horatio B. Cushman, *A History of the Choctaw, Chickasaw and Natchez Indians* (Greenville TX: Headlight, 1899), 262; and John Barker, "We Are *Ekelesia:* Conversion in Uiaku, Papua New Guinea," in *Conversion to Christianity: Historical and Anthropological Perspectives on a Great Transformation,* ed. Robert Hefner (Berkeley: University of California Press, 1993), 206–7.

8. Barker, "We Are *Ekelesia,*" 200.

9. James Taylor Carson, "State Rights and Indian Removal in Mississippi, 1817–1835," *Journal of Mississippi History* 57 (February 1995): 30–33.

10. Alexander Talley to William Winans, 27 August 1828, box 1, folder 10, Winans Papers.

11. Russell Thornton, "Boundary Dissolution and Revitalization Movements: The Case of the Nineteenth-Century Cherokees," *Ethnohistory* 40 (summer 1993): 359–409.

12. *Missionary Herald* 27 (May 1830): 156.

13. Adam Hodgson, *Letters from North America Written during a Tour in the United States and Canada,* 2 vols. (London: Hurst, Robinson, 1824), 1:239; emphasis added.

14. Thomas L. McKenney, *Memoirs, Official and Personal; with Sketches of Travels among the Northern and Southern Indians; Embracing a War Excursion,*

and Descriptions of Scenes along the Western Borders, 2 vols. (New York: Paine and Burgess, 1846), 2:120.

15. Alexander Talley to William Winans, 27 August 1828, box 1, folder 10, Winans Papers.

16. Cushman, *History*, 262; *Missionary Herald* 27 (January 1830): 21 and 27 (May 1830): 156.

17. Cyrus Kingsbury to Jeremiah Everts, 24 July 1826, ABCFM, 756.

18. *Christian Advocate and Journal, and Zion's Herald* 3 (24 October 1828): 30.

19. *Missionary Herald* 25 (April 1829): 122.

20. Alexander Talley to William Winans, 28 October 1829, box 1, folder 11, Winans Papers.

21. *Missionary Herald* 26 (April 1830): 112; emphasis in the original.

22. William Ward to John Eaton, 11 October 1829, M234, 169; *Christian Advocate and Journal, and Zion's Herald* 3 (26 December 1828): 66 and 3 (15 May 1829): 145; Cyrus Kingsbury to Jeremiah Everts, 23 July 1829, ABCFM, 756; John Terrell to John Coffee, 13 September 1829, box 2, folder 5, Coffee Papers; and *Missionary Herald* 26 (January 1830): 11.

23. John Terrell to John Coffee, 13 September 1829, box 2, folder 5, Coffee Papers.

24. *Niles' Weekly Register* 38 (3 July 1830): 345; *Missionary Herald* 25 (December 1829): 383, 24 (December 1828): 380, 25 (April 1829): 121, and 25 (October 1829): 320–21; John Terrell to John Coffee, 13 September 1829, box 2, folder 5, Coffee Papers.

25. *Missionary Herald* 26 (May 1830): 156.

26. *Missionary Herald* 26 (April 1830): 114.

27. Calvin Cushman to David Greene, 23 June 1829, ABCFM, 756; *Missionary Herald* 25 (October 1829): 321–22 and 26 (October 1830): 322.

28. *Missionary Herald* 25 (April 1829): 121.

29. *Missionary Herald* 24 (September 1828): 283.

30. *Missionary Herald* 25 (August 1829): 252.

31. *Missionary Herald* 24 (September 1828): 283.

32. John G. Jones, *A Complete History of Methodism as Connected with the Mississippi Conference of the Methodist Episcopal Church, South*, vol. 2 (Nashville: Methodist Episcopal Church, South, 1908), 178–79.

33. Robert Smith to William Winans, 3 November 1828, box 1, folder 10, Winans Papers.

34. John Terrell to John Coffee, 13 September 1829, box 2, folder 5, Coffee Papers.

35. Cyrus Kingsbury to Jeremiah Everts, 23 July 1829, ABCFM, 756; *Christian Advocate and Journal, and Zion's Herald* 4 (30 October 1829): 34; *Missionary Herald*

26 (May 1830): 156 and 26 (June 1830): 182; William Ward to John Eaton, 1 October 1829, M234, 169.

36. *Missionary Herald* 25 (December 1829): 379 and 26 (March 1830): 84; Loring Williams to David Greene, 23 June 1829, ABCFM, 756.

37. *Missionary Herald* 26 (May 1830): 157.

7. REMOVAL CRISIS

1. "The General Deposition of Greenwood LeFlore . . . ," 24 February 1843, box 3, folder 23, Claiborne Papers.

2. *Journal of the House of Representatives of the State of Mississippi, at Their Twelfth Session, Held in the Town of Jackson* (Jackson: Peter Isler, 1829), 214–16.

3. *Register of Debates in Congress*, 21st Cong., 1st sess., 1829–30 (Washington DC: Gales and Seaton, 1830), Senate, 305–17, and House, 994, *Register of Debates in Congress*, 21st Cong., 2d sess., 1830–31 (Washington DC: Gales and Seaton, 1831), 1024–30, 1095.

4. Cyrus Kingsbury to Jeremiah Everts, 23 July 1829, ABCFM, 756.

5. Alexander Talley to William Winans, 19 July 1830, box 2, folder 12, Winans Papers.

6. *Register of Debates in Congress*, 21st Cong., 1st sess., 1829–30, appendix, 14–16.

7. *Register of Debates in Congress*, 21st Cong. 2d sess., 1830–31, appendix, 9.

8. *Natchez*, 13 February 1830.

9. *Woodville Republican*, 3 March and 20 March 1830.

10. *Woodville Republican*, 14 August 1830.

11. *Natchez*, 17 February 1832; emphasis in the original.

12. *Journal of the Senate of the State of Mississippi at Their Thirteenth Session, Held in the Town of Jackson* (Jackson: Peter Isler, 1830), 9.

13. *Laws of the State of Mississippi, Passed at the Thirteenth Session of the General Assembly, Held in the Town of Jackson* (Jackson: Peter Isler, 1830), 5.

14. *Niles' Weekly Register* 38 (21 August 1830): 457–58 and 38 (26 June 1830): 327; James McDonald to Alexander McKee, 30 March 1831, box 1, folder 22, Peter Perkins Pitchlynn Papers, Western History Collections, University of Oklahoma, Norman.

15. *Niles' Weekly Register* 38 (10 July 1830): 362–63.

16. John Terrell to John Coffee, 13 September 1829, box 2, folder 5, Coffee Papers.

17. Speech by Greenwood LeFlore, April 1830, M234, 169, and Cyrus Kingsbury to Jeremiah Everts, 25 December 1830, ABCFM, 758.

18. William Ward to John Eaton, 4 November 1829, M234, 169.

19. William Ward to John Eaton, 1 October 1829, M234, 169.

20. Alexander Talley to William Winans, 28 October 1829, box 1, folder 11, Winans

Papers, and excerpt from *Hamilton County Herald* (Chattanooga), Greenwood LeFlore File, Greenwood Public Library, Greenwood MS.

21. Mushulatubbee to John Eaton, 28 September 1829, M234, 185.

22. Folder 89, microfilm reel 4, Halbert Papers, and Mushulatubbee to Andrew Jackson, 16 May 1829, M234, 169.

23. William Ward to John Eaton, 29 December 1829, M234, 169.

24. Cyrus Byington to Jeremiah Everts, 18 March 1830, ABCFM, 756; Cyrus Kingsbury to David Greene, 13 April 1830, ABCFM, 756; Alexander Talley to William Winans, 20 March 1830, box 2, folder 12, Winans Papers; *Missionary Herald* 26 (August 1830): 253; and Greenwood LeFlore to Mushulatubbee, 7 April 1830, M234, 169.

25. Greenwood LeFlore to Mushulatubbee, 7 April 1830, M234, 169.

26. Greenwood LeFlore to Mushulatubbee, 7 April 1830, M234, 169.

27. Cyrus Kingsbury to David Greene, 13 April 1830, ABCFM, 756, and Alexander Talley to William Winans, 20 March 1830, box 2, folder 12, Winans Papers.

28. Greenwood LeFlore and David Folsom to Andrew Jackson, 18 March 1830, microfilm reel 15, *Papers of Andrew Jackson* (Washington DC: Library of Congress, 1967), William R. Perkins Library, Duke University, Durham NC.

29. Cyrus Kingsbury to Jeremiah Everts, 6 May 1830, ABCFM, 756.

30. Greenwood LeFlore to Mushulatubbee, 7 April 1830, M234, 169; manuscript on the administrations of Chiefs Greenwood LeFlore, David Folsom, and John Garland, box H57, folder 67, Hargrett Papers; Alexander Talley to William Winans, 5 July 1830, box 2, folder 12, Winans Papers, and Andrew Jackson to the Senate, 6 May 1830, *A Compilation of the Messages and Papers of the Presidents, 1789–1902*, ed. James D. Richardson (Washington DC: Bureau of National Literature and Art, 1903), 2:478-79.

31. *Missionary Herald* 26 (August 1830): 253.

32. Unknown to David Folsom, 19 May 1830, 1830 box, folder 6, Peter Pitchlynn Papers, Thomas Gilcrease L. Institute of American History and Art, Tulsa OK.

33. Choctaw National Government to John Eaton, 10 August 1830, M234, 169.

34. Harriet Wright to Jared Bunce, 17 March 1829, ABCFM, 756.

35. William Ward to John Eaton, 14 July 1829, Nittakaichee, Yack Hopia, Hopia Tubbee, et al. to John Eaton, 20 November 1829, and William Ward to John Eaton, 29 December 1829, all M234, 169.

36. Cyrus Kingsbury to Jeremiah Everts, 23 June 1830 and 6 May 1830, ABCFM, 756; and Cyrus Kingsbury to Henry Hill, 19 April 1830, ABCFM, 764.

37. Cyrus Kingsbury to Henry Hill, 26 July 1830, ABCFM, 756.

38. Robert M. Jones to Peter Pitchlynn, 6 August 1830, box 1, folder 18, Pitchlynn Papers, Western History Collections, University of Oklahoma, Norman.

39. Middleton Mackey to John Eaton, 27 November 1829, M234, 185.

40. R. D. Hallin to Peter Pitchlynn, 13 July 1830, box 1, folder 16, and J. C. Hastings to Peter Pitchlynn, 13 June 1830, box 1, folder 17, both Pitchlynn Papers, Western History Collections, University of Oklahoma, Norman; Alexander Talley to William Winans, 5 July 1830, box 2, folder 12, Winans Papers.

41. *Missionary Herald* 26 (August 1830): 254.

42. *Missionary Herald* 26 (August 1830): 253–54.

43. Chiefs, Captains, and Warriors of the Southeastern and Northern Districts to John Eaton, 2 June 1830, M234, 169.

44. Peter Pitchlynn to John Coffee, 21 June 1830, box 2, folder 6, Coffee Papers.

45. Alexander Talley to William Winans, 5 July 1830, box 2, folder 12, Winans Papers.

46. John Pitchlynn to John Terrell, 3 May 1830, folder 2, John Terrell Papers, Alabama Department of Archives and History, Montgomery.

47. *Missionary Herald* 26 (August 1830): 253.

48. David Haley to Andrew Jackson, 12 August 1830, M234, 169; Thomas Clark to Gustavus Pope, 27 September 1830, Pope-Carter Papers, Special Collections, William R. Perkins Library; and Henry S. Halbert, "Story of the Treaty of Dancing Rabbit Creek," *Publications of the Mississippi Historical Society* 6 (1902): 374–77.

49. Halbert, "Story of the Treaty of Dancing Rabbit Creek."

50. "Journal of Proceedings at Treaty of Dancing Rabbit Creek, 1830," Senate Document 512, *Public Documents Printed by Order of the Senate of the United States,* 23d Cong., 1st sess., 1833–34 (Washington DC: Duff Green, 1834), 256–57.

51. Halbert, "Story of the Treaty of Dancing Rabbit Creek," 382.

52. Halbert, "Story of the Treaty of Dancing Rabbit Creek," 384–91. None of the federal documents describing the treaty negotiations mention the seven women.

53. Cyrus Kingsbury to Jeremiah Everts, 29 September 1830, ABCFM, 758.

54. Cyrus Kingsbury to Jeremiah Everts, 29 September 1830, ABCFM, 758, and Choctaw Nation, *Papers relating to the Claims of the Choctaw Nation against the United States, Arising under the Treaty of 1830* (Washington DC: A. O. P. Nicholson, 1855), 24.

55. Cyrus Kingsbury to Jeremiah Everts, 29 September 1830, ABCFM, 758.

56. Basis of a Treaty to Be Submitted to the Commissioners of the United States on Behalf of the Choctaw Nation, 25 September 1830, 1830 box, folder 11, Pitchlynn Papers, Thomas L. Gilcrease Institute of American History and Art, Tulsa OK.

57. Treaty of Dancing Rabbit Creek, M668, 6.

58. Cyrus Kingsbury to Jeremiah Everts, 29 September 1830, ABCFM, 758.

59. Cyrus Kingsbury to Jeremiah Everts, 17 November 1830, ABCFM, 758.

60. Southern Division Council to John Eaton, 16 October 1830 and 22 October 1830, both M234, 185; *Missionary Herald* 27 (January 1831): 18; and Cyrus Byington to David Greene, 1 December 1830, ABCFM, 758.

61. Thomas Wall to Alexander McKee, 28 April 1831, box 1, folder 23, Pitchlynn Papers, Western History Collections, University of Oklahoma, Norman.

62. Proclamation, 23 October 1830, M234, 169.

63. Answers of Greenwood LeFlore to cross interrogatories propounded to him by Choctaw claimants, 24 February 1843, box 5, folder 23, Claiborne Papers.

64. William Ward to Samuel Hamilton, 21 June 1831, 1831 box, folder 8, Pitchlynn Papers, Thomas L. Gilcrease Institute of American History and Art, Tulsa OK.

65. Answers of Greenwood LeFlore to the interrogatories propounded on his direct examination before the board of commissioners, 24 February 1843, box 4, folder 23, Claiborne Papers.

66. Cyrus Byington to David Greene, 1 December 1830, ABCFM, 758.

67. D. W. Haley to Andrew Jackson, 10 March 1831, M234, 169.

68. *Missionary Herald* 27 (January 1831): 19.

69. Loring Williams to Jeremiah Everts, 16 October 1830, ABCFM, 758.

70. *Missionary Herald* 27 (January 1831): 18.

71. *Missionary Herald* 27 (January 1831): 19.

72. Cyrus Kingsbury to Jeremiah Everts, 25 December 1830, ABCFM, 758.

73. John Pitchlynn to Peter Pitchlynn, 23 December 1832 and 21 February 1833, folder 31, box 1, Pitchlynn Papers, Western History Collections, University of Oklahoma, Norman.

74. *Woodville Republican*, 6 November 1830, and *Journal of the House of Representatives of the State of Mississippi, at Their Sixteenth Session, Held in the Town of Jackson* (Jackson: Peter Isler, 1833), 141.

75. *Natchez*, 3 February 1832.

THE RETURN OF OAKATIBBÉ

1. William Gilmore Simms, "Oakatibbé, or The Choctaw Sampson," in *The Wigwam and the Cabin* (New York: Redfield, 1856), 207.

2. Simms, "Oakatibbé, 200.

3. Simms, "Oakatibbé, 208.

Index

William Bartram on the Southeastern Indians
Edited and annotated by Gregory A. Waselkov
        and Kathryn E. Holland Braund

Deerskins and Duffels
The Creek Indian Trade with Anglo-America, 1685–1815
By Kathryn E. Holland Braund

Searching for the Bright Path
The Mississippi Choctaws from Prehistory to Removal
By James Taylor Carson

Cherokee Americans
The Eastern Band of Cherokees in the Twentieth Century
By John R. Finger

Choctaw Genesis, 1500–1700
By Patricia Galloway

The Southeastern Ceremonial Complex
Artifacts and Analysis
The Cottonlandia Conference
Edited by Patricia Galloway
Exhibition Catalog by David H. Dye and Camille Wharey

An Assumption of Sovereignty
Social and Political Transformation among the Florida Seminoles,
1953–1979
By Harry A. Kersey Jr.

Milton Keynes UK
Ingram Content Group UK Ltd.
UKHW040304120124
435845UK00008B/290

9 780803 264175